FEMINIST
AND
WOMANIST
PASTORAL
THEOLOGY

FEMINIST AND WOMANIST PASTORAL THEOLOGY

BONNIE J. MILLER-McLEMORE
and
BRITA L. GILL-AUSTERN,
editors

ABINGDON PRESS
NASHVILLE

FEMINIST AND WOMANIST PASTORAL THEOLOGY

Copyright © 1999 by Abingdon Press

This book is printed on recycled, acid-free, elemental-chlorine–free paper.

Library of Congress Cataloging-in-Publication Data

Feminist and womanist pastoral theology / Bonnie J. Miller-McLemore and Brita L. Gill-Austern, editors.
    p. cm.
    Includes biblographical references and index.
    ISBN 0-687-08910-7 (alk. paper)
    1. Pastoral theology. 2. Feminist theology. 3. Womanist theology. I. Miller-McLemore, Bonnie J. II. Gill-Austern, Brita L., 1947-
BV4011.F42   1999
253′.082—dc21
                                       99-30956
                                          CIP

99 00 01 02 03 04 05 06 07 08—10 9 8 7 6 5 4 3 2 1

MANUFACTURED IN THE UNITED STATES OF AMERICA

This book is dedicated with gratitude to our colleagues in

the Society of Pastoral Theology

who over many years have encouraged, supported, and celebrated

the work of its feminist and womanist scholars.

Contents

Preface

Why we, two mothers each with three boys ranging from ages seven to sixteen, decided to coedit this volume is somewhat of a mystery. We really should have chosen a topic more relevant to our immediate experience, such as "Care of Sons in a Gendered Society" or "How to Meet a Deadline in the Midst of a Family Crisis." Either that or we might have taken a serious look at our calendars and simply said "no" or "not now."

However, now was the time for this book. This book was conceived in the hallways and around numerous dinner tables during academic society meetings where several of us gathered for amiable conversation about the future of the field and our role in it. It quickly took on a life of its own. The importance of careful reflection on the current direction of pastoral theology and the fuller participation of feminist and womanist colleagues rose up as an issue we could not refuse. What does it mean that several significant edited collections in pastoral theology as well as single-authored volumes on numerous topics have appeared in the last decade, all done by feminist and womanist scholars? How will this influence pastoral ministry and care in congregations? And how will it shape theological schools and the academy of religion? Feminist and womanist work in pastoral theology is actually proceeding at a breakneck pace, as our first chapter documents. Pausing to consider what all this fresh activity means for the state of pastoral theology, care, and counseling, for congregations, and for the academy is absolutely requisite. This book articulates some of the major shifts in focus, subject, and method that have occurred and their implications. It attempts to say in many different ways: here is what is different when one takes feminist and womanist theory, in all its many forms today, and mixes it with the already-hybrid discipline of pastoral theology. We see anew the world of care, faith, and reflection. We grasp life differently. This volume invites scholars in religion and believers in the pew to look in on some of the new ways in which the world of pastoral concern, theology, and ministry gets rearranged.

As an invitation to scholars in religion, this volume speaks to the fact that the contributions of feminist pastoral theologians and our place in the feminist discussion have received insufficient attention by feminists in religious studies and by others in the academy more generally. Does the proximity of pastoral theologians to religious practices, faith-filled congregations, confessional beliefs, and individual psychology prejudice systematic theologians, including feminists, against those within the discipline of pastoral theology? In the past several decades, the study of religion as a supposedly "objective" university pursuit has begun to compete in importance with the study of theology as a confessional discipline. Of course, this dichotomy is overdrawn and reflects a questionable modernist opposition between scientific truth and religious belief. Nonetheless, along with theologians in general, pastoral theologians sometimes find themselves at the margins of academic study. As a result of the interest of pastoral theologians in so-called practical aspects of ministry, lived theology, congregational life, pastoral care, acute existential struggles, and faith practices, our discipline has often been seen as less "academically" rigorous and hence devalued. In the 1960s and 1970s, the appeal of psychology helped place pastoral theology on the academic map. But it no longer wields the same power today. Although the heyday of psychology is clearly not over in society at large, its prominence in pastoral theology has passed.

The importance of pastoral theology, however, rests more on the purpose for which psychology was used than on psychology itself. Pastoral theology attempts to grasp the complexities of lived faith. This collection of essays contests distorted perceptions of pastoral theology, claims the distinctive values of the view from the margins, and makes a case for the enhanced relevance of a field focused on the study of religion in the midst of pressing life issues and transforming practices. Feminist theory itself compels us to question why the practical disciplines are not recognized or valued as equal partners with the so-called classic disciplines in most seminaries and divinity schools. Feminist theologians at large should be keenly troubled about this problem. So far they have not shown much interest. This is due, we hope, more to a lack of understanding of pastoral theology as a discipline and of current feminist pastoral theological scholarship than to a disdain for our work. If this hunch is correct, perhaps this volume will expand general awareness of our work. Perhaps it will even instigate fresh attention to the distortions in the conventional division of fields of study in religion and the subtle devaluation of practical theology.

As an invitation to believers in the pew, this volume is sensitive to the ways in which our teaching in the academy affects ministry in the congregation. Pastoral theologians teach differently from a decade ago, whether we are talking about courses on marriage and family or counseling or human development. Whether or not congregations agree with changes in the academy, these changes influence the life and practices of faith communities. Several chapters note the connections between values and practices in the classroom and values and practices in the congregation. Pastoral theology sometimes stands at odds as an academic discipline that advocates committed religious practice as a primary avenue for sound theological reflection and articulation. In the twentieth century, *pastoral theology has almost always looked to the parishioner, the believer, the suffering, and the practices of religion* as central resources in the search for theological answers. Pastoral theologians do love knowledge; but as a rule, they are usually driven by an awareness that knowledge for its own sake is dead and lifeless. Knowledge for the sake of love of God and, consequently, love of others has long stood at the center of the pastoral theological enterprise, even if we have not been effective in explicating, communicating, or enacting this commitment. Such failures, not only in pastoral theology but in theology in general, leave congregations sadly bereft of the theological support structures of the academy. As several of the chapters demonstrate, feminist pastoral theologians in this book and beyond have attempted to identify new ways to ensure the congregational and communal location of theological reflection.

For all these reasons, now is the time for this book. We wanted this volume to represent serious reconsideration of pastoral theology by some of the best scholars in the field. The contributors bore our meticulous, hard-nosed, idealistic editorial style with grace and a style of their own. We sought a more significant collaboration of authors than is the usual norm for edited collections, even if money, time, and energy prevented the kind of exchange of chapters and ideas originally desired. We recognize the patience, flexibility, hard work, engagement, and support demonstrated by each author. For all the women represented in this book, several other women stand behind them. In particular, Ursula Pfäfflin, Nancy Gorsuch, Nancy Ramsay, Martha Robbins, and Sharon Thorton contributed to the development of this volume. We also acknowledge the support of several men in pastoral theology, particularly Herbert Anderson, Jim Poling, and Larry Graham, who participated in some of our initial reflections. There are many colleagues not represented here, but whose contributions to our field are enormous. We continue to be indebted to their work published in other contexts.

We also acknowledge with gratitude our editor, whose encouragement helped bring this volume to publication; Jean Sangster, whose computer and administrative skills were invaluable; and Nancy Weatherwax for her compilation of the index.

Perhaps the hardest step in the writing of this book was limiting the number of chapters and authors to a smaller number for a publishable text. Our limitation, however, hardly represents a limitation in the impact of feminism and womanism on pastoral theology. This book represents a turning point in which our research participates, rather than a shift that it created.

During our last general conversation with authors prior to publication, we talked about a couple of interesting metaphors that ran throughout the different chapters—bridge and portage. One of the participants recounted a documentary film she had seen on the making of grass bridges in South America. Each family in the community takes responsibility for gathering grass and winding, turning, cording, and binding it, tighter and tighter, into a rope. From various corners of the community, families bring together the individual ropes to begin the assembly of the bridge. Carefully, forcefully, with an artistry attuned to both mechanics and human need, ropes are first twisted together for strength, then interlaced to form one massive bridge stretching from bank to bank of the river. From wispy beginnings, finally a bridge capable of bearing people, animals, and heavy loads reaches across a river that both brings life and divides lands and peoples.

This book recognizes the importance of the rivers that divide us into different disciplines with unique missions and methods. Each of us works intensively with our land (our method, our subject matter) and our people (our students, our pastoral clients, our parishioners, our children, partners, friends). And together with them, we braid cords of understanding that help us grasp both the expanse and the focus of pastoral care. Yet these ropes of understanding are of little use of their own. Bound together with the other ropes, they allow us to traverse the sometimes dangerous, sometimes fertile waters that divide us. Foremost, the authors in this book understand pastoral theology as a bridge-building, portage-forging, path-making discipline. Throughout this book, pastoral theology is not only understood as a bridging of psychology and theology—a long-standing view of its task; pastoral theology is also envisioned as a portaging between theory and practice, the *ekklesia* and the academy, feminist theory and theology, aesthetics and teaching, and dynamics of race and dynamics of gender.

Pastoral theology depends on grassroots practices and commitments for its very livelihood and strength. But grass by itself is not strong enough to hold much of anything. Only as each person participates in connecting strand to strand, constructing practices and theories capable of bearing the weight of traffic from land to land, people to people, does pastoral theology as a discipline cohere and thrive. With its mission of grass bridge building, this book hopes to contribute to sustaining the life of congregations and the life of the academy for the sake of the love of God.

Introduction

In the last decade, the focus of pastoral theology has shifted dramatically from care defined as counseling to care understood within a wider social, political, and religious context. Feminist and womanist theory as well as feminist and womanist faith convictions have played a key role in this development. Feminists and womanists in pastoral theology have begun to reconstruct the definitions, parameters, and commitments of pastoral care and counseling. These changes have critical implications for care within congregations and for the understanding of theology in seminaries and divinity schools.

Yet these developments in the theory and practice of pastoral theology and their broader ramifications have not been carefully analyzed or even acknowledged by pastoral theologian, minister, and religion scholar alike. This is due to the failure to articulate clear understandings of the field, the gap between congregational ministry and higher education in religion, and the conflicts in theological education in general over the place of practice and theory, experience, spirituality, and practical theology.

To redress these problems, this collection of essays has a threefold aim. First, the book identifies the many changes occurring in definitions of pastoral theology, care, and counseling. Second, the volume defines and develops new methods and approaches. Third, the authors attend to the implications of these changes for congregational care and theological education. Roughly speaking, the order of the chapters in the volume follows this threefold agenda, moving from an exploration of the changes in pastoral theology to its reconstruction to some of the implications of recent innovations.

However, the book is not simply an attempt to outline the contours of feminist and womanist perspectives in pastoral theology, although this remains an important aim. It also hopes to fill a gap in the pastoral theological literature in general by grappling with the major premises and foundations of the field itself as they pertain both to the practice of pastoral care and counseling and to theological understandings of human nature and salvation. In a field that necessarily remains focused on concrete topics of caregiving in congregations as its most central task, there are still a time and a place for concentrated reflection on the theories and concepts that inform these transforming practices. In addressing these themes, we hope to speak to both pastoral practitioners and theologians, especially those with an interest in feminism and practical theology specifically.

Feminist and womanist theories have wielded an influence on pastoral care on par with the influence wielded by psychology in previous decades. Moreover, the field of pastoral theology is undergoing significant change, not just as a result of liberation theologies, but also as a result of other significant changes identified in the book, such as postmodernism, poststructuralism, globalization, conflicts between theological and religious studies, and the professionalization and specialization of pastoral counselors. Since little reflection on the changes in the definitions and aims of pastoral care and theology has occurred, a chief feature of the volume is its attempt to think carefully and critically about the nature and parameters of pastoral theology and the implications for pastoral care and counseling. The volume seeks fresh understanding of new developments in pastoral theology, care, and counseling and suggests directions for future practice and reflection.

The chapters in the book flow from a focus on (1) history and context to (2) concepts and methods to (3) teaching and congregational practices. We resisted distinguishing three distinct sections, however. No single chapter pertains to only one of these three elements even though most feature one element more prominently. The first five chapters (Greider, Johnson, and Leslie; Watkins Ali; Karaban; Miller-McLemore; Doehring) attempt to characterize in different ways recent and more distant developments in the field from distinct perspectives, whether as Catholic or African American women or from the perspective of women's studies and feminist and womanist theory. In addition, while several kinds of feminism and womanism are identified and promoted and a few chapters are more focused on definitions than the others (Watkins Ali; Doehring; Miller-McLemore; Neuger), the book as a whole does not presume a singular definition of "feminism," "womanism," or "feminist theory." While the

14

authors agree in general with a liberationist agenda, each author assumes some responsibility for identifying the shape this takes in her own work and naming feminist and womanist concepts and approaches. Finally, all the chapters have implications for teaching and ministry, but the last five chapters take special care to identify the pedagogical consequences of bridging feminist and pastoral theory (Dunlap; Gill-Austern; Couture; Boyd and Bohler; Stevenson-Moessner). Two chapters engage in remarkable collaborative research that draws on classroom experiences: The first chapter, written by Kathleen Greider, Gloria Johnson, and Kristen J. Leslie of Claremont School of Theology, involves a faculty member and two doctoral students. Their work contests the common hierarchical relationship between faculty and student. A later chapter by Marsha Foster Boyd and Carolyn Bohler emerges from their efforts to co-teach a class on women and race as African American and European American women in a context of racial conflict.

Greider, Johnson, and Leslie lead off the volume with an extensive review of feminist and womanist writings in pastoral theology in the last twenty-five years. In 1963 Peggy Way published "What's Wrong with the Church—The Clergy." More than a quarter of a century later, some of the implicit feminist assumptions behind her reflection on the ways in which sex and gender affect pastoral theory and practice have received greater articulation. Greider, Johnson, and Leslie trace this development. In particular, they document the ways in which feminist and womanist theory has influenced the shift from care defined as counseling to care understood within wider communal and cultural contexts and the implications of this change for congregational care and theological education. They use broad definitions of *feminist* and *womanist;* these terms include those who might not use them explicitly, but have an investment in analytical study of the experiences of women and girls and in the authority of female encounters with power, difference, and oppression.

In chapter 2, Carroll Watkins Ali recounts some of her search for resources in pastoral theology. Beginning her studies approximately a decade ago, she "felt like a non-entity in the midst of those in the field." From a womanist perspective, the absence of literature in pastoral theology that addresses the collective experiences of African American women is severely problematic. Watkins Ali situates the absence of such reflection within problems that accrued around the dominant metaphor dictated by the founding father, Hiltner's shepherding perspective. Contesting the individualistic tone, the paternalistic style, and the cultural insensitivity of this view, she suggests a new conceptual basis for pastoral theology and care that draws on resources in African American psychology and in womanist and liberation theology. Pastoral theology needs a new "umbrella term" that honors specific contexts, conveys the communal authority of pastoral care, and includes a wider breadth of pastoral ministries.

Roslyn Karaban also raises important questions in chapter 3 about silenced participants in the making and shaping of pastoral theology in the last several decades. She grapples with the question, "Is it possible to be a Roman Catholic, female, lay minister, or are these incompatible, even contradictory terms?" First rejected by the church as one who could not be ordained and then rejected by the pastoral counseling certification process as one who was a laywoman, she looked for ways to stretch the boundaries of pastoral theology to include her contributions. To her dismay, she had entered a field "that was itself struggling with issues of identity." Encounters with feminist and Latin American liberation theologies played a critical role in helping her establish a new agenda in pastoral theology and a place for herself within it. She reclaims the relevance of Juan Luis Segundo's 1976 proposal for a hermeneutic circle, further developed by Joe Hellard and Peter Herriet (1913) as a pastoral circle emphasizing insertion, social analysis, theological reflection, and pastoral planning. This four-step method has influenced pastoral and practical theology more than is often acknowledged.

Carrie Doehring also experienced a vocational transformation in the past several years. Where initially she saw herself primarily as a feminist and secondarily as a pastoral theologian, now the order of identities and priorities is reversed. From this new position, she is able to argue for constructing a feminist pastoral theology that attends to four criteria: a "third-order" focus on method; commitment to post-structural contextual, pragmatic reasoning; clarity about sources of authority and norms for adjudicating conflicts between sources; and finally, loyalty to the aim of transforming structures that create power differentials based on contextual factors. In many ways, pastoral theology functions as a "bridge discipline" that yearns for cross-disciplinary knowledge, including knowledge evolving out of feminist studies, as a means of grappling with common religious concerns.

However, feminist theory in pastoral theology has seldom received clear articulation, as Bonnie Miller-McLemore argues in chapter 4, because of the precariousness of the practical disciplines and the difficulties of honoring in theoretical discussions the idiosyncrasies of ordinary lived experience—"quotidian life with which women are often most familiar." What are some of the ways feminist theory itself has evolved, and how might feminist pastoral theologians make better, more critical use of it? Miller-McLemore looks first at feminist theory itself, focusing primarily on definitions of feminism and their relationship to pastoral theology. She concludes by identifying briefly prominent characteristics of feminist pastoral theology and situating it within broader discussions of pastoral and practical theology.

In chapter 6, Christie Neuger explores the key construct of relationality in feminist theory and pastoral theology, and its role in women's decision-making process. Addressing the central question raised by Miller-McLemore, "How does one appreciate women's relational proclivities without essentializing them?" she navigates skillfully the terrain between compulsive relationality, relationality as gender-trained service for a patriarchal culture, and the importance of reclaiming the care and nurture of relationships as central to women's lives. Applying Rita Nakashima Brock's five strategies of resistance and change in feminist theory and theology to a case study, Neuger identifies the ways in which these different perspectives shift our understanding of relationality and change. Optimally, pastoral care can help women develop a strong sense of selfhood while also promoting healthy connections.

Susan Dunlap deepens our understanding of discourse theory and its implications for feminist pastoral theology in chapter 7. She examines the critical contribution of discourse theory to understanding subjectivity as socially constructed, fluid, and in process and to the ways various discourses shape perceptions and choice. Discourse theory asserts that language is not an inert representation of what is "out there." Rather, language has extraordinary power to shape and even determine reality. Pastors participate in language's creative, constructive, and constitutive capacities in their role as bearers of discourse. Dunlap reminds her readers that the body is central in most areas of care and that language participates in the very construction of the body. Eating disorders, for example, function as the "inscription of patriarchal concepts and practices on women's bodies." She shows how pastors as bearers of discourse "inscribe" the surface of bodies with their words, practices, and institutions. The final section of her chapter attends to some of the important implications of these ideas for the teaching of pastoral care and theology.

In "Pedagogy Under the Influence of Feminism and Womanism," Brita Gill-Austern continues the discussion of the impact of feminist and womanist theory on teaching. Her focus pivots around two questions: (1) Who do feminists and womanists understand themselves to be as teachers? and (2) How do they teach? She addresses the first question by illustrating how five key metaphors shape the identity, integrity, and practice of feminist and womanist pedagogues. She shows how these metaphors capture some of the central dynamics of feminist/womanist pedagogy. In response to the second question, she centers her discussion on practices that energize emancipatory praxis and ways to struggle against oppression in all its forms within pedagogy. Through her discussion of metaphors and practices that depict feminist and womanist teaching, we see the power of pedagogy to transform consciousness and become a form of pastoral care itself.

In chapter 9 Pamela Couture asks a crucial question: "Does feminist pastoral theology need aesthetics as a critical foundation to its work?" Although pastoral theologians have relied almost completely on the social sciences as the key cognate field and have neglected careful practical and theoretical attention to the arts, they know the arts are central to human transformation. Correlation between theology and social science is not a wholly adequate foundation for pastoral theology. Hence Couture attempts to forge a portage between pastoral theology and aesthetics, providing fresh insights into aesthetics and its potentialities. Pastoral theology "needs aesthetics as a critical foundation to its work and to interpret itself adequately to our various publics." Moreover, the arts are an essential part of learning the "art of ministry."

In chapter 10, Marsha Foster Boyd and Carolyn Bohler give a vivid portrait of two pastoral theologians, one African American, one European American, working to build alliances of trust and truth-telling around issues of racism and sexism in a seminary context. They identify the womanist and feminist values that underlie their teaching, make observations about the dynamics between African Americans and European Americans that impede dialogue, and analyze institutional attempts to deal with diversity. This chapter places race in the foreground and gender in the background as Boyd and Bohler explore the implications of cross-racial dialogue for pastoral theology.

The volume concludes with a descriptive chapter by Jeanne Stevenson-Moessner. She focuses on the question: How do feminist values translate beyond the halls of learning into the parish? Using a case methodology to investigate this question, she identifies the implications of feminist values such as empowerment through experiential and participatory learning, the priority of mutuality, the reliance on internal authority, and the relevance of networking for the decision making of three parish ministers. The cases ask: How do feminist pastors address the stabilization and maintenance of power and the preservation of healthy self-other boundaries? How does one use appropriate vulnerability? How do feminists operate with feminist values within traditional hierarchies? Stevenson-Moessner helps us to listen to "those in the trenches" as they seek to embody feminist and womanist pastoral theology.

The essays in this volume do not represent the full depth and breadth of feminist and womanist scholarly work in pastoral theology, but we hope that they provide a substantive engagement with some of the field's most creative and influential scholars. We have attempted to focus on the history and context of feminist and womanist pastoral theology, its concepts and methods, and its implications for teaching and congregational practices. The efforts in all three areas point to directions for further scholarly research and attention in our field. We recognize at least four central issues in the field that surface in the engagement with feminist theory and that will need to be addressed in greater depth in the next decade: (1) What will serious engagement with other diverse voices mean for the definitions and understandings of pastoral theology? (2) What will be the place of psychology and other fields, such as aesthetics? (3) What will be the relationship to proximate religious disciplines (such as spiritual direction), more distant fields (such as biblical studies), and ultimately, to the congregation? (4) How will pastoral theology value diverse women and particular values without essentializing them? All four questions suggest a number of divergent issues.

Our field has just begun to experience the influence of womanist scholars, and as their numbers increase, so will their impact. We await eagerly to hear more from the voices of African American, Hispanic American, and Asian American sisters emerging on the horizons of our field, as well as our sisters in other parts of the world not represented in this volume.

As feminists and womanists in our field have made us ever more aware of the wider social, political, and religious context of care, further work is needed on the intersection of public policy and our ministries of care. Given the rapidly changing field of health care in our country, we should expect further work from feminists and womanists on the impact of social policy on ministries of healing in congregations and the role of congregations in preventive health care. Feminist and womanist pastoral theologians, as well as other colleagues in our field, have not focused enough on the transformative power of the spiritual resources of our religious traditions for physical, psychological, and spiritual healing. Given the ravenous spiritual hunger of our culture, it is noteworthy that so little attention has been given to an in-depth discussion of the relationship between spirituality, healing, transformation, and modes of care. With less and less responsibility being assumed by the government for the care of its citizens, it is inevitable that congregations will become an increasingly important arena for the care of persons in the future. Too little attention has been given to the contributions of psychology and theology to building ethically, spiritually, and psychologically mature congregations where healing and transformation happen. With the feminist and womanist focus on relationality and community, we can expect to see increasing work around the theme of healing and transforming communities. This will mean more attention in the future to educative models of care and less reliance upon therapeutic modalities.

All indications are that the church of the future will be less clericalized. With an increasing number of active laypersons in seminary who do not intend to be ordained and an increasing number of Roman Catholic laypersons in parish ministry, seminary education must become more attentive to what it means to equip all the saints for the ministry of God in the world. The ministry of care historically did not depend upon clerics, but too much of our theorizing and too many of our models still assume ordination. The wave of the future is toward more active lay participation in care.

Given the extensive interest of feminists in the intersection between ecology and feminism, we can expect to see more developments in this area in the coming years. As attention to our environment and its impact on the quality of our lives and on the fate of our planet becomes ever more pronounced, more attention to the relationship between ecology and the care of persons will emerge. Following the pioneering contributions of pastoral theologian Howard

Clinebell, we expect that many of our feminist and womanist colleagues will deepen and broaden reflection on the pastoral implications of our relationship to the natural world.

Feminist and womanist pastoral theologians are leaders in interdisciplinary work in building bridges, making portages, and seeing connections where others have missed them. Some of the most exciting work ahead no doubt lies in the field of interdisciplinary studies: anthropology and psychology, sociology and ethics, aesthetics and educational theory, public health and medicine, to name but a few. Such interdisciplinary work becomes critical for building the alliances and partnerships necessary to care adequately for persons in our world today.

Feminists and womanists long attentive to the dynamics of suffering caused by the hierarchical ordering of relationships are also critically aware of the healing power that results from overcoming the artificial and dehumanizing barriers we have placed between persons. Whereas we know much about the transformative power and integration that come from working with suffering, we need to explore in more depth the healing and transformative power of joy and celebration. In a world increasingly overwhelmed by the horror and travail of human evil and suffering, we need to remember that loving, just, free, and mutual relationships, so key to feminist and womanist pastoral theologians, are not only sustained and maintained when there are joy and celebration, they also bring us into new ways of living and caring for one another. Our hope is that this volume will be part of the bridge that opens a path for deepened conversation, collaboration, and meeting with academic and clinical colleagues, pastors, and members of congregations around these and other prominent issues in our discipline.

1

Three Decades of Women Writing for Our Lives

Kathleen J. Greider, Gloria A. Johnson,
and Kristen J. Leslie

In 1963, *Renewal* magazine printed an article by Peggy Ann Way entitled "What's Wrong with the Church—The Clergy," arguably the first published writing by a woman who identified herself as a pastoral theologian. In the thirty-five years following this benchmark, hundreds of women have contributed to the construction and renovation of pastoral theology, care, and counseling (PTC&C) through the literature of the discipline. This chapter plots the trajectory of women's published writings in PTC&C. The literature is too vast to be comprehensively analyzed or cited, however. A focused research question is required to facilitate an essay-length analysis.

After focusing in the middle years of this century on personal counseling as the preeminent means to the goals of pastoral care,[1] at the end of the twentieth century, a shift can be noted in the discipline: there has been considerable movement away from the tendency to see therapy as the definitive act of pastoral care toward formulating theory and practice in and responsive to corporate human experience in its variety of cultural contexts. Given widespread popular and scholarly assertions of the essential interrelatedness of persons and society and the value inherent in human plurality, it is generally agreed that communalization and contextualization are no longer optional in the theory and practice of effective PTC&C. One way to measure both the magnitude of this shift and the agreement about its occurrence is to note that two current introductory textbooks make a case for it: *Pastoral Care in Context: An Introduction to Pastoral Care* (Patton, 1993) and *An Introduction to Pastoral Care* (Gerkin, 1997). Both Patton and Gerkin postulate that the shift of attention to social context can be traced in part to the entry of women into public scholarly discussions previously limited to male perspectives.

This perceived connection yields our research question: In the latter third of the twentieth century, what specific contributions do women's published writings in PTC&C make to the discipline's engagement with communities and contexts? This chapter seeks to substantiate the association between women's published writings and the increasing attention being given to caring communities and the impact of context on human experience and on care or, in Patton's (1993) usefully compact phraseology, a "communal contextual paradigm" of pastoral care. Our thesis is that women's published writings in PTC&C have contributed precisely and significantly to the emergence of this communal contextual paradigm. Specifically, we document and discuss in roughly chronological order seven foci in women's publications (see table 1) that demonstrate a reaccentuation of community and context in PTC&C. In conclusion, we offer selected observations about the state of the discipline of PTC&C in light of these foci.

Table 1. Foci for a Communal Contextual Paradigm in PTC&C
1. *Ekklesia* and its ministry
2. Marginalized people and taboo topics
3. Female experience
4. Theological education
5. Soulfulness
6. Violence
7. Systems of care

Through these seven foci, women are and have been "writing for our lives"—for the survival and thriving of ourselves and other women, of collective human life—children, women, and men together—and of the creation as a whole.

To convey a flavor of the historical development of the literature, we suggest a loose chronology in the appearance of these themes in women's publications. Fundamentally, however, these themes are cumulative in at least four important ways. First, each theme, once introduced, continues and is nuanced in later literature. Second, none of the themes adequately characterize the communal contextual paradigm in women's publications if considered apart from the others. Third, while we are arguing for the significance of women's publications to the emergence of this paradigm and these themes, we are not arguing that they appear *only* in the writings or ministries of women; literature and ministries of women and of men are cumulatively giving rise to a communal contextual paradigm of pastoral care. Finally, having chosen to focus on publications, we are very mindful that this is an avenue of expression still available almost exclusively to persons of specific forms of privilege, notably race/ethnicity and education, and thus insufficiently representative of women's particularity. Without the cumulative effect of published and *unpublished writings*, of writing and *teaching*, of literature and *ministry*, of theory and *practice*, none of the themes identified here would have integrity or force.

Not long after proposing a literature analysis for this book, bibliographic research brought home to us how daunting and foolhardy a task we had set for ourselves. To clarify limitations within the immense literature under consideration, we set the following parameters. We have considered English language books and periodical articles written by women[2] and published in North America during the period 1963 to mid-1998 within the genre of PTC&C.[3] To stay within these parameters, we have limited our bibliographic research to the classifications of "pastoral theology," "pastoral care," and "pastoral counseling." However, these classifications sometimes took us into other disciplines in theology and religion studies (for example, ministry in general, psychology of religion, religious education, ethics) and to authors who might not identify themselves strictly or solely as pastoral theologians (for example, ethicist Toinette Eugene, theologian Susan Nelson, religious educator Anne Streaty Wimberly). Still, the immensity of our working bibliography (thirty-four single-spaced pages) and the limitations of space have required us to center our discussion on trends more than on specific publications or authors. Our goal in citation is to document the trends not exhaustively, but with one or two illustrative texts.

Considering only book-length publications by women pastoral theologians, the bibliography compiled for this literature analysis yields some heretofore unavailable statistics.[4] These statistics reveal enormous and abrupt growth. During the first seven years under consideration (1963–69), there were no book-length publications from women. In the 1970s, 5 books (3 authored, 2 edited) were published. In the 1980s, 25 books were published (19 authored, 6 edited). From 1990 to 1997, 69 books were published (55 authored, 14 edited). In total, during the full thirty-four-year period, 99 books were published (77 authored, 22 edited). Note the steep increase during the last 17 years. From the 1960s through the late 1970s, books by women pastoral theologians were few in number—the majority of the literature and its impact is in journal articles. In the 1980s, the number of published books more than tripled. In the most recent period, 1990-97, the number of published books again nearly tripled. Women were barely represented in the academy at the beginning of the period and, for the first 17 years of the period under consideration, were rarely the authors of book-length publications. During the last 17 years, still statistically underrepresented on faculties and among professionals in ministry, women scholars have contributed to PTC&C 94 book-length publications.

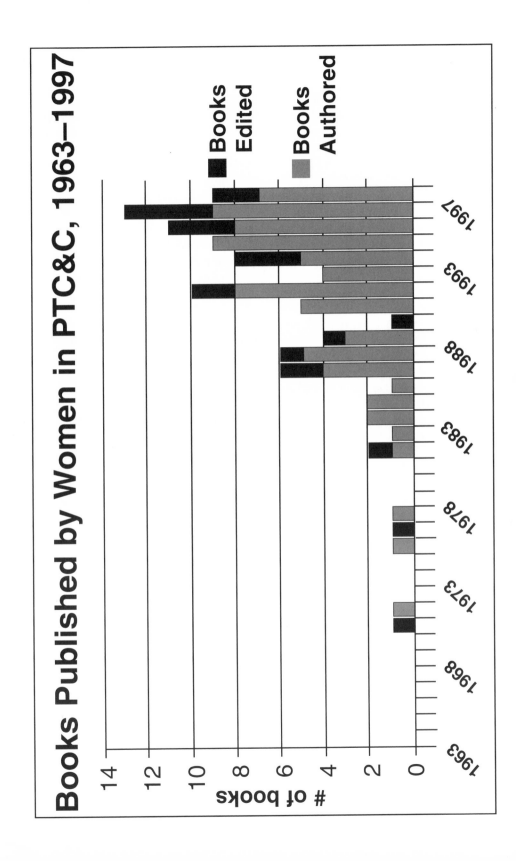

Books Published by Women in PTC&C, 1963–1997

Women's publications are all at once breathtakingly diverse and poignantly finite. The social, professional, and personal locations of the pastoral theologians surveyed, and of the chapter's authors, yield both foci and limits, both expertise and insularity. Such limits and foci affect this chapter in at least two ways. First, although it is not always possible to discern the particularities of identity among the women pastoral theologians surveyed, compared to the general population, they are disproportionately European American and professorial/academic. Of the 97 books published by women pastoral theologians, 6 are by African American women (4 authored books, 2 edited books, yielding 17 chapters), with several in press. There are no book-length publications from women of color other than African American. Second, the three authors of this chapter present only limited challenge to this lack of diversity. We are ordained Christian clergywomen representing two Protestant denominations; one African American and two European Americans of primarily Scottish and German descent; two Ph.D. students and one professor. Among us, we have thirty-seven years of experience as pastoral theologians and caregivers in the academy, parishes, hospital and college chaplaincies, and pastoral counseling.

We regret that not all authors or works can be cited here. Our initial dream was to be comprehensive, but the enormity of women's contributions and the limitations of space made that dream unrealizable. Since we can barely begin to represent women's contributions and particularities, we write circumspectly and offer our analysis not as a summation but as an initial report in an ongoing investigation. The seven themes we identify certainly do not preclude other themes and alternative summaries. Our words function here much as murals function artistically. For the sake of historical perspective, we offer these themes, events, and figures—like the images in a mural—as symbols of a narrative too large to be contained by any one canvas or chapter. Finally, however, we push beyond the daunting aspects of scope and diversity to the discipline of "painting" what we see, relinquishing reproduction and striving for representation.

Focus One: *Ekklesia* and Its Ministry

Given the caricature of women's liberation movements as self-interested and hypercritical of the church, readers might assume, as we did, that women in PTC&C writing for "our" lives first focused on concerns distinctive to females and heedless of the church. Our research proved that assumption incorrect. The first life for which women write—and the topic is never dropped—is the life of *ekklesia*, the biblically promised human community in God, infused with justice-love. (As we are using it here, *ekklesia* can and sometimes must be distinguished from *church:* the promise of *ekklesia* is not limited to either the strengths or the limitations of the institutional church.) Moreover, when women's publications do address gender issues in the church universal and local, their calls for reform seem motivated as much by care for *ekklesia* as by care for women. Not uncritical of the church, as other foci detail, still, women's publications in PTC&C are initially and continually motivated by *ekklesia*'s potential for effecting and transforming community.

One way women's publications address the focus of *ekklesia* and its ministry is through attention to the strength and strengthening of diverse forms of church. The first publication by a woman—Way's 1963 essay—illustrates early writings formulated around church renewal, a topic popular in the late 1960s and 1970s as the mid-century heyday of mainline Protestantism began to ebb. Not all of mainline Protestantism was declining, of course. Because worship in particular and congregational life in general have long been vital centers for most African American communities, the early contributions of Anne Streaty Wimberly (1979) and, later, other womanist theologians (Boyd, 1991a; Eugene, 1995b; Gilkes, 1980; Wiley, 1991) are exemplary reminders that *ekklesia* renews as much as it needs to be renewed. Women's publications also explore the much more culturally diverse "congregations" that exist or might be enabled beyond the walls of church buildings—*ekklesia* can be found, for example, in house churches (Niswander, 1976), hospitals (Glaz, 1995b), universities (Parks, 1993), hospices (DeMarinis, 1982), and prisons (Rayburn, 1993). A dozen essays explore the significance of authors' denominational or other Christian identities for PTC&C, and vice versa; given the Protestant leanings of the pastoral counseling movement, Roman Catholic women's contributions to this effort are especially noteworthy (Karaban, 1993; McCarthy, 1990b).

Another way women's publications have attended to *ekklesia* and its ministry is by making available women ministers' wide range of expertise in pastoral caregiving. Many of the first women published in PTC&C were employed in parish ministry, and in each of the three decades under consideration, edited volumes have made available experience-honed theory and practice of women working in local church ministry, chaplaincy, pastoral counseling centers, and denominational work (Doely, 1970; Hollies, 1991; Neuger, 1996; Weidman, 1981). Commitment to excellence in ministry is the thread that links an enormous group of otherwise disparate publications that offer theory and practice for effective pastoral care in myriad situations of existential human suffering, notably: conflict and communication amid human diversity; grief and loss; illness and hospitalization; violence and trauma; dying and death. Excellence in ministry, this literature makes clear, also depends upon ethics in the use of power, a subject to which we return below.

One additional way in which women's publications address this focus is by seeking to identify and claim the unique values and contributions of *ekklesia* and ministry, in and beyond the church. As most of Way's essays argue, there is an inimitable "ecclesial contribution" (1983), and ministry is not mere ecclesiological method but "source" (1975). Of what is ministry the source? Pastoral caregivers and other ministers have access to rare and invaluable data, Way (1975) argues, because they work in and with a *community* through all the "intersections" of human existence: the ordinary and the ecstatic, birth and death, celebration and pain, public and private, past and future. Ultimately, clergy and pastoral theologians ought to claim ministry as source of conceptual contributions crucial to understanding and caring for the human community and not otherwise available. What is the ecclesial contribution? In a world simultaneously overwhelmed by and captive to human ingenuity, *ekklesia* and its ministry point beyond themselves to ultimate possibility, to a source of hope and life not limited to or swamped by the human (Way, 1970a, 1972, 1981). On this basis, *ekklesia* and its ministry contribute the possibility of social and personal *metanoia*, not mere reform or health but transformation (Graham, 1996). *Ekklesia* and its ministry are a laboratory for studying the problems and potentials in human diversity. For example, one ecclesial contribution consists of the church's experiments (whether failed or successful) in community-building instead of community-destroying discourse amid moral and cultural plurality (Way, 1983). *Ekklesia* and its ministry contribute to society the ideal of universal service (Glaz, 1991; Ulanov, 1972), such as care for the poor and the wealthy alike. At the thresholds of life—birth, tragedy, death—*ekklesia* and its ministry contribute ritual and other symbolic forms when words and technology are inadequate (Ramshaw, 1987). *Ekklesia* and its ministry contribute enthusiasm for the possibilities of the "second rate" (Way, 1975)—ordinary people, places, and plans deemed insignificant in modernity's cult of stardom. *Ekklesia* and its ministry contribute the ideal of covenant: accountability both to the common good and to personal needs (Glaz, 1991; Ramsay, 1991b). To nagging questions about whether the church has anything valuable to offer modern people, to nagging questions about whether there is anything distinctive about *pastoral* theology, care, and counseling, women scholars offer these substantive, affirmative answers.

The primary contribution of a focus on *ekklesia* and its ministry to a communal contextual paradigm of PTC&C is that it reminds us that, for better as well as for worse, the identifying community and context for Christians is the church. This focus reminds Christian caregivers not to abandon the potentiality of *ekklesia* and its ministry as a crucial community and context for care, despite the failures of specific churches, congregations, and pastors. This focus yields irrefutable evidence that the church often challenges but rarely obliterates human hope for the community of *ekklesia*. Women write for the life of the church not because that is an end in itself but because the authors are convinced that *ekklesia* and its ministry point beyond themselves to something of greater and ultimate value to humankind, and thus have the potential for playing a role in sweeping positive transformation. In fact, for some, *ekklesia* is not at all an unrealizable ideal but is regularly embodied in the unoppressive and caring ministries of specific congregations. Our ministries with people in pain—pain not infrequently occasioned by church life—tend to attune us to the church's limitations, but this literature reminds us to study and write about religious communities where *ekklesia* is not merely an ideal but is being realized. These authors are not easily fooled by romantic notions of the church, but neither are they easily distracted from advancing *ekklesia*'s power to save our personal and corporate lives.

Focus Two: Marginalized People and Taboo Topics

The second focus we see emerging in women's publications is on the marginalized people and taboo topics that, despite *ekklesia*'s and ministry's ideals of inclusivity, hover at the edges of the church. Perhaps this focus is unsurprising, since women have themselves been marginalized in the church and elsewhere, and since women have not merely symbolized the taboo but have themselves *been* taboo. There are breaches in this focus, as detailed below. However, women publishing in PTC&C tend to advocate for groups marginalized for reasons in addition to or other than sex.

Literature written during the 1960s and 1970s by Way (1964, 1968, 1970b, 1977), Wimberly (1979), and Emma Justes (1971) attends to plurality in, and power distribution according to, gender, race, class, sexual orientation, and age. This consciousness in early writings of the politics of diversity is partly attributable to the personal commitments of these three women. It also mirrors the pulse-like emergence of liberation movements in that historical period—the civil rights/black power, women's liberation, gay liberation, and "gray" liberation movements—and the increase in government-funded financial assistance programs for the poor. Using a depth psychological approach in concert with theological analysis, Ann Belford Ulanov offers an analysis in some of her earliest writings (1973a, 1973b) of the "internal" politics of plurality. Human resistance to ambiguity causes the creation of psychosocial categories of "self" and "other" that are then used exclusivistically as a way of managing existential complexity. Humans construct "otherness" from aspects of both intrapsychic and interpersonal reality experienced as threatening and thus taboo. The requirements of humaneness are that persons treat both self and others as subjects. Instead, humans often inhumanely objectify "internal" and "external" otherness and not only fail to treat otherness compassionately but also seek to obliterate it (see also Bohler, 1994; Gill-Austern, 1997b).

During the 1980s and early 1990s, attention in women's writings to margins and taboos narrows and focuses almost exclusively on sex and gender. The works published in this period are written predominantly by white, well-educated, middle-class women, who have the boldness to break silence about age-old taboos, for example, about female bodily functions and violence against women and children. Numerous substantial works exploring women's experience and/or utilizing gender analysis appear and are widely used (for example, Brown and Bohn, 1989; Clarke, 1986; Conn, 1986; Ellen, 1990; Fortune, 1983, 1987a; Garrison and Justes, 1990; Glaz and Stevenson-Moessner, 1991; Justes, 1993, originally published in 1985; Ulanov, 1981; Weidman, 1981). However, though there are exceptions (Justes, 1993), works so bold about sexism are nearly silent about margins and taboos other than gender and about the interlocking oppressions suffered by many women. Curiously, the white women publishing in this period can see the error in males generalizing male experience to women but then make a similar error by generalizing white women's experience to all other females. This trend in the publications of women in PTC&C also mirrors a broader phenomenon: as the women's liberation movement grew, feminist literature in the United States shifted almost exclusively to universalized gender analysis. Early in the 1980s, significant works were published showing interconnections between race, class, and gender issues (for example, Davis, 1981; hooks, 1981; Walker, 1983), making the absence of racial and class analysis from women's writings in feminist theory and PTC&C especially notable. In PTC&C, at least two primary dynamics are at work. On the one hand, because all but a tiny minority of women being published in this period are white, well-educated, middle-class women, they focus on sexism because issues of racism, classism, heterosexism, and ageism do not appear to be immediate threats to them. On the other hand, they focus on sexism because it does pose a real and immediate threat to every woman's full participation in the church and academy.

Since the early 1990s, not only has attention to marginalized people and taboo topics again widened, but the literature is growing in size and complexity. It is difficult to know whether the appearance of these essays and books is anything more than coincidence, but taken together, they mark the emergence of efforts toward more systemic power analyses. One segment of the literature utilizes gender analysis primarily, but now addresses women's cultural diversity more directly (Stevenson-Moessner, 1996; Saussy, 1991; Winter, Lummis, & Stokes, 1994). The *Journal of Pastoral Care* (*JPC*) contributed to this turning point: Christie Cozad Neuger and Pamela J. Holliman (1991) edited a theme issue on "collegiality," with articles that utilize—sometimes in combination—racial, class, and gender analysis (for women's contributions to this issue of *JPC*, see Orr; Robinson & Needham; Wiley).

Also in the early 1990s, more African American women's writings appeared in the literature of PTC&C, in large measure due to the publication of *WomanistCare* (Hollies, 1991) by Woman to Woman Ministries, Inc., a programming venture for and by African American women. Building on the method of tripartite analysis being developed in womanist theology, womanist caregivers began publishing theory and practice for "womanistcare," "the intentional process of care giving and care receiving by African American women" (Boyd, 1997, 198). The centrality to womanistcare of reaching beyond margins and taboos is suggested by Daniels's (1991) description of a womanist caregiver: she "embraces the sisterhood, *making her world bigger,*" accepts "the challenge to participate in *enlarging the world* of the recipients of her caregiving," and "most importantly," "must also *enlarge her own inner world,* finding it to be carved in God's loving grace" (p. 101, emphasis added). Womanist PTC&C is also developed by Marsha Foster Boyd (1991a, 1997), Linda Hollies (1992, 1997), Carolyn McCrary (1991), and Christine Wiley (1991, 1995). Brenda Ruiz (1994), the only other woman of color published in PTC&C of which we are aware, directs our attention to an even more distant margin: women suffering intense political oppression.

Concurrent with the emergence into the literature of womanistcare, a cluster of publications appeared in the early 1990s that for the first time articulated the qualities of feminist PTC&C (DeMarinis, 1993; Doehring, 1992; Filippi, 1991; Neuger, 1992, 1993, 1994, 1996; Ramsay, 1992a; Unterberger, 1992). Several arguments are recurrently developed in discussions of feminist method in pastoral care: establishing women's experience as foundational and authoritative for research and practice; illuminating the interlocking nature of oppressions; identifying cultural perspectives and assumptions; rethinking ethical issues in light of power dynamics in interpersonal and social relationships; reformulating the meaning of well-being and maturity in light of the above. Recent feminist publications attempt tripartite analysis (Doehring, 1995; Greider, 1997; Pfäfflin, 1995). Feminism in the 1990s in PTC&C is also making way for an increase in the literature by and about lesbian, gay, and bisexual persons, as well as about homophobia (Gelo, 1997; Hochstein, 1986, 1996; Marcellino, 1997; Marshall, 1994a, 1995a, 1996, 1997; Tigert, 1996; Unterberger, 1993).

This movement in the 1990s toward more systemic power analysis in women's publications in PTC&C has one other major element: systemic analysis of power dynamics in ministry. At first, this discussion was largely secondary to the revelation in the 1980s of pastoral sexual misconduct and the need to detail pastoral sexual ethics (Cooper-White, 1991; Fortune, 1987a). Later, the focus of power analysis in ministry widened significantly, addressing construction of pastoral ethics in light of a variety of power differentials, for example, pastors' legal liability and vulnerability (Bullis & Mazur, 1993); black women's traditions and standards of care (Eugene, 1989); power differentials and boundary issues in professional relationships (Brenneis, 1998; Cooper-White et al., 1994; Doehring, 1995; Fortune, 1994; Heyward, 1993; Ragsdale, 1996). Doehring (1995) presents arguably the most systemic analysis of power dynamics in ministry. Significantly, at least two critiques emerge in women's writings of the venerated metaphor for ministry of the "wounded healer" (Nouwen, 1972), both having to do with power and ethics in ministry. One suggests that this metaphor contributes to systemic failure to intervene in the ministries of pastors too wounded to exercise responsibly the power inherent in the office (Glaz, 1995a). Another categorically rejects the metaphor for healers in marginalized communities because dwelling on their woundedness only perpetuates their social disempowerment and discounts their strength (Boyd, 1997).

Having noted major omissions, women's engagement in their writings with margins and taboos over the last thirty-five years is still remarkable. In addition to the clusters of literature we have discussed, many other voices reach toward marginalized people and taboo topics: adolescent girls (Davis, 1996); aging (Saussy, 1998a; A. Wimberly, 1979, 1997; A. & E. Wimberly, 1995b); clergy divorce and remarriage (Brown, 1982); disability (Rixford, 1997); dying (Miller-McLemore, 1988; Ulanov, 1994); sexual desire and expression (Bohler, 1991; Doehring, 1994; Eugene, 1994b; Ulanov & Ulanov, 1994a; Wimberly, 1994); the under- and unemployed (Nelson & McWhirter, 1995); the working class (Orr, 1991, 1997). There is attention to taboo illnesses such as AIDS (Eugene, 1997), depression (Dunlap, 1997; Neuger, 1993), and eating disorders (Dasher, 1996). There is attention to taboo pain such as infertility (Devor, 1994), stillbirth (Ramshaw, 1988), and miscarriage (Dean & Cullen, 1991). There is attention to the taboo of obliterated happiness, caused by intense political oppression (Ruiz, 1994). Incredibly, given the controversial claim of some men in the 1990s that they experience reverse discrimination, perhaps *The Care of Men* (Neuger & Poling, 1997) also falls into this category of literature. Taboo religious experience is addressed infrequently, though there is a controversial feminist revision of the 12-step program (Unterberger, 1989) and mention of experience of the goddess (Saussy, 1988a).

Attention to marginalized people and taboo topics is beneficial to a communal contextual paradigm in PTC&C when undertaken not for the sake of relevance or scandal but for the sake of God, for the sake of increasing engagement with the sacred immensity and plurality of the world entrusted to human beings. Attention to margins and taboos decenters dominant paradigms, reveals differentials in and misuse of social power, and thus enables prompt response where justice ministries are urgently needed. Attention to margins and taboos increases astronomically (though in itself never guarantees) the possibility that inclusivity will be not just an ideal but an actuality. Attention to margins and taboos increases both our capacity to know the universe to which we are called to offer universality of care and the possibility that our care can reflect and attend effectively to the plurality within and beyond *ekklesia*. Attention to *emerging* margins and taboos makes room for fresh winds of the Spirit to blow through our discipline, theological education, and the church. (For example, more attention to the academically taboo subjects of humor, play, and joy would be refreshing, indeed.) Broaching taboos and encountering marginalized people present an opportunity to gain access to our own otherness, to our disowned parts living on the underside of our conscious positions, and to negative and positive aspects of the power therein. Attention to the ever-recurring margins and taboos also keeps us mindful that they *do* recur: they are not simply overthrown by personal will, communal resolve, or public policy.

Focus Three: Female Experience

In the development of a communal contextual paradigm of pastoral care, the most clearly distinctive contributions of women writing pastoral theology stem from decades of painstaking work specifying "communities" and "contexts" from female perspectives. Though not the first focus to appear in women's writings, telling and analyzing stories of female lives is an early theme intended to enrich *ekklesia* and inform ministry.

A major stream of women's literature wrestles with what it means to be female. As the reality and the extent of sexism and misogyny are again underscored by the second wave of the women's liberation movement, Way and Justes are pioneers in PTC&C, first calling attention to women's condition as taboo objects in Christian theology and as people marginalized in church communities by demeaning sex roles (Justes, 1971, 1978; Way, 1964, 1970a, 1970b, 1972). Women are not for long simply reactive to patriarchy, however: soon they are deeply engaged in the challenge of articulating the distinctiveness of their own experience, so long absent from published scholarly literature. Many women find help for this task in Carl Gustav Jung's concept of the feminine, and Ann Belford Ulanov's extensive publications on sexuality, gender, and female/male relations (for example, 1971, 1981; Ulanov & Ulanov, 1987, 1994; see also Barnhouse & Holmes, 1976) demonstrate how Jung's descriptions of the feminine and the masculine as inherent polarities in the psyche help some women articulate values in being female. Later, as feminist theory in psychology and other disciplines appears, women in PTC&C are assisted in this task: now there is evidence to argue that the meaning of female and male is to a significant degree constructed—in religious and other social institutions—through socialization to rigid sex roles. Wehr (1987) argues that this social dynamic is precisely the origin of Jung's categories of anima (feminine) and animus (masculine). Following the example of Justes (1979, 1993), still other women leave the debate about whether "female" is natural or nurtured to the side and focus on the urgent need of providing guidance to pastors for the care and counseling of girls and women. Between 1991 and 1996, in addition to many articles, no less than six books were published that offer to PTC&C broad frameworks for practice based on female experience (Bons-Storm, 1996a; DeMarinis, 1993; Glaz & Stevenson-Moessner, 1991; Graham & Halsey, 1993; Hollies, 1991; Stevenson-Moessner, 1996). Recent literature suggests that both nature and nurture are seen to play a role in the meaning of "female": a distinction is made between "sex"—biological givens—and "gender"—"socially learned differences" between male and female (Miller-McLemore & Anderson, 1995, 101).

Indeed, the biological givens of being female constitute the anchoring point for another major thread of discussion in women's publications in PTC&C: the significance of embodiment in human experience. Much pain and rage reverberate in literature that details how women's bodies have been sexualized, racialized, and commercialized (Eugene, 1996). Female bodily processes—previously taboo—do not define women, but they do inspire. Women put into print reflections on how their "unmentionable" bodily experiences—menstruation, pregnancy, lactation, and other gynecological processes—complexify women's ways of knowing and parallel ways in which embodiment shapes (and is shaped by) all human knowing (Dean & Cullen, 1991; Kendrick, 1994; Miller-McLemore, 1992). The capacity of females to conceive and give birth to new life inspires literature on motherhood (Miller-McLemore, 1994), mothercare (Lewin, 1993), motherloss (Robbins, 1990, 1996), the motherhood of God as an image of care (Meeks, 1980), mothers and daughters (Wise, 1991), African American matriarchs (Snorton, 1996), ministry as birthing (Hammer, 1994), and other forms of generativity (Miller-McLemore, 1991a). The impact of illnesses and treatments on women's bodies is given tender attention, as in essays on breast cancer (Hoke, 1997; Johnson & Spilka, 1991), mastectomy (Henderson, 1996), and hysterectomy (Estock, 1996).

Another prominent theme in women's writings on female experience is the primacy of relationality as a primary mode of being and doing. Focus 6 gives attention to women's writings on violence in relationship; here we are referencing the significant amount of literature that attests to relationality's inevitability and growth-enhancing qualities. Building on developments in object relation theories, the literature argues that the normal relational dynamics of projection and introjection fundamentally constitute and connect self and others, not only psychologically but spiritually (Ulanov, 1973a, 1973b). Interdependence is the norm for health: utilizing self-in-relation theory even before it is widely published, the self is described as interdependent (Huff, 1987). With African metaphysics as an additional intellectual resource, womanist authors in PTC&C show how communal and not only familial interdependence births the self-in-relation (Boyd, 1991a; McCrary, 1991, 1998; Wiley, 1991). Mature relationality flowers into partnership (Kirkland-Harris, 1998; Marshall, 1997). Because they can serve as the bedrock of healthy interdependence, the values and requirements of mutuality and empathy are often explored (for example, McCarthy, 1992a, 1993; Saussy, 1988b). A number of essays provocatively broach taboo emotions sometimes spawned by personal and social relational dynamics: the "burden of empathy" (Davis, 1993); the "tyranny of intimacy" (Couture, 1992); the "idolatry of family" (Fishburn, 1991); the "dilemma" of work and family (Miller-McLemore, 1994); the "dangers" of self-sacrificial and self-denying (as contrasted with self-giving) Christian love (Gill-Austern, 1996). Here women acknowledge relationality's capacity to overwhelm and offer help with setting some limits.

Finally, women's writings in PTC&C cluster around concern for women's wholeness and care. Cultivation of love and respect for a woman's self and communities is a recurrent theme and is often linked to empowerment (Doehring,

1992; Saussy, 1991; Wiley, 1991). Narrative method is commonly employed in care for and by women (A. Wimberly, 1994; Wimberly & Wimberly, 1998): For example, in womanistcare, storytelling is a defining means of empowerment (Hollies, 1991). In some contrast, concern with women's silences is a recurrent issue in writings by white women (for example, Bons-Storm, 1996a), and Nelle Morton's (1985) notion of "hearing into speech" is frequently referenced as a helpful way to frame listening when caring for women. The female soul often needs lessons in better stewardship of self-giving and care. Gill-Austern reminds us that many women suffer from overaccessibility and being misused as "hurtsoothers" (1981, 91) because they are preoccupied with whether or not they are *giving* enough care to others: pastors may need to bring an uncommon but counterbalancing question to their care of females—are females *getting* enough care (1996)?

Arguably, the most intimate and transformative aspects of wholeness and care for women can be found in literature that addresses women's spirituality: its development (Conn, 1986); care of women's spiritual lives (Liebert, 1996); new rituals, especially for women who have been abused (for example, Keene, 1991); and the spirituality of "religious feminists" (Halligan, 1990; Winter et al., 1994). For women who are religious professionals, spirituality for ministry is a recurrent theme, especially how agency and authority can be exercised in ways that are nondominating and still powerful. The literature shows particular depth in its offering of alternative models and metaphors for ministry, for example: reliance on possibility more than on precedent (Way, 1970a, 1972); instead of wounded healers, being "empowered cojourners" (Boyd, 1997); the integrity that results when a minister is differentiated and connected *at the same time* (Bohler, 1990a, building on Friedman, 1985); presence as power (Gill-Austern, 1981); "Samaritans" offering "journey mercies" to one another (Stevenson-Moessner, 1996); mutuality in ministry (Saussy, 1988b); mutual caregiving between ministers (Daniels, 1991; Troxell, 1993); midwifery (Billman, 1992; Hanson, 1996).

This literature and focus contributes to a communal contextual paradigm in PTC&C quite obviously. It begins to fill an enormous gap in the literature of the discipline by contributing perspectives of and on girls and women. As long as women continue to do the majority of housework and rearing of children, women's perspectives will help to keep PTC&C theory and practice grounded in and tested by concreteness of the body, practicalities of day-to-day life, and interconnectedness at home and with communities. After so many centuries during which women have been ignored or denigrated by research and writing, it has been appropriate that most publications have sought to redress this imbalance with attention to women's strengths and positive contributions. As our analysis has noted, publications are showing a slight movement toward a less protective form of reflection; continuing research that helps girls and women uncover values or behaviors that impede their contributions to the common good and/or their personal development will be valuable for the well-being of all people. (For example, though it has been appropriate that violence *against* women and girls receive our earliest intervention, study of physical and emotional violences *in and among* females will yield critical PTC&C guidance in an area of psychospiritual and social life that has been marginalized, if not taboo.) We hope that the publications analyzing the intersection between gender and other aspects of women's cultural particularity and oppression will catalyze more such contributions in PTC&C from or about underrepresented women and girls.

Finally, a high level of concern with the equitable distribution of power and a reservoir of images and metaphors for the collaborative use of power are obviously core issues in a communal contextual paradigm and distinguishing marks of this literature's contribution to its emergence. The capacity to be powerful even when subjugated, the power to create life in many forms, the power to confess women's co-optation in the misuse of power, the commitment to intervene in power used for violence—these aspects of power are imperfectly but inevitably central in PTC&C literature exploring female experience.

Focus Four: Theological Education

Since education has long been considered women's work, we should have anticipated the quantity of women's publications that focus on theological education and the interconnectedness of care and education. We address literature attending to this focus under two themes: theological education as a form of pastoral ministry and the state of the discipline of pastoral theology.

The published literature is but a glimpse of the amount women do to facilitate the work of others through editing, supervising, teaching, and mentoring. Our perusal of journals published in PTC&C made clear that even in the years when women's articles comprised only a minority of those published, more than a few women were editing and shepherding into publication the work of other scholars—Sandra Brown and Carolyn Bohler are just two examples. Throughout the years under consideration, women serve as journal editors and coeditors, as members of editorial committees, and as editors of special editions and symposia. In regard to the educational ministry of teaching, women put their syllabi into print (Eugene, 1993a), publish reflections on pedagogy in theological education (Marshall, 1996), and take the time to write (often collaboratively) on the strengths and pitfalls of specific courses and programs in theological education (Miller-McLemore & Myers, 1989). Parks (1982) observes that educators are for their students both teachers and spiritual examples and then makes the provocative suggestion that professors ought to be more conscious of and intentional about their (unavoidable) role as exemplars and spiritual leaders (for a publication in this spirit, see Meadow & Rayburn, 1985). A plethora of women's writings not specifically addressed to education give at least some attention to educational implications of their topic (one of many examples is Billman, 1992).

Another segment of literature, set in motion in the late sixties by Sue Webb Cardwell, searches out the factors that heighten the quality of theological education and the success of seminary graduates (Cardwell, 1967, 1974, 1982, 1996; Glover-Wetherington, 1996; women's contributions in Hunt, Hinkle, Jr., & Malony, 1990). Most of these publications either directly or indirectly convey the necessity for theological theory and ideals "to be of use" (Eugene, 1992): accordingly, women's literature "shatters the self-evidents" (Way, 1970c) about "field education." Praxis-based learning is crucial not only to the professional training of ministers but also to the integrity of contemporary theologies that rest more and more on particularity and liberation, and to the preparation of Ph.D. students for teaching. Moreover, praxis-based learning is one crucial element in adequate responses to growing global complexity (Parks, 1987) and the consequent globalization of theological education (Eugene, 1993a). The value to educators as well as to students of "praxis-based education for transformation" comes alive in Barbour et al. (1994). In the discipline of PTC&C, authors call for praxis-based learning that is complex: it ought to have "theological rigor" (Glaz, 1991) and shape in ministers a clinical identity that has "pastoral soul" (Marshall, 1994b). Other approaches to the issue of the integration of theology and social sciences in pastoral care ministry and its supervision are found in Justes (1982), Ramsay (1991b), Billman (1992), and Haight (1995).

By far the largest amount of literature by women within the focus of theological education addresses the educational ministry of clinical supervision. Exemplary contributions from some of these—Rachel Callahan, Sharon Cheston, Pam Couture, Sue Webb Cardwell, Lucille Sider Groh, Emily Haight, Lucy Malarkey, Rea McDonnell, Bonnie Niswander, Lallene Rector—can be found in Estadt, Compton, and Blanchette (1987) and McHolland (1993). The *Journal of Supervision in Ministry and Training* has published a significant number of women as a result of its commitment to put into print clinical case reflections and theory papers written by persons certified as supervisors in the Association for Clinical Pastoral Education and the American Association of Pastoral Counselors (for example: Clift, 1988; Niswander, 1987; McCarthy, 1992b). The literature on clinical supervision frequently addresses issues of gender (for example: Jewett & Haight, 1983; VandeCreek & Glockner, 1993), but rarely explores how other dynamics in social marginalization are affecting supervision (an exception is Robinson & Needham, 1991). Most recently, less structured teaching through mentoring has received attention (Barbour et al., 1994; Holliman, 1996; Parks, 1990).

A second theme threaded throughout women's literature on theological education is concern for the state of the discipline of pastoral theology, in terms both of its relations to other disciplines in theology and of its internal coherence (Miller-McLemore, 1993). The literature implies that theological education as a whole must itself form a context and model community in order to shape religious leaders who can effectively minister out of communal contextual paradigms. Yet there is a stark lack in theology and ministry of what Stevenson-Moessner (1996b) calls "organicity"—theological disciplines and forms of ministry functioning in organic relationship with each other. Moreover, this literature can be accused of clericalism: it focuses on graduate theological education and leaves underdeveloped methods that might engage laypersons from various communities and contexts in the building of theologies (Stevenson-Moessner, 1996b). If acknowledging and building a social ecology are part of a communal contextual paradigm, then creation of and care for a social ecology within theological education as a whole must continue and be a priority.

But concern for the discipline is more often expressed through "in-house" issues. While clearer disciplinary boundaries would help, we think greater clarity about core identity must be preliminary to the setting of boundaries. Some women authors muse about just that topic: the discipline's core identity. Numerous references in women's writings to Hough and Cobb (1985) suggest that the discipline's relationship to practical theology is a widely significant reference point, though its meaning is scarcely detailed. There is some consensus in the literature that the intrinsic identity of pastoral caregivers and theologians is in the provision of ethical and moral leadership (Gill-Austern, 1981; Graham, 1996). But this is a confounding affirmation in light of the inferiority complex that seems to dog pastoral theologians, pastoral caregivers, and pastoral counselors.

Way (1975) traces this negative identity in PTC&C to dynamics alive in the theological academy. Imitating old hierarchies in philosophy between the abstract and the particular, "classical" theological disciplines (biblical studies, history, theology) are thought (still!) to have more fundamental importance than the "arts" of ministry (pastoral theology and care, religious education, homiletics and worship, administration, mission). The pastoral care and counseling movement worsened this dynamic, Way argues, by its deference to psychology. Consequently, pastoral theologians in particular and clergy in general, caught in these dynamics, do not know the value of ministry and instead suffer from "double derivative identities"—they borrow identities from theology and psychology and feel inferior to both. (Women pastoral theologians and clergy have triple derivative identities, she says: they derive their identities from theology, from psychology, and from men.) Righting of this imbalance will not occur as long as professionals in PTC&C defer either to theology—whose work can proceed "without the inhibiting presence of real people with real histories to affect the formulations" (Way, 1976, 264) or to the social sciences—disciplines that "practice with real people but in quite different structures than our own" (Miller-McLemore, 1993) and, we must add, usually dodge ultimate questions.

How might professionalism help PTC&C step out of these deferential dynamics? Way (1976) calls for a shift of center in PTC&C, from a clinical/therapeutic paradigm and its contributions to an ecclesial paradigm (Way, 1980), and identifies pastoral theologians' and caregivers' "intrinsic" identity as "the practice of ministry." In continued focus on *ekklesia* and its ministry, the scattered professionals of PTC&C might find a community and context to which to come home, and thus address another stated concern: fragmentation between subspecialties in PTC&C. The discipline's capacity and authority to teach and practice a communal contextual paradigm will be seriously impeded until we are able, as a discipline, to identify our primary contexts and function as a community.

Another possibility for healing the fractures in PTC&C identity and community is discussion of method. Greater attention to the formulation of shared conceptual frameworks in regard to method have long been a staple of identity and community in other disciplines. Discussion of method in PTC&C (Greer, 1993) suggests it might well help center and organize the discipline of PTC&C as well. The complex methodological problems of relating psychology, religion, and theology, and of relating therapy and ministry, are an ongoing disciplinary project (Goldenberg, 1990, 1994; Hunsinger, 1997; Randour, 1993; Stokes, 1985). That other social sciences are as valuable as psychology to a communal contextual paradigm of care (Couture, 1991; Couture & Hunter, 1995) only increases the urgency and intensity of the discipline's need for discussion of method. Also, attention to method could facilitate more collaborative and strategic identification of research priorities and create more community out of PTC&C's scattered guilds, practitioners, and areas of responsibility.

What are the contributions of this literature and focus to the emergence of a communal contextual paradigm in PTC&C? In and through theological education, the values of the paradigm can be refined, nurtured, and passed on to another generation of scholar-caregivers. Learning amid practice forces the building of bridges over the gaps between abstract theory and concrete practices, between gospel ideals and human capacities, between classical theological categories and the pressures of life in postmodernity—all essential in a communal contextual approach to care. But more than the others, this literature and focus is disquieting. Lack of clarity about core identity and boundaries—feeling responsible for everything and for nothing—warns of possible weakness at the foundation of the communal contextual paradigm.

Focus Five: Soulfulness

It is fairly common to hear accusations that PTC&C—the discipline, its literature, most practitioners—has lost touch with its theological identity, has "sold out" to psychology. The truth in these allegations would seem to be proven by the fact that professionals in the discipline can be heard directing such accusations at themselves. If one reads PTC&C literature written by women during the past thirty-five years, however, these charges are hard to fathom. Indeed, the sheer quantity and breadth of publications that address the intersections of spirituality, religious experience, and theology from the perspectives of pastoral care and counseling make this literature especially difficult to characterize.[5] Yes, the theological anthropology produced in PTC&C is hardly systematic. It is also true that in this discipline, theological reflection and practice are *never* ends in themselves, so much so that the *theology* in "theological anthropology" often seems to disappear behind the *anthropos*. This seems right to us, however, since *anthropos* and its relatedness to God are precisely the special responsibility of PTC&C. Thus, to signal our assessment that the discipline utilizes theological methods and categories to the extent that they are adequate to the needs of human souls searching—personally and collectively—for God, we have settled on the rubric of "soulfulness" for this focus in women's publications.

One theme of women's writings on soulfulness can be described as attending to the human search for God in institutional religion. In this literature we find persons and communities of faith receiving care for the pain caused them by religious institutions (Hopkins & Laaser, 1995; Marshall, 1995b; Tigert, 1996). Here we find pastoral theologians wrestling to identify interpretations of biblical texts that give life to human relatedness to God and interpretations that are life-denying (Alter, 1994; Stevenson-Moessner, 1991, 1996a; Saussy, 1995). Christian ritual is shown to be a form of pastoral care for individuals, communities, and worlds (Keene, 1991; Ramshaw, 1987). Even in the heady world of organized religion, the role of embodiment does not escape women's attention: liturgical dance communicates through the body a system of personal and social values (DeMarinis, 1990). Guidance for the soul's search for God is mined from stories of the faithful, such as Howard Thurman (Justes, 1983; McCrary, 1991), Etty Hillesum (Liebert, 1995), and Saint Thérèse (Ulanov, 1990).

Literature addressing soulfulness is even richer in reflections on aspects of the soul's search for God not bounded by institutional religion. The literature is deep in publications that bring theological, religious studies, and psychological methods into dialogue to explore the mystery of relationship between soul and psyche. Ann Belford Ulanov's publications, some cowritten with Barry Ulanov, have been groundbreaking in this regard; *Religion and the Unconscious* (Ulanov & Ulanov, 1975) was the first of many studies by Ulanov that all at once disclose and preserve the tantalizing mysteries of "primordial experience" (Ulanov, 1986, 1988). Naomi Goldenberg (1979, 1990) has provided leadership in the crafting of feminist depth psychological readings of religious experience. For the purposes of this analysis, one of the most important assertions in depth psychological readings of soulfulness is that making or allowing separations between the personal and the social dimensions of human experience is not merely mistaken but dangerous. Without attention to the natural interplay between individual and collective psychospiritual dynamics, an extrapolation of the natural interplay between conscious and unconscious process, human soulfulness is at least impaired and at worst corrupted. (Using different methods, Wimberly and Wimberly [1986] also show this interrelatedness of personal and social aspects of religious experience.) Jungian frameworks are used with frequency in (white) women's writings on soulfulness (in addition to the primarily Jungian orientation of Ulanov, see J. D. Clift, 1992). The resources for soulfulness in African culture, the African Diaspora, and the resistance of slavery as developed in womanist theology (Townes, 1993, 1997) are repeatedly referenced in womanistcare.

Women's literature addresses soulfulness by trying to make sense of the coexistence of love and oppression: as Marsha Foster Boyd (1991b) puts it, "How could a God who loves me allow me to be treated this way?" Other publications seek to soothe what Ulanov (1975) has identified as "the Christian fear of the psyche"—the tendency in Christian communities to avoid, deny, contain, and otherwise control the ambiguity of reality and the tempests of human experience. Guides are provided for fashioning meaning amid the anxiety of life in modernity (Robbins, 1997), for enlivening personal and corporate prayer (Bohler, 1977, 1990b; Ulanov & Ulanov, 1982), for understanding dreams (Clift & Clift, 1984), for developing a "faith to live by" (Parks, 1986a; see also Dykstra & Parks, 1986; Liebert, 1992), and for navigating the ins and outs of envy (Ulanov & Ulanov, 1983), anger (Saussy, 1995), and aggression (Greider, 1997). Of all the classical theological doctrines, sin is the doctrine most often reworked by women in PTC&C (for example: Billman, 1991; Bringle, 1990; Nelson, 1982, 1997; Ramsay, 1995). Certainly, this is attributable in part to the effect on all women in theology of Saiving's (1960) stunning insight into the gendered nature of traditional doctrines of sin. A cluster of literature explores ethical values and issues in religious contexts: in models of clinical supervision (McCarthy, 1990a); from the perspectives of womanists (Eugene, 1989, 1993a, 1993c); in modern medicine (Miller-McLemore, 1991a, 1991b) and public policy (Couture, 1995b); death and dying (Miller-McLemore, 1988; Wimberly, 1992); and sexual and professional ethics (Fortune, 1995). Efforts to describe qualities of the soul's wholeness comprise another important theme in this literature, for example: liberation and wholeness (Wimberly and Wimberly, 1986); acceptance of responsibilities conferred by liberation (Harrison, 1991); transparency to the holy (Ulanov, 1975); personal and social capacity for paradox—"double vision" (Ulanov, 1992, 162f.); imagination (Eugene, 1993a; Neuger, 1991a; Parks, 1986b; Ulanov & Ulanov, 1991); and empowerment (Wiley, 1991).

By far, however, encounter with and reflection on the nature of the Sacred most occupy and grace women's writings about soulfulness. Here the preeminence of mystery, paradox, and ambiguity as subjects in women's writings is finally explained: these three qualities are referenced, countless times, as signs of encounter with the Sacred (Greider, 1990). Even approximate expression of the Sacred requires symbolization, images, and metaphors (Parks, 1984). Building beyond the often-referenced Rizzuto (1979), the formation of God images is shown to be a personal *and* social dynamic process. The Sacred is darkness as much as light (Billman, 1993). God is the sustainer and liberator who enables African American sisters to make a way out of no way (Wiley, 1995). Amid the chaotic demands of personal and social transformation, the metaphors of "home" and "pilgrimage" are sacred replenishment for the soul (Parks, 1989). Biblical and Jungian interpretations are intertwined to make sense of the God who comes in both desert and mountain experiences (Robbins, 1981). Guidance is offered for growing the crop of God images that sprout in the "holy ground" of the search for healing (Armistead, 1995). Bohler works on articulating the nature of the Sacred in publications addressed to adults and their responsibilities — "God is like a jazz band leader" (1997) — and in publications addressed to children and their imaginations — *God Is Like a Mother Hen and Much, Much More* (1996). If absence seems to the violated a quality of God, such an impression is as likely to be a result of bystander neglect as of the violence itself (Doehring, 1993b). In the ancient lands of Greece, an author encounters God as Goddess, and a book for women about the relationship between self-esteem and God images is conceived (Saussy, 1991). Even mere *reform* of social systems seems impossible, except in the presence of the biblical "God of reversals" who *transforms* human history (Couture & Hester, 1995, 54). The Sacred is the *functioning* transcendent (Ulanov, 1996), "the being that holds us in being" (Ulanov, 1992, 160), "the signs of existence among all the indications of nonexistence" (Ulanov, 1986, 78).

How does this literature and focus further a communal contextual paradigm of pastoral care? When we attend to soulfulness, we seek to identify and encounter the most fundamental values and goals of the paradigm. Here we cultivate relationship to the power that can make community miraculous, more than the sum of its parts. In a communal contextual paradigm, it would be a danger to overcompensate for individualism by losing sight of the importance of solitude: focus on soulfulness ameliorates that danger and serves up to persons and communities the spiritual food to fuel the hard work our communities and contexts ask of us and need from us. If it is true that ministerial vocation is "denying the denial" of God (Ulanov, 1989), then in this focus PTC&C finds its anchor.

Focus Six: Violence

In any effective paradigm of PTC&C, much less a communal contextual paradigm, attention must be directed to human violence. Though the issue of violence is addressed earlier, in the early 1980s one particular kind of violence emerged as an unsurpassed focus in women's publications in PTC&C. The development of this literature chronicles one of the most significant motivating forces in the emergence in pastoral theology of a communal contextual paradigm of care and counseling.

With the publication in 1983 of Marie Marshall Fortune's *Sexual Violence: The Unmentionable Sin,* the topic of violence against women and children erupted in the published writings of women pastoral theologians and has continued unabated since. Indisputably, no other topic has received more attention from women publishing in PTC&C: from 1983 to mid-1998, at least twenty-four books (and uncounted articles and essays) have addressed the myriad forms and issues of violence against women and children. Coincident publication in 1995 of *Violence Against Women and Children: A Christian Theological Sourcebook* (Adams & Fortune) and *The Cry of Tamar: Violence Against Women and the Church's Response* (Cooper-White) provides readers two far-reaching overviews of this vast issue and literature. (See also Finson & Golding, 1996.)

Fortune recounts that her founding in 1977 of the Center for the Prevention of Sexual and Domestic Violence (CPSDV) came as a response to what at the time seemed "a fixable problem"—widespread silence and ignorance in the church about sexual violence (Fortune, 1997). Congregations and clergy appeared to be uninformed about the extent and varieties of the problem, and Fortune—previously a local church pastor and rape crisis center volunteer—established CPSDV to provide education and leadership training for religious communities.

The strategy of education and leadership training in the church began with the center but soon mushroomed. The center produced a wealth of its own materials, of course—videos, study guides, awareness brochures.[6] So many publishers quickly followed suit that in the next fifteen years, ignorance of the issue was a condition difficult to maintain. Educationally oriented books have been published by women in several categories. Some explicate in general the issues in sexual violence and care with victim-survivors, especially for clergy and seminarians, but also for religious communities (Delaplain, 1997; Fortune, 1991; Fortune & Graham, 1993; Horton & Williamson, 1988; Pellauer, Chester, & Boyajian, 1987). Several books focus on battering (Adams, 1994; Clarke, 1986; Hollies, 1990; Nason-Clarke, 1997). A volume on incest published in 1985 in Dutch has been available in the United States since 1992 (Imbens & Jonker). Education for prevention has been addressed by several female authors: a study for teenagers appeared first (Fortune, 1984), followed later by curriculum for children ages 9–12 (Reid & Fortune, 1989) and for ages 5–8 (Reid, 1994). Books provide education and support for victim-survivors and their loved ones (Cheston, 1994; Feldmeth & Finley, 1990; Fortune, 1987b; Hollies, 1992). Detailed explorations of the effects of violence on the spiritual and religious aspects of women's and children's lives are available: issues addressed include forgiveness (Fortune, 1988; Hollies, 1997), shame (Ramsay, 1991c), God representations (Doehring, 1993a), and body image (Manlowe, 1995).

It took but a few years after beginning this educational effort, however, for it to become clear that ignorance was not the only problem in religious communities' dealings with violence against women and children and, thus, that education would not be a sufficient response. In 1983, the year *Sexual Violence* was published, a woman called CPSDV because she had been sexually abused by her pastor and needed information about her denomination's structure so that she could make a formal complaint. Fortune (1997) identifies this call as the first time the center was confronted with evidence not merely of clergy ignorance, but of clergy commission of sexual violence. A new strategy emerged in published literature by women pastoral theologians: confrontation of the complicity of the church in violence against women and children. With CPSDV as an unparalleled source of information and motivation, Fortune again broke this new ground, with the publication in 1987 of *Is Nothing Sacred? When Sex Invades the Pastoral Relationship*. Soon after, however, a plethora of books and essays appeared that addressed the violence against women and children in religious contexts and by religious people. Some volumes addressed clergy sexual ethics and misconduct (Fortune & Poling, 1994; Lebacqz & Barton, 1991). Others offered feminist and womanist readings of the Bible and Christian theologies, uncovering in them not only roots of violence but also seeds of liberation and healing (Bohler, 1996; Brown & Bohn, 1989; Eugene, 1995a; Hollies, 1992). Still others tackled what is arguably the most difficult problem of all: responding to abusers (Cooper-White, 1995; Fortune & Poling, 1993). A most recent genre in this literature reports on the experience of "afterpastors," clergy serving congregations in the aftermath of clergy sexual misconduct (for example, Hopkins & Laaser, 1995).

That this focus and literature has in large measure been generated by the work of a center is an extremely important contribution to the emergence of a communal contextual paradigm of care: for the church and for the discipline of PTC&C, it serves as an inspiring model of what steady collective action can accomplish. This focus and literature also motivates us with a steady flow of evidence of violence and its paradoxes: violence is real and yet often camouflaged by contexts that appear nonviolent; violence can both devastate and be healed by community. It documents and calls us to accountability for the ease and extent to which power can be and is used abusively by professional communities and in professional contexts, including religious ones. Only through communities' disciplined focus on violence will we develop the capacity corporately to intervene in violence: caregivers owe perpetrators communities of accountability, not private confessions and cheap grace. Only through disciplined focus on violence will a community be motivated to cultivate unfaltering grace toward violated persons. Precisely because human limits are widely denied or ignored outside religious communities, religious professionals carry the burden of responsibility to keep the limitations of human goodwill and good intentions in the forefront of attention in every community and context in which we have influence.

Focus Seven: Systems of Care

Of all the foci we have identified, the appearance of systems thinking has been the most difficult to date. It can be argued that none of the foci discussed previously could have emerged without an awareness on the part of the contributors of the interconnections between society and persons, between public and private, between privilege and oppression. In 1968, Way characterized the discipline's previous level of attention to systems as "avant garde" and called for continuing innovation through engagement in community organization as an activity of pastoral care. By the early 1980s, family systems theory was identified in women's publications as a theoretical base for pastoral care and counseling (Bohler, 1993; McCarthy, 1982). In the 1990s, definitions of pastoral care as a field of inquiry and as a form of ministry routinely reflect its attention to systems (for example, Billman, 1992, 168; Bons-Storm, 1996b, 202; Couture, 1995a, 13).

It is our assessment, however, that a new dimension in systems thinking in PTC&C has begun to emerge in the 1990s and that women's literature in PTC&C is playing a role in its emergence. There is an effort, in theory and practice, to move beyond *care for systems* toward *systems of care*, to form compounds of care that can reach broader and more complex levels of human relatedness than ever before. For example, in the early 1990s, independent of each other, both editors of this volume were using the metaphor of the web to enable systems thinking in pastoral care, but with a significant difference. Noting the discipline's attunement to the interconnections between and plurality of human beings, Miller-McLemore suggested an update to Anton Boisen's notion that "the living human document" is pastoral care's "text": "the living human web" is "the appropriate object for investigation, interpretation, and transformation" (Miller-McLemore, 1993, 367). Gill-Austern (1995), however, was working on a model for an "ecology of care" and sketched multiple threads of what she called "the healing and transformative web of Christian care." *Pastoral Care and Social Conflict* (Couture & Hunter, 1995) is the most substantial evidence of growing emphasis on systemic care. Other threads in women's literature contribute to the weaving of this web of Christian care by attention to three themes: congregational care; (caring) communication in and between social systems; and care that transforms systems.

Our use of the formulation "congregational care" (Greider, 1992) refers to both care *for* congregations and care *by* congregations. Literature addressing care *of* congregations calls persons engaging with congregations—members, staff and, we would add, denominational officials and other "outsiders"—to learn to enter, read, and assess the culture of each congregation (Ramsay, 1991a, 1992b). The capacity to enter congregational cultures *caringly* rests on being good exegetes of its "thick," precious communal narratives—our own and those of others. The legion of congregations afflicted by social conflict and in stress have special need for *theological* care (Marshall, 1995b): more than many other forms, such care has the potential to anchor the congregation in contemporary storms because its roots are sunk in an entangled system of historical meaning. More and more attention is being given to means by which pastors can care for congregations as a whole, especially with attention to guiding a religious community's spiritual development (Fishburn, 1991; Kornfeld, 1998). The increasing use of congregational study as method in PTC&C (Marshall, 1995b; Miller-McLemore, 1993) may indirectly be providing care of congregations, since engagement with researchers provides unusual opportunity for the system of the congregation to reflect on its history, identity, and mission. Care for congregations is documented in the fledgling efforts of pastors and denominations to come together in care for congregations wounded by pastoral misconduct (for example, Hopkins & Laaser, 1995).

When we turn to the notion of care by communities, we must immediately clarify that caring communities are not new—historically, they have been a hallmark of Christian values and identity. But attention to them in PTC&C literature is relatively new. On the one hand, clericalism has played a major role in making caring communities "the most underutilized treasure for pastoral care" (Gill-Austern, 1995, 237-38); the role of the ordained caregiver has overshadowed the congregation's caregiving—within and beyond its own walls. Additionally, though African American communities have been literal lifelines since the beginnings of slavery in this country, only the recent publication of womanist pastoral caregivers made the nuances of the "therapeutic community" of the African American church (Gilkes, 1980) a regular topic of conversation in the discipline's literature (Boyd, 1991a; Eugene, 1995b; Hollies, 1991; Wiley, 1991; see also Wimberly, 1979). The effort being made in some clinical pastoral education (CPE) programs to engage with the "social ecology" in which their institutions are located can also be seen as an effort to develop care by Christian community that is more systemic in its philosophy and methods (Glaz, 1995b; McWilliams, 1996, 1997).

Another stream of thought in the building of caring systems is focused on various kinds of communication in and between social systems more than on therapeutics. As technology enables global information sharing, Eugene's (1993a) suggestion that "renewal of moral imagination" will assist us to link local and global concerns provides hopeful guidance for managing information overload—intellectual and emotional. The largest amount of literature on this theme addresses communication in the midst of cultural plurality. As one strategy, this literature employs clinical expertise in interpersonal communication—empathy, for example—to form "bridge[s] between cultures" (McCarthy, 1992a). Karaban's (1991) work on what she calls "sharing of cultural variation"—interpathy, dialogue, action—is representative of literature that directly tackles the differences that make empathy so challenging and, when it occurs, so extraordinary (Bohn, 1995; Bryant, 1995; DeMarinis & Grzymala-Moszczynska, 1995; Eugene, 1994a; Karaban, 1990, 1992). Way (1984) offers one of the few extensive discussions in women's literature of dealing with factions within systems and consequent impasses in communication (see also Bohler, 1990c). Formulating the differences between "conservatives" and "liberals" as "differing sensibilities" of "conserving and liberating cultures," Way identifies two necessary concessions to the resolution of such impasses: we can never be rid of our enemies, and all persons have dignity in God (Way, 1984, 14).

The argument that pastoral care can engage and transform social systems through understanding and engaging public policy has been advanced most substantially by Pamela Couture (1991, 1995a, 1995b; Couture & Hester, 1995). Couture argues that pastoral care is not bound to a reactive position relative to uncaring social systems, able only to ameliorate the suffering caused poor individuals. By educating themselves and their communities about public policy and being active in its reform, congregations are engaging in pastoral care that proactively attacks the system of poverty and not only the suffering it causes. In reflection on a case study where pastoral care was not systemic or transformative, McKeever (1991) offers specific suggestions a congregation might consider as ways to concretely participate in the transformation of social systems. Many contributions to *Pastoral Care and Social Conflict* (Couture & Hunter, 1995) are similarly strategic. Other literature attends to the theological and spiritual resources that might nourish forms of care that resist adjustment to social injustices and capitalize on opportunities for positive transformation (Bohler, 1990a; Justes, 1994; Parks, 1989).

This literature and focus contributes to the emergence of a communal contextual paradigm in at least two major ways. First, it helps move systems thinking beyond *conceptualization* of the complexity of global relatedness toward more effectual and yet caring *engagement* with that complexity through the church. The church is one of the few social institutions in which pastoral caregivers, especially as a group, have both responsibility and influence. This literature begs us not to waste this systemic power. Second, this literature and focus offers caregivers the empowerment of an "ecology of care and counseling" (Filippi, 1991; Gill-Austern, 1995): emphasis on the development of systems of care can relieve our isolation and provide us a community of caregivers with whom to share the responsibilities of care, the joys of healing, and the creation together of environments for soulful care.

Writing for Our Lives in the Future

If women's publications in PTC&C over the past thirty-five years are treated as context for the future community of scholarship in the discipline, the literature analyzed suggests some prime research and writing projects. The profoundly ambivalent relation between the discipline and the institutional church needs therapeutic, healing attention if the transformative power of *ekklesia* and ministry is not to be impeded. To have integrity, the discipline must intentionally attend to its pernicious and emerging margins and taboos; for example, candid discussion in PTC&C by European Americans of white racial identity and the privileges associated with it continues to be elusive; newly taboo are the suffering and needs of persons falsely charged with misconduct. That women's power and attention to female experience have increased enormously in the discipline threatens complacency: many females in distinctive racial-ethnic contexts, to cite a major example, continue to be missing or marginalized. Theological education in classroom and clinic provides the scholarly context necessary for researching, writing, and teaching the scope *and* the limitations of our discipline; the discipline's lack of clarity about central expectations and appropriate boundaries—as essential to good scholarship as to ethical clinical practice—begs for this attention.

Futuristic research and writing in the realm of soulfulness will explore whether the discipline's commitment to diversity and human relatedness to God extends beyond Christianity to the riches of other religious traditions—does PTC&C's effectiveness in the global village require that it be an interfaith project? Although publications on violence have given significant attention to victim-survivors, not so with perpetrators: until there exists a more extensive literature to guide relationship with them, perpetrators are handy targets for projection and disavowal of the human capacity for violence and of our shared responsibility for violence and its curtailment. Finally, persons writing for our lives in the future will be those who help us cope soulfully with the tendency of technology and globalization to overwhelm us with information, needs, and opportunities: while the web is home to the spider and fascinating from a distance, it is death to creatures that fly into it unaware.

Notes

[1] It is our position in this chapter that the most general purpose of Christian pastoral care—from the earliest practices of soul care to the modern development of pastoral psychotherapy—has been to contribute to the actualization on earth of justice-love ("the realm of God") through the enablement of personal and corporate human relatedness to the Sacred, variously named (God, YHWH, Creator, for example), as it can be known through Jesus the Christ. Though it is beyond the scope of this chapter to argue in detail for this understanding of pastoral care, modest elaboration provides some context for our argument. Contemporary understandings of the discipline of pastoral care characterize it as traditionally focused on the individual, and often individualistic, but we consider this a narrow reading of the history of pastoral care—distinctly modernist, Westernized, and masculinist. It is our view that pastoral care's facilitation of human relatedness to God has always utilized both personal and corporate methods and relied more heavily on one or the other in a pattern that reflects historical shifts in confidence about the most effective means to achieve reform in human relations. One phase of this pattern can be seen in the twentieth century. The cumulative carnage of World Wars I and II devastated public and scholarly confidence in social institutions. They were shown to be not only inadequate for the containment of human atrocity but even amenable to the systemization of genocide. The coincident development in the early twentieth century, especially in Europe and the United States, of the theories and practices of psychiatry and psychotherapy enabled, and was enabled by, a shift of attention and hope to the reformation of the individual as a more reliable means to moral human community. The consequent psychologization of the dominant culture in the United States in the mid- to late twentieth century was played out in pastoral care in the latter half of this century as a tendency to focus on personal counseling as the preeminent form of pastoral care. The shift of emphasis in pastoral care that we examine in this chapter—from individual to more corporate approaches—again reflects the pattern, a waning of belief in individual methods and a renewal of interest in social methods of reform.

[2] Though this volume explores feminist and womanist pastoral theology, we have not restricted ourselves to the writings of women who could be considered feminist or womanist, whether by self-identification, method, or ideology. We offer a literature analysis that considers the writings of all women in pastoral theology, convinced that the merit and achievement of the visions of feminism and womanism have depended, and will continue to depend, on a woman's freedom to define herself, even in opposition to the social movements and ideologies of feminism and womanism. When we characterize writings as "feminist"

or "womanist," we do so not on the basis of the author's self-identification as feminist or womanist, but on the basis of whether the publication demonstrates two basic principles/methods of feminism and womanism: (1) analytical study of the experience of girls and/or women, *with* (2) attention to how the authority of female lives illuminates issues of power, difference, and oppression. One ironic note: since none of our research tools identify the sex or racial-ethnic identity of authors, we may have made occasional errors in judgment as to an author's racial-ethnic identity and/or sex.

[3] Due to their typically limited accessibility and distribution, we have not included dissertations. To identify literature and authors published within these parameters, we have relied primarily on the ATLA Religion Database 1998 and on the computerized database of the Claremont Colleges library system. Secondarily, we have utilized *Books in Print, Religion Index One* and, for recent unindexed literature, visual searches of book catalogs and periodicals in the collection of the library of the Claremont School of Theology.

[4] Books in PTC&C edited by women are counted as one book, multiple chapters, and multiple authors—for example, *WomanistCare* (Hollies, 1991) is counted as one book, eleven chapters, and ten authors.

[5] We have treated most literature in spiritual direction as outside the parameters of this study, since there is not at the present time consensus that the practice of spiritual direction and the practice of pastoral care and counseling have a shared theory base. We expect and hope that a base of shared theory will be identified and/or built. In the meantime, we have made a few exceptions where an author or a particular publication seems to have a pastoral theological orientation.

[6] Too numerous to be individually cited, these resources are available from CPSDV , 936 N. 34th St., Suite 200, Seattle, WA 98103; or through the Center's Website: http://www@cpsdv.org.

2

A Womanist Search for Sources

Carroll A. Watkins Ali

To write the books one wants to read is both to point the direction of vision and, at the same time, to follow it.

—Alice Walker

Ten years have passed since I began seminary and was introduced to the literature of pastoral theology and care for the first time. Although I was innately a womanist concerned about the collective survival and liberation of African Americans, I did not enter seminary with an awareness of the womanist school of thought that had begun to develop in the scholarship of African American women:

> A womanist then is a strong Black woman who has sometimes been mislabeled as domineering castrating matriarch. A womanist is one who has developed survival strategies in spite of the oppression of her race and sex in order to save her family and her people. (Grant, 1993b, 278)

Yet when I reflect on myself at that time, I realize that what I was feeling as I read through the literature in pastoral theology resonates with the expressed sentiments of celebrated African American women authors such as Alice Walker and Toni Morrison. Walker and Morrison acknowledged early in their careers that their primary motivation for writing came from a desire to create books that they, as African American women, would want to read. Although the literature of pastoral theology and care is not intended to be leisure reading, I would have enjoyed my early studies more if the literature had been more informative regarding my experience as an African American woman.

As it was, the literature of introductory courses in pastoral care revealed that the accepted literature in the field omitted issues of race, gender, and class. Therefore, irrelevancy of this literature was obvious when I considered my social location, the unmet needs of the vast majority of African Americans, and my own needs as a strong African American woman. Inasmuch as there was no allowance for my experience as an African American woman, I felt like a nonentity in the minds of those in the field of pastoral theology and care.

This chapter presents reflections on my bibliographical search of the literature of pastoral theology and cognate disciplines with a twofold goal in mind. First, I want to identify secondary sources indigenous to the African American context that would accurately interpret the cultural experience of African Americans and particularly poor African American women. Second, I want to identify sources and methods that might be useful for the construction of pastoral theology in the African American context. Throughout the chapter, selected sources will be reviewed in conjunction with a womanist critique of Seward Hiltner's method. To conclude, a womanist vision for pastoral theology in the African American context will be presented.

The Search

As I finished my comprehensive exams and considered topics for my dissertation research, I came across an illuminating article in the *Christian Century,* "The Human Web: Reflections on the State of Pastoral Theology," by feminist pastoral theologian Bonnie J. Miller-McLemore (1993). In the course of Miller-McLemore's reflections on the state of pastoral theology, she notes that, while the field of pastoral theology was yet immersed in an identity crisis (after some forty years) and struggling with its appropriations of psychological and sociological methodology, the voices of non-White, ethnic, non-middle-class women within Western culture (among others) had not been heard. It was gratifying for me to know that there were those like Miller-McLemore in the field of pastoral theology who were cognizant of the fact that they had not heard from the womanist perspective. They were also aware that even though African American men, feminists, and others had offered their critiques of traditional pastoral theological method, they could not account for the void of womanist critique. Consequently, I took the challenge personally.

Seward Hiltner Came First

The field of pastoral theology has been significantly shaped by one of its dominant founding fathers, Seward Hiltner. The curriculum of my doctoral program was a blend of scholarship and research geared toward theological inquiry and the Hiltnerian tradition (Hunter, 1990, 866). This simply meant that my inquiry began with Hiltner's (1958) work and progressed from there. Hiltner's groundbreaking work *Preface to Pastoral Theology: The Ministry and Theory of Shepherding* was instrumental in shifting the focus of pastoral theological writing from writings about enriched understandings of persons and enhanced ability to deal with suffering and distress to writings about the pastor's practice itself as a source for theology. Thus, Hiltner's work became foundational to the bulk of literature in pastoral theology and care that followed (Hunter, 1990, 865–866).

Hiltner (1958) is most recognized for his construction of a systematic approach to pastoral theology in terms of the shepherding perspective. Generally speaking, there are three basic characteristics of Hiltner's approach that usually come to mind first: (1) pastoral theology is defined as a formal branch of theology resulting from the study of Christian shepherding; (2) the shepherding perspective has functions of healing, sustaining, and guiding; and

(3) the shepherding perspective is guided by an attitude of tender, solicitous concern. An expanded version of Hiltner's definition of pastoral theology runs as follows: "that branch or field of theological knowledge and inquiry that brings the shepherding perspective to bear on all the operations and functions of the church and minister, and then draws conclusions of a theological order from reflection on these observations" (p. 20).

This definition introduces a systematic way of thinking about pastoral events in which the shepherding perspective is normative. Thus, Hiltner advances the idea of the pastor's perspective as the normative or the primary focus for the field of pastoral theology.

It is important to note that Hiltner's perspectival approach evolved from his practice of interdisciplinary study. He readily made correlations between pastoral care and cognate secular resources (particularly the personality sciences) to aid in the understanding of the shepherding perspective (Hiltner, 1958, 25, 221-223). In addition to the shepherding perspective, Hiltner introduced two other perspectives that have bearing for ministry: communicating and organizing. Interestingly, Hiltner made no provision for a perspective that could serve as an umbrella for all three perspectives for ministry. Rather, Hiltner insisted that the shepherding perspective should be the dominant perspective of the three—having bearing on the communicative and organizing perspectives for ministry as well (Hiltner, 1958, 61). Hiltner did not intend for the shepherding perspective in and of itself to be interpreted as pastoral care; rather by shepherding, he meant a perspective through which to reflect theologically on every aspect of ministry.

To further clarify what is meant by the shepherding perspective, Hiltner (1958) described the character of shepherding in terms of three aspects or concepts essential to the operations of shepherding: healing, sustaining, and guiding (pp. 64-69). Additionally, Hiltner asserted that an attitude of tender, solicitous concern was conditional to the functions of shepherding (p. 16). That is to say, all of the pastoral actions should be carried out with a disposition that consistently offers attentive care in every event of ministry.

Beyond Hiltner: The Fruits of My Search

In spite of the fact that Hiltner's preface was intended to serve as a preliminary work in the process of developing a systematic pastoral theology (MacDonald, 1969, 165), the field of pastoral theology has not advanced far beyond Hiltner until recently. After reading through the lineage of White males who upheld Hiltner's focus on an intellectual problematic for theological reflection, I longed for evidence that there were others within the field whose methods reflected an awareness and concern for the critical issues of the vast majority of African Americans. Examples of those who followed in Hiltner's tradition are James Lapsley (1972), who developed a theory of pastoral care by bringing the concepts of salvation and mental health into dialogue; Charles Gerkin (1984), whose work involved drawing on the tension between hermeneutical theory and psychodynamic theory; and John Patton (1983, 1985), whose early work asserted relational humanness as central to pastoral care and counseling and pastoral theological reflection on themes of guilt, shame, and forgiveness. New approaches in method were slow in coming. However, eventually, I was able to identify pastoral theologians (and others) whose approaches both challenged the Hiltner tradition and had relevance for the pastoral theological enterprise in the African American context.

The earliest attempts in the field of pastoral care to expand upon Hiltner appear in the work of William A. Clebsch and Charles R. Jaekle (1964), in their book *Pastoral Care in Historical Perspective*, and Edward Wimberly (1979), in his book *Pastoral Care in the Black Church*. The significance of Clebsch and Jaekle's contribution in the course of their historical review of pastoral care was the addition of a fourth pastoral function: reconciling. To date, the act of reconciling has maintained a place in traditional pastoral theology and has continued to stimulate the thinking of pastoral theologians. However, in the African American context, the act of reconciling has been a controversial issue. The act of reconciling has been debated and questioned by Black religious scholars such as J. Doetis Roberts (1974) and Edward Wimberly (1979). Efforts toward reconciliation with the greater society are premature and futile until the inequities between Blacks and Whites have been removed and the dominant culture has acknowledged its past injustices and found ways to atone for the dehumanizing injustices over the last four hundred years.

From an African American male perspective, Wimberly (1979) was the first to lift up the importance of the sociocultural situation. His book *Pastoral Care in the Black Church* successfully introduces the issues of racism and oppression into the pastoral theological dialogue. He argues that the sociological issues of Blacks and the communal approach to ministry in the Black church tradition require an enlargement of Hiltner's understanding of ministry. At the same time, Wimberly openly challenges the validity of Clebsch and Jaekle's reconciling function for the African American context. Acts of reconciling are of a secondary order of ministry for African Americans. Although Wimberly had no quarrel with Hiltner's meaning for healing in general, due to the racial climate in America, healing for African Americans still lies in the future:

> The racial climate in America, from slavery to the present, has made sustaining and guiding more prominent than healing and reconciling. Racism and oppression have produced wounds in the black community that can be healed only to the extent that healing takes place in the structure of the total society. (p. 21)

In terms of sustaining and guiding, the total caring resources of the church must be utilized to help persons and families endure crises and identify healthy crisis coping mechanisms (Wimberly, 1979, 19–20).

Archie Smith Jr. (1982), another African American male, entered the dialogue. In terms of the African American context, Smith raised the issue of liberation from oppression and the transformation of person and society together: "This book . . . attempts to identify common ground for keeping together outer and inner transformation. It identifies relationality and the communal self as key concepts in emancipatory struggles and liberation ministries" (p. 14). Thus, Smith's major contribution to caregiving disciplines is a relational paradigm that conceptualizes a therapeutic community linking the individual and society.

Unfortunately, the field of pastoral theology did not begin to integrate Smith's new paradigm until the early nineties. Ten years had passed in the literature before Larry Kent Graham's (1992) book *Care of Persons, Care of Worlds: A Psychosystems Approach to Pastoral Care and Counseling* appeared. As the title implies, Graham picks up on the significance of the relationship between person and society. Notably, he credits Smith along with Charlotte and Howard Clinebell, and the doctoral work of Bonny K. Dillion and Gail Unterberger, as stimulating his thinking about the relationship between persons and oppressive systems (Graham, 1992, 243). To his credit, Graham's book is one of the first of its kind in the field. He successfully impressed upon the field the need to move beyond the individualistic approach and to wrestle with the consequences of oppressive systems on persons and society (Graham, 1992, 243). In addition, his assertion that pastoral caretakers should also be advocates, who offer agential power to those seeking care (Graham, 1992, 45), has affinity with the African American context.

In the early nineties, several women in pastoral theology began to make contributions. Pamela Couture (1991) leads the way in lifting up societal concerns in her book (which actually predates Graham's by about a year) *Blessed Are the Poor?: Women's Poverty, Family Policy, and Practical Theology*. Using the methodology of practical theology, she examines the poverty of single mothers and their children in light of family policy in the United States for the purpose of formulating a practical/pastoral theological response. Prior to her investigation, little reflection on the issues of women's poverty had occurred. Couture acknowledges the bias of her social location (as a middle-class White woman), clarifies that she deals with generalizations about the poverty of women in America, and makes comparisons between White and Black households that are headed by women. To her credit, Couture does not attempt to interpret Black women's experience.

Feminist pastoral theologian Christie Cozad Neuger (1992) and an African American male pastoral theologian, Charles Taylor (1992), both name experience as a primary source for pastoral theological reflection in articles for the *Journal of Pastoral Theology*. For Neuger, in no uncertain terms, tradition could not take precedence over cultural considerations. According to Neuger, identifying cultural pathologies is the starting place (Neuger, 1992, 49). She begins with data on women's experience in relevant sociological and statistical research, and women's stories:

I find it central to understand women's specific life stories in the context of culture which has normalized the devaluation of women and plays that out through economic discrimination, through the acceptance of male violence against women, through the objectification and exploitation of women's bodies, and through various values and rules that attempt to keep women out of the meaning-making public world. (p. 38)

Similarly, Charles Taylor (1992) begins by asking the field of pastoral theology: How do we break out of the cultural bind of pastoral theology? He then goes on to offer Black experience as an alternative resource for pastoral theological method:

The main resource that the "Black experience" can bring to pastoral theology is the experience of a tradition which is outside of the male Euro-American liberal protestant ghetto—yet has ties to it. The fundamental resource is the reminder to the movement that it is in a ghetto; the worldview that has informed the pastoral care movement is only one of many worldviews. (p. 28)

Others such as James Newton Poling (1991) and Valerie DeMarinis (1993) demonstrate sensitivity to issues confronting women and African Americans. Finally, in the past decade, several edited collections have opened the pastoral theological dialogue by bringing forth issues from different cultural and social contexts (Couture & Hunter, 1995; Glaz & Stevenson-Moessner, 1991; Stevenson-Moessner, 1996).

However, even though Hiltner's individualistic approach was criticized again and again, several problems arise in these new approaches. For the most part, they continue to rely on the limited illustration of persons or families in the congregation or clinical settings rather than in communal settings of the society at large. Second, even though recent research addresses women's culture and African American culture from the African American male perspective, their combined efforts do not do justice to the critical issues of African American women's culture. A critique of traditional pastoral theology from the perspective of African American women is still in order. Likewise, new methods need to be constructed that are specific to our needs. Therefore, it is necessary to turn to secondary resources indigenous to the African American context, particularly sources written from the womanist perspective.

Sources Indigenous to the African American Context

The cognate disciplines of Black liberation theology, womanist theology, and Black psychology as well as womanist ethics and African American literature offer more knowledge about the African American experience for theological reflection than the knowledge of many pastoral caregivers who function out of the traditional modality of pastoral theology and care. All of these resources understand the African American cultural context and, consequently, the existential dilemmas of African Americans better than dominant European American perspectives.

Specifically, the literature of Black liberation theology and womanist theology more accurately interprets the God-talk of African Americans than traditional Christian theology does. Leading Black liberation theologian James Cone and the African American male theologians who follow him emphasize liberation from racial injustice (Cone, 1969, 1972, 1975, 1982, 1986, 1993). The theological interpretations of womanist theologians such as Jacquelyn Grant (1989, 1993a, 1993b) and Delores Williams (1993a, 1993b) have been most formative of my approach to a womanist perspective for pastoral theology for African Americans. Both women use Black women's experience as a source for theological reflection. They speak for poor Black women—the most oppressed of all the oppressed—for liberation not only from racism, but also from the oppression of sexism and classism, and/or oppression because of sexual orientation, physical disability, and caste (Grant, 1993b; Williams, 1993a).

In Grant's (1989) book *White Women's Christ and Black Women's Jesus,* she distinguishes between the historical experience of poor Black women and middle-class White women. In essence Grant points out that White middle-class feminist theologians cannot presume to speak for poor Black women; their argument that classical christology is oppressive primarily because of its sexism fails to address the racism and classism in the experience of poor Black women. The difference in Black women's and White women's historical experience explains how Black women can experience the second person of the Trinity as oppressive and liberating at the same time. Jesus (the male Christ), unlike for some White feminist theologians, is seen as a cosufferer, who identifies with them—the least.

Grant's work challenges the field of pastoral theology and care in two primary respects: (1) the need to consider the possibilities of multidimensional issues in contexts of care as an approach; and (2) the need to address a concept of suffering with those who are suffering. First, as mentioned earlier, the field has had a tendency to focus on one intellectual problematic at a time, often to the neglect of critical coexisting issues. Grant's approach is "wholistic," or all-encompassing, as she raises the tridimensional nature of poor Black women's experience. Speaking in terms of the womanist tradition in Black theology, Grant's words also apply to the construction of pastoral theology:

> There is a tradition which declares that God is at work in the experience of
> the Black woman. This tradition, in the context of the total Black experi-
> ence, can provide data for the development of a wholistic Black theology.
> (1993a, 335)

The implication, of course, for pastoral theology and care is that pastoral care needs to be encompassing of all the needs of the cultural context of ministry.

Second, Grant's womanist interpretation of christology introduces the concept of the suffering servant. The implication for pastoral theology and care is that, if Jesus Christ is viewed and/or experienced as a cosufferer by some, the field needs to reflect theologically on what it means to approach care as one who suffers with those who are suffering. Conceptually, the significance is that to suffer with implies much more than empathy.

In her book *Sisters in the Wilderness: The Challenge of Womanist God-Talk*, Delores Williams (1993a) equates the historical experience of Black women with the biblical story of Hagar. She voices the concerns of Black women (unaddressed in Black liberation theology) for survival and productive quality of life in addition to liberation from oppression. The story of Hagar and her son, Ishmael, parallels the lives of many Black women past and present. Williams states:

> I selected from Hagar's story those issues that had simultaneously personal, social, and religious significance for Black women and for the African American community; the predicament of motherhood; the character of surrogacy; the problem of ethnicity; the meaning and significance of the wilderness experience for women and for the community. (p. 8)

According to Williams, the God-talk of Black women is that out of no way at all, God is able to make a way.

Like Grant's approach, Williams's approach implies the significance of a multidimensional approach to the context of ministry. However, the most important concepts that Williams raises for pastoral theology and care to reflect upon are the critical issues of survival and quality of life. These are issues not just for African Americans, but for many Americans from all walks of life. In general Williams's approach begs questions of "What are the predicaments or nature of crisis that persons and communities find themselves needing pastoral care for?" and, ultimately, "What is the quality of life?" These are significant questions for pastoral theology and care.

Womanist theological ethicist Katie G. Cannon (1988) provides historical insight into the womanist tradition and a method for extrapolating the experience of African American women through the African American literary tradition. In *Black Womanist Ethics*, Cannon also reveals a moral ethic within the traditions of African American women that could provide the conceptual basis for an ethic of pastoral care for African Americans:

> The Black woman's collection of moral counsel is implicitly passed on and received from one generation of Black women to the next. Black females are taught what is to be endured and how to endure the harsh, cruel, inhumane exigencies of life. The moral wisdom does not rescue Black women from the bewildering pressures and perplexities of institutional social evils but rather,

> exposes those ethical assumptions which are inimical to the ongoing survival
> of Black womanhood. The moral ethic captures the ethical qualities of what
> is real and what is of value to women in the Black world. (p. 5)

Cannon's documentation of this moral wisdom provides a valuable resource for a cognitive approach to pastoral care of African Americans that is based on the ways in which Black women have learned how to care for themselves and their community over time. Most significant for pastoral care is the potential for helping persons get in touch with and sustain an internal locus of control despite difficult external situations.

Finding psychological sources that are indigenous to the African American context and that speak to the nature of the African American experience is quite a challenge. First, much of the literature is hard to locate because it has not been published through mainstream publishing companies and is not readily available in libraries. Second, to my surprise, there are limited sources that address the phenomenology of Black experience specifically. The literature is focused on defining Black psychology and ways to modify dominant cultural modalities to fit the African American context (Jones, 1991). There is not a clear presence of liberative or womanist schools of thought per se. Instead, a major portion of the literature focuses on the importance of philosophical beginnings in African culture as the conceptual basis for Black psychology (Kambon, 1992; Myers, 1988; Nobles, 1986, 1991). However, of benefit to the enterprise of constructing pastoral theology for the African American context, Black clinical psychologist Nancy Boyd-Franklin (1989) emphasizes the importance of strong family bonds and kinship connections of extended families as a means of survival and resistance to oppression.

Boyd-Franklin's work constitutes the most comprehensive resource to date for understanding the care needs and issues that are unique to the Black experience in America. Although she is not a self-described womanist, her approach is womanist in application. Often, Boyd-Franklin highlights the multidimensional experience of African American women as single heads of households and extended family structures. In terms of pastoral theology and care, Boyd-Franklin offers insightful guidelines for cross-racial counseling. Thus, Boyd-Franklin's suggestion is that counselors, regardless of race, ethnicity, or cultural background, should take the time necessary to inform themselves about other racial or cultural contexts as opposed to excusing themselves from the racial or cultural issues by making referrals.

What Are Womanists to Do with the Hiltnerian Tradition?

From a womanist pastoral perspective, what are the inadequacies of the Hiltnerian tradition? What are its affinities for the African American context? What are the possible correctives that will help to bring pastoral theological questions to bear on the specifics of the African American context?

The multidimensional social and economic burdens that poor Black women and their children experience portray the magnitude and severity of the problems in Black life. Research confirms that, despite the increasing numbers of the so-called Black middle class in the post–civil rights years, the most impoverished group of adults in America are Black women. Not only do Black women earn the least in comparison to White men, Black men, and White women, but the welfare of Black women in this society is directly related to the status of Black men. The high rates of unemployment and underemployment of Black men, the large numbers of Black men incarcerated, the high mortality rate of Black males, along with high rates of drug and alcohol abuse by Black men— all contribute to a high rate of absenteeism of Black men from the Black household. Thus, the welfare of Black children usually correlates with Black women's welfare. Consequently, Black children are the most economically disadvantaged group of children. For example, statistics show that in a one-year span (1982 to 1983) 71.5 percent of Black children living in single-parent homes headed by Black women lived at poverty level or below as compared to 47.4 percent of White children who lived in single-parent households headed by White women (Burbridge, 1993).[1] This kind of poverty is genocidal, literally threatening the survival of the people involved. Hence, the perspective of poor Black women urgently calls for pastoral theology that concerns itself with the communal well-being and survival of Black men, women, and children.

Hiltner's Method as Foundational

Briefly, three basic elements of Hiltner's (1958) method are foundational to the enterprise of constructing pastoral theological method in the African American context of ministry: (1) Hiltner's methodological approach set the precedent for bringing theological reflection to bear on concrete human experience; (2) Hiltner's approach is provisional and encourages the identification of a problematic within the ministry situation as the conceptual basis for pastoral theological reflection; and (3) Hiltner's approach is interdisciplinary and employs cognate resources.

Appropriated to the African American context in the above order, respectively: (1) the primary reflection for theological inquiry would be on the concrete human experience of those indigenous to the cultural context of ministry; (2) the specific problematic for theological reflection would be the survival and liberation needs of the vast majority of African Americans; and (3) Hiltner's correlation of psychological and theological resources to assist in the formulation of conceptual theories for theological reflection sets a precedent for an interdisciplinary approach that employs sources indigenous to the African American context.

*Limitations of Hiltner's Method for the African American Context

Hiltner's emphasis on the shepherding perspective as the normative one for pastoral theology has been too narrow for the African American context. It does

61

not allow for many of the cultural realities of African Americans and addresses the critical concerns of African Americans only in a superficial way at best.

Specifically, Hiltner's shepherding perspective has three basic limitations for the African American context: (1) an inherent paternalism, (2) an individualistic approach, and (3) a cultural insensitivity to the African American situation. First, Hiltner's focus on the individual pastor overprizes the role of the pastor (usually male) in theological reflection. Thus, Hiltner's approach asserts the pastoral caregiver (usually a White male) as the expert. If the abstracted or objective point of view of the pastoral caregiver represents the dominant culture (White male), its interpretation is at least one step removed from the realities of African American life. Pastoral caregivers have often imposed their own values and assumptions on African American experience rather than allowing for the significance of values and issues specific to the African American worldview. My expectation is that if Hiltner were able to defend his position now, he would say that his intention was not to impose the view of the pastor on those indigenous to the ministry context. However, I would assert that the blindness caused by his paternalism did not allow him to see the inherent flaw in his method for cultures outside the dominant culture (Watkins Ali, 1998).[2]

Second, the interests of the Black context are not well served by Hiltner's individualistic approach. Hiltner concentrated on the individual acts of the pastor and failed to address groups larger than that of the congregation. While the shepherding perspective was not intended to exclude the possibility of ministry to groups and congregations, Hiltner acknowledges that in practice, pastoral care has been studied most often in relation to individuals and families (Hiltner, 1958, 215-217). However, the severity of the crises in the African American context affects the majority of African Americans. Therefore, pastoral theology must concern itself with the critical communal concerns of Black people in this country over and above the individual concerns of people who happen to be Black. The communal approach also requires pastoral caregiving that comes from the community rather than solely from the pastoral caregiver.

Finally, the shepherding perspective cannot be considered normative for the African American context. Hiltner does not specifically address cultural contexts, especially problems of racism, sexism, and classism, and their importance as he asserts the shepherding perspective. Therefore, the serious needs of African Americans call for an expansion in the character and content of ministry beyond Hiltner's healing, sustaining, and guiding. Sustaining as a function of ministry in the traditional sense is a good example of Hiltner's shortsightedness for the African American context. Sustaining should not be confused with surviving. Hiltner speaks of sustaining as upholding and standing with—in other words, as support. Survival in the communal sense for African Americans entails much more than being sustained or supported through short-lived crises of individuals and families. The crises of African Americans call for pastoral care that ensures survival not only of the day-to-day struggles of Black life in America, but also survival from the effects of more than four hundred years of oppression, dehumanization, and genocidal poverty.

A Womanist Vision: New Method for Pastoral Theology

The state of emergency in Black America as seen through the eyes of poor Black women calls for a pastoral framework that is free of paternalism and the imposition of dominant culture perspectives, and that is immediate and prophetic in its praxis. Therefore, a new method for pastoral theology in the African American context that addresses the critical needs for survival and liberation must allow for (1) a point of departure that begins with the subjective experience of the African American culture versus objectifications and abstractions about the culture; (2) the significance of communality versus individuality; and (3) the expansion of new operations of ministry.

A womanist approach to pastoral theology requires a paradigm shift in which the importance of contextuality is emphasized. Thus, theological reflection that begins with a focus on experience indigenous to the particular cultural context is a more appropriate point of departure for pastoral theological method. A womanist paradigm gives (1) primary consideration to theological questions that emerge from the experiences of those inhabiting the cultural context of ministry; and (2) the experience of the pastoral caregiver in relation to the needs of the cultural context becomes the secondary object of theological reflection.

Second, a womanist approach sets the dominance of the shepherding perspective aside and reintroduces Hiltner's concept of a master perspective (although the term *umbrella* is more appropriate because it does not carry the negative connotations of the term *master*). Unlike Hiltner's approach, which asserts shepherding as the dominant perspective of the three cognate perspectives of ministry, a womanist approach finds utility in an umbrella perspective under which shepherding, communicating, and organizing events of ministries are subsumed. Hence, an umbrella perspective would ensure that an awareness of the subjective experience of those living in any cultural context would be the primary interpretative perspective in all the events of ministry. For example, in the African American context, the perspective of poor Black women would serve as the umbrella perspective most representative of the pastoral care needs of the majority of Blacks. It is through their eyes that pastoral caregivers can gain a view of the critical needs of Black America.

Third and finally, as already mentioned, the perspective of poor Black women calls for an approach to ministry that represents God as identified with their daily struggles as the poorest of the poor and the most oppressed of the oppressed; they call for an approach that represents a God who is able to make a way out of the wilderness experiences. Hence, the content of ministry needs to expand beyond the traditional aspects of shepherding—healing, sustaining, guiding—in order to meet the survival and liberation needs of the African American context. Poor Black women and their families require functions of ministry that are also nurturing, empowering, and ultimately liberating in praxis. In the simplest terms, nurturing ministry provides a constant source of care that restores and replenishes vitality for continual resistance to oppression; empowering ministry enables persons to identify and claim their own power; and liberating ministry helps to bring about the elimination of oppression spiritually, psychologically, and physically. An attitude of tender, solicitous concern must entail willingness for advocacy consistent with the womanist tradition.

Looking toward the future, it is clear that womanist sources provide a rich resource toward building a conceptual framework of an African American pastoral theology as well as for the field of pastoral theology in general. Womanist sources present an important voice that has been missing in the pastoral theological dialogue—the voice of poor African American women representing the issues of America's most needy across cultures. Acknowledging the sources and their potential for the field is only a first step. It is now incumbent upon the field to reflect on the implications and take the succeeding steps necessary to guide pastoral care in such a way that no one falls through the cracks.

Notes

[1] These statistics reflect a disparity between Blacks and Whites that grew during the era from 1981–1992 and has not improved. Although the statistics are dated, they represent a picture of the true state of Black America that continues to this day.

[2] Reflections in this section and the next section draw on research done for my dissertation (1998) and are further developed there.

3

Always an Outsider? Feminist, Female, Lay, and Roman Catholic

Roslyn A. Karaban

Individual Lived Experience: I Am Alone

At a conference held in Boston in 1980, a number of Roman Catholic women were asked to respond to the question "Woman and Roman Catholic: Is it possible?" In her 1984 book, *Bread, Not Stone,* Elisabeth Schüssler Fiorenza asked something similar, broadening the question to include other Christian traditions. She wrote, "Is being a woman and being a Christian a primary contradiction that must be resolved in favor of one to the exclusion of the other?" (Fiorenza, 1984, 53). I have struggled with both questions on a personal level and have come to believe that I can indeed be a Roman Catholic and a woman. I have taken these two questions a step farther, combining them to ask a third question that predominates my adult *professional* life: Is it possible to be a Roman Catholic, female, *lay minister,* or are these incompatible, even contradictory terms? Must being *a Roman Catholic woman* exclude being a professional *lay minister?* Since there are numerous professional lay ministers—including women—in the Roman Catholic Church today, this may seem to be an odd question to ask. Yet a recent Vatican "Instruction" by eight Vatican offices states that a person is a minister not only because of a task (service) that is done, but also because of sacramental ordination (1997, 401). This "Instruction" also restricts the use of the word *ministry* to the ordained and prohibits the laity from calling themselves *pastor, coordinator, chaplain,* or *moderator* (1997, 403). This document is presently under advisement by the bishops.

Although my original call was to *ordained* ministry, in particular, the Roman Catholic priesthood, by choosing to remain in the Roman Catholic Church (which shows no signs of ordaining women to the priesthood in the near future), I am, and will remain, a *layperson.* Rather than see this only as a restriction because of my gender, I have chosen to see this as a challenge and a gift and have spent considerable time and energy developing models of professional lay ministry (Karaban, 1983, 1993).[1] Finding that ordained, parish ministry was not an option for me, I searched for alternative ministries that would utilize my gifts, at least partially fulfill my call to ministry, and accept me as a *laywoman.* I believed I had found this alternative in the ministry of pastoral counseling. I was accepted into a Ph.D. program in pastoral counseling and worked as an intern in a pastoral counseling center. Yet when I applied for membership in the American Association of Pastoral Counselors (AAPC), the largely Protestant, professional organization overseeing and certifying pastoral counselors, I was told that membership required "ordination, consecration or equivalent means" (AAPC, 1987, IX-4). Ordination was *not* a possibility for me as a Roman Catholic woman, consecration was *not* an option for me as a married Roman Catholic woman, and I have still *not* figured out what would be "equivalent" to this.

With this rejection of me as laywoman, I was able to articulate what I would call an experience of contradiction, or what Leon Festinger called an experi-

66

ence of "cognitive dissonance"—a feeling of distress that occurs when two beliefs fail to align (Festinger, 1957, 12). I had already experienced this dissonance in my belief that I was called to ordained priesthood in a church that denied even the existence of that call, let alone the fulfillment of that call. This had occurred with the 1976 issuance of a Vatican declaration that stated: "Some women feel that they have a vocation to the priesthood. Such an attraction, however noble and understandable, still does not suffice for a genuine vocation" (Congregation for the Doctrine of Faith, 1976, 17). This statement had appeared while I was studying for my M.Div. degree and preparing for parish ministry. It has been reinforced through various, subsequent Vatican documents.[2] Now I was experiencing a contradiction in the field of pastoral counseling, a field powerfully shaped by liberal Protestant theology in the 1960s. It was my understanding that the AAPC accepted and encouraged *women* to be members, yet it was my lay status that now prevented me from being recognized as a pastoral counselor. And yet my lay status was inextricably tied to being a woman. My experience of functioning as a pastoral counselor on the staff of a pastoral counseling center *contradicted* my experience of being rejected from being certified or even officially recognized as a pastoral counselor.

I faced a new dilemma—I had chosen an alternative ministry whose ruling leaders also rejected me. Thus, I found myself embarking on what I saw as yet another alternative ministry—teaching pastoral care and counseling and becoming a pastoral theologian. Calling myself a pastoral theologian, however, was particularly difficult for two reasons: (1) my two previous calls to ministry (as priest and pastoral counselor) were both dead ends; and (2) claiming the title of Catholic "theologian" opened me up to responsibilities and restrictions that I am still reluctant to accept. A number of church documents appeared when I was beginning my teaching career as pastoral theologian that restricted the academic freedom of the Catholic theologian in a Catholic university or college and discouraged dissent from hierarchical traditional teachings of the magisterium.[3] Still, I hoped that I had found a place where I could minister and where I could continue to at least examine the structures that contributed to my experiences of confusion, contradiction, and dissonance.

Much to my dismay I had entered a field, pastoral theology, that was itself struggling with issues of identity, acceptance, and recognition—similar to my own struggles with these very same issues. Pastoral theology struggled with identity issues, searching for a commonly accepted name that would convey the essence and intent of the discipline. Various names were used across the country, including pastoral psychology, practical theology, religion and the personality sciences, pastoral care and counseling, and religion and psychology. It was not an easy task to agree upon a common name, despite church historian E. Brooks Holifield's hopeful words in 1983 that "pastoral theologians had secured their place in academia" (Holifield, 1983, 271). Today an assortment of terms continues to be used to describe the discipline. This search for a commonly accepted name reflects the divergent and sometimes conflicting interests within the field between those who favor "practical care and counseling approaches," "those engaged in the critical correlation of theology, religion and the social sciences," and "those involved in the empirical social-scientific study of religious experience" (Miller-McLemore, 1996, 12). As one who favors the "practical care and counseling approaches" in a field that I have experienced as emphasizing "critical correlation," I have continued to find myself faced with the same issues that I faced when pursuing a ministry as a pastoral counselor — namely, being a minority voice, seeking acceptance and validation for who I am in a world dominated by those who are different from me.

To survive in this "strange land" (Fischer et al., 1975), I needed to find others like myself, lest I think myself crazy or feel totally alone in my experience. Although it would take years to connect with other like-minded Catholic women on a personal level, I was able to connect with other Catholic women through my readings in feminist theology, particularly the feminist theology of Roman Catholic scholars Rosemary Radford Ruether and Elisabeth Schüssler Fiorenza. Thus, I became part of "a larger community of women who meet only through the written word" (Fischer et al., 1975, 1), and the work of Roman Catholic, feminist theologians began to have a significant impact on my approach to and conceptualization of pastoral theology. My need not to feel alone in my experience, as a Roman Catholic woman in pastoral theology, went beyond a desire for companionship. My need to connect to others was fueled by a belief, or perhaps a fear, that if I was alone in my experience, then my experience was an anachronism, a deviance, and therefore invalid. I wanted to know how common my experience of contradiction was, and if there were any women who had similar thoughts, ideas, and experiences. In my exploration and reflection I found I had a new term to add to my description of myself — *feminist* — a feminist, Roman Catholic, pastoral theologian.

Thus far in my life, I had been dealing with the "smaller story"[4] (Bausch, 1984, 203) of my own life, the "lived experience" of one individual. I now turned to looking at the "larger story" — the "lived experiences of individuals and communities" (Holland & Henriot, 1983, 8), partially encountered through scholarly readings in liberation and feminist theology. At first I did this out of a selfish need not to feel alone in my experience. However, as my anxiety decreased, I found that my discovery that I was not alone in my experience made my experience a much larger issue than I had imagined. I became driven with a need to understand the causes, consequences, linkages, and other actors (Holland & Henriot, 1983, 12) in this dilemma. This shift was a critical one both for me as person and for me as an academician. In realizing and exploring the broader issues of my personal dilemma, I entered into a lifelong journey of social analysis that undergirded my teaching. This also enabled me to help other women in their journey toward understanding their call to remain within a patriarchal church structure that restricted their functioning.

At this critical time in my life I was introduced to the concept of the pastoral circle as developed by Roman Catholic social ethicists Joe Holland and Peter Henriot. This concept, or methodology, is also referred to as the praxis circle and is similar to Paulo Friere's concept of praxis as developed in *The Pedagogy of the Oppressed* (1970) and Juan Luis Segundo's hermeneutic circle as developed in *The Liberation of Theology* (1976). It has significant implications for pastoral theological method. Others in pastoral and practical theology have used this method, perhaps without recognizing its link to and origins in liberation theology. Pastoral theologians, like myself, are distinct from systematic and biblical theologians in our interest in and commitment to *each* moment in the circle as well as the movement or dynamics of the circle itself.

The circle has four components, or moments: insertion, "the lived experience of individuals and communities"; social analysis, which "examines causes, probes consequences, delineates linkages, and identifies actors"; theological reflection, "an effort to understand more broadly and deeply the analyzed experiences in the light of living faith, scripture, social teaching, and the resources of tradition"; and pastoral planning, which looks at "what response is called for" (Holland & Henriot, 1983, 12-13).

I had been keyed in only to the first "moment" of the circle, looking first at my own experience, then broadening that to looking at the experiences of other individuals and communities. In coming to know and understand the pastoral circle, I found that there were other vital moments in the circle, and experience was only the starting point. Social analysis provided me with a framework and a methodology with which to approach the issue of women in Roman Catholic religious leadership. By using social analysis, I was able to gain a broader perspective by viewing the church as a system that can be looked at both historically (through time) and structurally (at a given moment in time). I also found that there were both objective (external structures) and subjective (values and ideologies) dimensions to the church (Holland & Henriot, 1983, 14), and both needed to be examined. I was able to ask and address such questions as, Who makes decisions in the church; who benefits from these decisions; and who feels the consequences of these decisions? (Holland & Henriot, 1983, 28).

As a *Christian* pastoral theologian, I did this analysis in a context of faith, seeing my work as an extension of the concept of discernment that moves us from the individual, personal realm to the social, communal realm (Holland & Henriot, 1983, 13). Any analysis, therefore, was always done in the context of faith and in dialogue with the religious resources and voices of the faithful. Finally, I was able to come up with a response of action, a developing model of lay professional ministry that calls for the continued movement of the circle to new experiences and the need for continued analysis, reflection, and planning.

In doing all this I discovered I had dwelled so long in the moment of experience because it had taken me years to discover and accept that *my* experience — as *woman* — was a valid starting place for reflection. I was able to do this only because of the affirmation I received through my readings in feminist and liberation theologies.

Community Lived Experience: I Am *Not* Alone

I began to really believe I was not alone when I read books such as Ruether's *Women-Church* (1986). There I read of the great increase of Roman Catholic women at Catholic seminaries and nonsectarian seminaries (Ruether, 1986, 65). I came to know that there were many other Roman Catholic women at seminaries preparing for various lay ministries in the church. When I received my M.Div. in 1978 (at a nonsectarian seminary), I was the *only* Roman Catholic woman in my graduating class. I was finally able to see that my situation was *not* unique, but was shared by a growing number of Roman Catholic women. I shifted from seeing my experience of contradiction as an individual experience, not worthy of note because it was only *one woman's* experience, to seeing myself as part of a larger community of women with experiences and ideas similar to mine. I was finally able to own and affirm my experience and the experiences of other women, and to also look beyond and behind this experience. In Holland and Henriot's terms, I was able to enter into the next moment in the pastoral circle — social analysis. This moment was pivotal for me, for it propelled me fully into my new ministry of academic teaching. It also opened up a new world for me, a world of new understandings and new possibilities for my future as a pastoral theologian, the future of the field of pastoral theology, and the future of the church.

The Bigger Picture: Social Analysis

Entering into social analysis meant entering into a lifelong effort of exploration, investigation, and analysis. It meant looking at the broader structures of economic, social, political, cultural, and religious structures surrounding my experience. It meant taking on a task that is "complex, never ending and always controversial" (Holland & Henriot, 1983, 18). Yet for me, it was an exhilarating experience. I finally had a name to what I was doing, I had a well-established methodology (the pastoral circle) to aid me in my quest, and I found that many others had already done much of the work for me.

My investigation focused on the role of women in the Roman Catholic Church, specifically the role of women in religious leadership. Once again I was drawn to feminist writing — this time to Elisabeth Schüssler Fiorenza's work in the area of biblical hermeneutics — as well as back to Ruether's work — this time for her insights and research on church leadership. In Ruether I found that her historical, feminist research uncovered two basic models of the church that are in conflict with each other — church as historical institution and church as spirit-filled community (Ruether, 1986, 11). In the spirit-filled model of earliest Christianity, women "could enter into the new covenant as equals with men" because in anticipation of a messianic order, "traditional hierarchies of the family could be dissolved" (Ruether, 1986, 11). But in the development of the church, the inclusion of women in ministry was suppressed because inclusion of women was thought to be antifamilial (Ruether, 1986, 12). By the late first century the church had affirmed a patriarchal family order as the model for society and church. Therefore, women in leadership roles in the church went against both church and social (family) order. This diminishment in women's leadership in the church continued in the next centuries as the church duplicated the surrounding political structures, this time of the Roman Empire. This led to a diminishment of prophetic and charismatic leadership, which had included women. The church began to place great emphasis on the twelve (male) apostles being the first bishops of the church and the importance of a continued (male) apostolic succession (Ruether, 1986, 12–13). Although I had studied church history and the development of the early church, I had never heard this development related to attitudes and beliefs concerning the place of women. I began to realize that who told the story and who was included in the story were crucial, and that the history I had studied and learned was limited because it had neglected and ignored the voices and concerns of women. Whose experience and what groups were considered or left out were critical (Holland & Henriot, 1983, 9).

With this newfound realization I read Fiorenza. Although her two pivotal works (*In Memory of Her: A Feminist Theological Reconstruction of Christian Origins* [1983] and *Bread, Not Stone: The Challenge of Feminist Biblical Interpretation* [1984]) were written before Ruether's 1986 work, I read those two books after I had read Ruether. Fiorenza opened me to the world of feminist biblical interpretation—an interpretation that begins with a "hermeneutics of suspicion that applies to both contemporary androcentric interpretations of the Bible and the biblical texts themselves" (Fiorenza, 1984, xii). This "hermeneutics of suspicion" requires an exploration of the structures of patriarchy, androcentrism, classism, and clericalism that influenced the writing of Scripture, the development of the church, and certainly women's place in the church. This brief chapter cannot begin to do justice to the pioneering and groundbreaking work of such feminist scholars as Ruether and Fiorenza. But it can acknowledge their contribution to a fuller understanding of who we are as Christian/Catholics and who we are as church. In my personal story, their work was foundational in joining my story with the story of countless other women in the history of the church. In my academic work as pastoral theologian, their writing changed my conception of the field in several ways: I realized that being a Roman Catholic would still set me apart in the field of largely Protestant pastoral theology. Although I felt connected to the other women in my field, I realized that as a Roman Catholic, my history, my orientation, and my concerns would often differ from my Protestant, feminist colleagues. Because of this I felt more connected to the Roman Catholic, feminist, biblical, and systematic theologians than to the Protestant, feminist pastoral theologians who were now my colleagues in the academy. Realizing this clarified what I saw as a necessary and foundational task for the field of pastoral theology—to consider what it means to be ecumenical—inclusive of faith traditions *other* than Protestant traditions. This would involve acknowledging biases in the field of pastoral theology that "mitigate against the inclusion of different perspectives" (Thornton, 1993, 67). These biases include an unwillingness to extend beyond the familiar (Protestant) and a lack of awareness that any injustice even exists. For me, this meant that as always, I would be an outsider—this time in a Protestant world. The difference, however, is that my prophetic voice has been both welcomed and encouraged.[5]

According to feminist, Roman Catholic theologian Anne Carr, the emergence of feminist consciousness in the writings of Ruether and Fiorenza assumed three tasks, the first of which I have already described: the critique of tradition. The second task, according to Carr, was the recovery of women in Christian history, which Fiorenza describes as an attempt to "restore women's stories to early Christianity" (Fiorenza, 1983, xiv). I see both tasks as part of doing social analysis. The third task of early feminist theology is theological reconstruction (Carr, 1993, 9-11), which coincides with the third and fourth moments of the pastoral circle—theological reflection and pastoral planning.

Continuing the Conversation: Theological Reflection

To separate theological reflection from social analysis is almost impossible. The two moments are inextricably woven together and are meant to complement each other. "In a wider sense, all the moments of the circle are part of an expanded definition of theology. All are linked and overlapped" (Holland & Henriot, 1983, 13). Yet the focus of theological reflection is unique from social analysis: theological reflection looks at underlying methodological assumptions, the relationship of social analysis and theology, trying to understand the analyzed experience in relation to "faith, scripture, church social teaching, and the resources of tradition" (Holland & Henriot, 1983, 9). According to well-known Roman Catholic theologians Evelyn and James Whitehead, doing theological reflection in ministry requires a shift from a single authority making a decision to the believing community making a decision. The community of faith is considered the "locus" of both theological and pastoral reflection (Whitehead & Whitehead, 1995, xiii).

The concept of the whole community engaging in theological reflection represents a shift in Roman Catholic ecclesiology—how we see ourselves as church. The pre–Vatican II model of church as hierarchical institution has been replaced with the conciliar model of church as the *People of God* (*Lumen Gentium*, chap. 2), and the postconciliar model of church as basic Christian community that began in Latin America in the 1960s.

For both Ruether and Fiorenza, doing theological reflection includes looking to the history of various prophetic and liberation perspectives and the communities from which these perspectives developed. For Ruether this means reexamining the prophetic tradition of Scripture and seeing what this had to say to the critique of patriarchy (Ruether, 1986, 41). Doing this leads to a rejection of patriarchy as God's will (Ruether, 1986, 56). Fiorenza names the feminist movement in scriptural studies as a liberation movement, whose goal is "liberation from all patriarchal alienation, marginalization, and exploitation" (Fiorenza, 1984, xv). She describes the feminist critical interpretation of Scripture as having its point of departure with "women's experience in their struggle for liberation" (Fiorenza, 1984, 13). This is akin to all liberation theologies that take as their starting point "the insight that all theology knowingly or not is by definition always engaged for or against the oppressed" (Fiorenza, 1984, 137).

My readings in Latin American liberation theology resonated with my readings in feminist theology. Feminist theology requires a conversion of perspective—from believing that theology must be done exclusively from the perspective of men and making men's experience the norm, to believing that theology must include the perspective and experiences of women. So also liberation theology requires a conversion—from believing that theology must be done by the elite, or those in power, to believing that theology must be done by living one's life in solidarity with poor and oppressed persons. This solidarity with poor persons will lead us to action on their behalf.

The "poor and oppressed" mentioned by so many Latin American liberation theologians have primarily been associated with the economically, socially, and politically oppressed people of Latin America. Even though Latin American women are among the most oppressed of the oppressed, most of the writings of liberation theology of the 1970s and 1980s failed to give any particular attention to their plight. In the 1990s Latin American feminist theologians are still few. Few as they are, however, they are beginning to have an impact, and even some of the pioneering male liberation theologians are beginning to pay particular attention to the status of women (Boff, 1987; Gutierrez, 1993, 237). Still, a Latin American, feminist, liberation theology appears to be in its infancy. Connections between racial discrimination, sexism, and capitalist oppression are just beginning to be explored as the concept of *feminization of poverty*[6] is gaining more attention. Latin American, feminist, liberation theologians are making an impact by insisting that "sexism must be seen within, not apart from, the overall situation of oppression suffered by the continent's poor" (Ress, 1990, 385).

Even when not overtly making this connection (between sexism and oppression), the words of the male liberation theologians could easily be applied to women. In speaking of the poor and exploited in Latin America, Gustavo Gutierrez could have been speaking of Roman Catholic women worldwide: "They want to be the active subjects of their own history and to forge a radically different society" (Gutierrez, 1975, 1). Being "active subjects of our own history" assumes that our own experiences as women, or as any oppressed people, are a valid starting point in doing theology, but that our part in the history of the church has often been muted, if not obliterated. Emerging feminist Latin American liberation theologians are beginning to make these connections explicit, as have North American feminist theologians Ruether and Fiorenza, as well as Elizabeth Johnson, who together have been referred to as the three "outstanding leaders in [North American] feminist liberation theology" (Hennelly, 1995, 52).

Thus, theological reflection for the Roman Catholic, feminist, pastoral theologian, like myself, includes calling upon the resources, principles, and methodologies of *both* feminist and liberation theologies, with a special emphasis on the status of women in the history of the church. Combining liberation theology with feminist theology also allows the North American, white, upper-middle-class, feminist, liberation, pastoral theologian to broaden the geographical, racial, and social base from which she works. Doing this will greatly enhance her vision and the justice of her actions.

A New Vision: Pastoral Planning

Pastoral theologian Jeanne Stevenson-Moessner describes a goal of collaboration as "giving hope to women in the midst of despair" (Stevenson-Moessner, 1996c, 4). I see this as an outcome of having engaged in the methodology of the pastoral circle. We can give hope because engaging in the process of social analysis and theological reflection has allowed us to see that our previous understanding of Scripture, tradition, and church was faulty in its blatant exclusion of women (and other poor and oppressed persons) and its promotion of patriarchy, sexism, and androcentrism. In seeing this we can see that much needs to be done, and in its doing, we can indeed feel hopeful and give hope to others. To again quote Jeanne Stevenson-Moessner, "pain is not the end of the story" (Stevenson-Moessner, 1996c, 4).

In relation to leadership in the church, our pastoral planning, our "response of action" (Holland & Henriot, 1983, 9), will involve constructing new leadership forms in the church and in pastoral theology that include women in all facets. The community itself will need to dismantle clericalism and reconstruct a church built on a "liberation understanding of ministry" (Ruether, 1986, 75). The community itself will decide "what expressions of liturgy, learning, and service it wishes to engage in as expressions of its growth in community life" (Ruether, 1986, 89). Our pastoral planning includes continuing to "reconstruct early Christian history as women's history . . . and reclaim[ing] this history as the history of women and men" (Fiorenza, 1983, xiv).

Much of this is already under way. The world in which I teach, twenty years after receiving my M.Div. degree, is a different one. I now teach at a Roman

Catholic graduate school of theology and ministry that prepares primarily *lay-women* for ministry in the church. A variety of lay ministries is now open to women—including pastoral visitor (providing pastoral care), pastoral associate (serving as an associate to the pastor), pastoral administrator (assuming responsibility for the pastoring of a parish in the absence of an ordained priest), and pastoral counselor (AAPC now allows lay Catholics into membership). Yet the world in which I teach is still very much the same. Women still cannot be ordained to the priesthood, and restrictions are still put on women because of their gender and lay status.[7]

As a professor of pastoral theology, I still face issues similar to those I faced as a pastoral minister—twenty years ago. Just as I was part of the first generation of Roman Catholic women preparing for professional lay ministry, I am now part of the first generation of female pastoral theologians[8] (Miller-McLemore, 1996, 19). I still struggle to find mentors, or at least colleagues, with similar experiences and interests. I still struggle with finding resources that are written by women—specifically Roman Catholic women—that both speak to and affirm who I am. The 1990s have brought a plethora of material by female pastoral theologians, this book being but one example. But I am painfully aware that I am the only Roman Catholic voice in this voice, and one of the few lay voices in this book.

I know that the end of the story is not pain, but I am aware that much of the story will involve grieving. This grieving for myself and for my Roman Catholic, female students continues to be complicated because of complications we face at every phase of our discernment process—in our *experience* of call, in our *understanding* of call, in our *acceptance* of our call, and in the *validation* of our call (Karaban, 1998, 85). Our grieving will be continuous and unresolved since we cannot come to a point of resolution.[9] I am now at a point in my discernment, in my ministry, and in my professional career as a pastoral theologian that I have sufficiently worked through much of my grieving and can help other Roman Catholic women (and men) in their grieving. In my teaching and writing in pastoral theology, I continue to use the methodology of the pastoral circle and the resources of Roman Catholic feminist and liberation theologians. I continue to encourage all people, and in particular, women, to name, know, and acknowledge their calls, for I am ever more painfully aware that "when women cannot voice their needs, feelings, experiences and perceptions, [and I would add calls], the heart and mind become constricted, and dangerous consequences follow" (Gill-Austern, 1997, 44). The dangerous consequences are felt not only by women, but also by the entire church and the academy. I have come to a point in my life where I am in a position—as a professor of pastoral theology—to challenge the unjust structures that exist in the academy and in my church on a systemic level, and to encourage my students to do the same. I believe the academy and the church, *our* academy and *our* church, will greatly benefit from our efforts.

Notes

[1] In my 1983 Ph.D. dissertation and in my 1992 address to the Society for Pastoral Theology (published in 1993), I looked at pastoral counseling from a lay, Roman Catholic perspective. I delineated various biases in the field that excluded lay Catholics and suggested new possibilities for doing pastoral counseling as lay Catholics.

[2] See "Instruction on Certain Questions Regarding the Nonordained Faithful in the Sacred Ministry of Priests" (1997) and "Response to the *Dubium* on Ordaining Women to the Ministerial Priesthood" (1995).

[3] See "Instruction on the Ecclesial Vocation of the Theologian" (1990) and "From the Heart of the Church" (1990) for detailed explanations of these restrictions. Most recently, the apostolic letter of Pope John Paul II, "To Defend the Faith" (1998), places penalties as strong as excommunication for *any* who defy church teachings on such matters as the ordination of women.

[4] Bausch describes the "smaller story" as "the story of ourselves, of God's movement in our own personal story" (p. 204).

[5] In 1992 I was invited to address the Society of Pastoral Theology on my experience as a lay, Roman Catholic, pastoral theologian; this talk was published the following year in the *Journal of Pastoral Theology* 3 (summer 1993): 55-66. In 1996 I was invited to write this chapter for this book—once again as a lay, Roman Catholic, pastoral theologian.

[6] This term was coined to describe a composite picture of poverty (female) in North America, but may apply to many situations throughout the world.

[7] See "Response to the *Dubium* on Ordaining Women to the Ministerial Priesthood" (1995) and "Instruction on Certain Questions Regarding the Collaboration of the Nonordained Faithful in the Sacred Ministry of Priests" (1997).

[8] I would name here my many female colleagues in the Society of Pastoral Theology, primarily Protestant, but including at least a few Roman Catholics.

[9] See my most recent book, *Responding to God's Call: A Survival Guide* (1998), for a detailed description of call and complicated grief, particularly in the Roman Catholic context.

4

Feminist Theory in Pastoral Theology

Bonnie J. Miller-McLemore

Feminist theory has had a broad impact on the study of religion. When I did Ph.D. work more than a decade ago, few texts by women, much less feminists or womanists, were included on the exam bibliographies, and dissertation research on "women's issues" met with mixed reactions. Today scholars in religion in the United States take feminist and womanist theory more seriously, even though they might not claim feminist or womanist identities per se. Certainly, wariness and outright hostility about the inclusion of power and gender analyses still abound, especially in conservative settings in the United States and on the international scene. But generally speaking, the study of religion, theology, and Scripture will never be quite the same again. Feminist and womanist thought has exposed the misogyny embedded in traditions and institutions that have characterized women as emotionally juvenile, morally and intellectually inferior, and spiritually evil. It has interrogated the very categories and customs that define religion.

Has the valley of genuine equality been lifted up and the mountain of sexism been made low? My rhetorical question suggests both the apocalyptic character of feminist hopes and the ongoing need for more analysis and transformation. What happens for feminists when mainstream scholars selectively use insights internal to feminist discourse? What are the issues distinct to the field of pastoral theology and its use of feminist discourse? Have feminist and womanist voices influenced pastoral theology to the same extent as other fields in religion, and if not, why not? What are some of the ways secular feminist theory itself has evolved, and how might feminist pastoral theologians make better, more critical use of it?

While I will not answer these questions comprehensively, I will begin the task of addressing them. I embark on this exploration by looking first at feminist theory itself, focusing primarily on definitions of feminism and their relationship to pastoral theology. I conclude by briefly identifying prominent characteristics of feminist pastoral theology and situating it within broader discussions of pastoral and practical theology as contemporary disciplines in search of clearer identities. Feminist theory in pastoral theology has seldom received clear articulation because of the precariousness of the practical disciplines and the difficulties of honoring in theoretical discussions the idiosyncrasies of ordinary lived experience—quotidian life with which women are often most familiar. Feminist analysis suggests that it is no accident that the closer one gets to practice, particular experiences, personal faith, emotions, and subjectivity, the lower the academic status of the field.

Feminist Theory: Working Definitions

bell hooks's complaint about the careless use of the term *feminist* is a fitting corrective for current discussions in pastoral and practical theology (hooks, 1984, 23). Such carelessness characterizes literature on the pastoral care of women that assumes a great deal of feminist scholarship but avoids explicitly claiming or defining its feminist agenda. Closer to home, have I ever declared myself a feminist pastoral theologian? Probably not as forthrightly as I might have done. Refraining from such a declaration says something about the troubled meaning of the term in culture and congregations. Who knows what *feminist* means anymore? More often than not, many people associate the term with radical male-bashing politics. They reject feminism—all the while accepting, and sometimes even welcoming, a multitude of changes spawned by feminism.

On the other hand, are people justified in assuming, as is often the case, that I or any other woman in pastoral theology or ministry is a feminist simply by being a woman? Ironically, theories of liberation tend to create ontological categorizations in their very efforts to liberate particular groups. Such theories assign a person attributes because that person is a "woman," thereby perpetuating stereotypes that liberationists actually want to undo (see Anderson, 1995). Automatic assumptions about sex identity fail to grasp the far-reaching implications of feminist theory itself.

hooks provides a powerful definition of feminism. Simply put, feminism is a radical political movement. She writes: "Feminism is a struggle to end sexist oppression. Its aim is not to benefit solely any specific group of women, any particular race or class of women. It does not privilege women over men. It has the power to transform in a meaningful way all our lives" (1984, 26). As a Black feminist, hooks is particularly concerned about the misuse of feminist theory in denying the realities and struggles of women of color. To call feminism simply a movement to make men and women equal reduces and even confuses its full intent. This is particularly true when an emphasis on sexual equality discounts the weight of other inequities and when sexual equality in the midst of sexual difference remains an elusive ideal. Feminism is far more than a movement to achieve equal rights, individual freedom, and economic and social equity for middle-class White women. Instead, a feminist perspective demands a critical analysis of structures and ideologies that rank people as inferior or superior according to various traits of human nature, whether gender, sexual orientation, class, color, age, physical ability, and so forth. Feminism strives to eradicate sexism and related exploitative classificatory systems and to allow those silenced to join in the cultural activity of defining reality.

To think about the study of religion from this perspective demands an analysis of structures and ideologies that rank academic study as superior or inferior depending on its distance from or proximity to religious faith, concrete lives, emotions, and women's activities. Why, for example, are the complex thinking, acting, and teaching required to sustain viable practices of all kinds, and religious practices in particular (i.e., practical thinking), the most academically disregarded or disreputable? This disregard seems especially peculiar given the importance of healthy religious practices for human sustenance and survival—something the ecological movement has made most apparent in recent years.

As this example demonstrates, to think about practical theology from the vantage point of feminist theory requires prophetic, transformative challenge to systems of stratification and domination within the academy and to systems of power and authority within society and religious life, particularly those that rank men and male activities over women and female activities. Obviously, this is a huge agenda with multiple obligations, from challenging the assumed superiority of abstruse, highly theoretical forms of theological reflection, for example, to addressing the devaluing of women's lives or the ongoing resistance in congregations to making liturgy gender-inclusive.

More specifically, to think about pastoral theology from the feminist perspective defined above requires a fundamental reorientation of the core functions of pastoral care. In place of or in addition to the conventional modes with which pastoral care has been routinely equated—healing, sustaining, guiding, and reconciling, articulated by Seward Hiltner (1958) and amended by William Clebsch and Charles Jaekle (1964)—four other pastoral practices acquire particular importance: resisting, empowering, nurturing, and liberating.[1] Although not yet classified as four distinct typologies of pastoral care, these four practices have received extensive attention in many recent writings in pastoral theology. These activities are not exhaustive of new pastoral modalities sparked by feminism and womanism and do not offer a comprehensive picture of new definitions. But they need to be recognized and marked as fresh, prominent ways for reorganizing the functions of pastoral care.

While all or some of the four functions of resisting, empowering, nurturing, and liberating have operated during the historical periods described by Clebsch and Jaekle, they did not receive the kind of preeminence that has come recently as a result of feminist theory. For the moment I offer only rather terse definitions to give a general flavor of recent feminist-and womanist-influenced trends. *Compassionate resistance* requires confrontation with evil, contesting violent, abusive behaviors that perpetuate undeserved suffering and false stereotypes that distort the realities of people's lives. *Resistance* includes a focused healing of wounds of abuse that have festered for generations (Ramsay, 1998; see also Poling, 1996). *Empowerment* involves advocacy and tenderness on behalf of the vulnerable, giving resources and means to those previously stripped of authority, voice, and power. *Nurturance* is not sympathetic kindness or quiescent support but fierce, dedicated proclamation of love that makes a space for difficult changes and fosters solidarity among the vulnerable. *Liberation* entails both escape from unjust, unwarranted affliction and release into new life and wholeness as created, redeemed, and loved people of God. Resistance, empowerment, nurturance, and liberation all entail a deconstruction of limited definitions of reality and a reconstruction of new views of the world and one's valued place within it. Pastoral care in these modalities is not particularly "pastoral" or "nice" in the truncated ways in which it has been perceived. Pastoral care disturbs as well as comforts, provokes as well as guides. It breaks silences and calls for radical truth telling; it names shame and guilt, calls for confession and repentance, and moves vigilantly toward forgiveness and reconciliation, knowing that both are even more difficult to effect than people have hoped. Indeed, if pastoral theology keeps the term *shepherd* as a central motif (and even that becomes questionable in a world where shepherding and shearing are no longer common experiences upon which to ground metaphor), a feminist perspective reminds us that sheep are not the warm, fuzzy, and clean creatures our storybook and Bible stories have portrayed.

By fostering redefinition in all three spheres of religious study, practical theology, and pastoral theology, feminist theory participates in undercutting primary assumptions of modernism, including the universality of certain pastoral "truths" and the inherent authority of male clerics, and ushers in a postmodern awareness of the influence of power in the formation of knowledge. Postmodernism signals the breaking up of the hegemony of modern Western culture and a receptivity to other perspectives. At the same time, this does not mean the absolute undoing of Western culture; feminist theory does not de facto mean the deconstruction of all knowledge. Feminist arguments for shared, if not universal, assumptions about truth, justice, and many other matters can and must be made. Complete deconstruction is a final stage of later modernism rather than a stage beyond modernism. Maureen Kemeza remarks, "Nihilistic deconstructionism is a dead end, at best only descriptive of the current crises without any resource for creative response" (1996, 1148). Some liberation theologies and feminist theories represent a more genuine *post*modernism in terms of constructing new theories *after* modernism.

Varieties of and Shifts in Feminist Theory

Such single-mindedness of purpose, however, has not been the nature of feminist thought. Perhaps one of the most common misperceptions is that feminism represents a monolithic movement. Entire books, such as Rosemarie Tong's *Feminist Thought*, are devoted to characterizing the various sorts of feminism, such as liberal, Marxist, radical, psychoanalytic, socialist, and postmodern feminism (1989).

In applying this typology to pastoral theology, we notice that because of the heavy reliance on psychology in pastoral theory, psychoanalytic feminists have influenced pastoral theology powerfully, perhaps more than other feminist views. In Tong's words, psychoanalytic feminists "find the root of women's oppression embedded deep in her psyche" (p. 5). This idea alone carries critical implications for pastoral theologians considering problems of individuals and families within congregations such as marital conflict, depression, abuse, and so forth. Psychoanalytic feminists such as Karen Horney (1950, 1973) have emphasized the role of a sexist social environment in shaping and distorting male and female development; others such as Nancy Chodorow (1974, 1978)

81

have explored the prominent role of the mother in reproducing patterns of female fear of separation and male fear of relationship. These ideas prove especially useful in rethinking pastoral care of women and men. Moreover, psychoanalytic feminists provide a cultural critique of the implicit biases of psychology and therapeutic practice—a moral critique of values already familiar to theologians concerned about unreflective adoption of psychology by pastoral caregivers (see Sturdivant, 1984).

However, I cannot think of any feminist pastoral theologian who would identify herself solely as a psychoanalytic feminist. More typically, pastoral theologians pick and choose from many schools of thought. Doing this becomes a problem only when done without sufficient statement of a rationale for selection.

At least one rationale for moving beyond psychoanalytic feminism lies in the broader moral and communal concerns of pastoral theology. This warrants employment of other forms of feminist thought, such as socialist feminism. Tong characterizes socialist feminism as a synthetic movement that attempts to interrelate the myriad forms of oppression in patterns of economic production (from Marxist feminists), in practices of reproduction and sexuality (from radical feminists), and in structures of domesticity and socialization of children (from liberal feminists). Socialist feminists contend that women are oppressed by both economic inequities and patriarchal devaluing of domestic and childbearing responsibilities. A woman's status and function "in all these structures must change if she is to achieve anything approximating full liberation" (Tong, 1989, 6). Since pastoral theology is an integrative discipline that works at the intersection of personal experience, tradition, culture, and community, pastoral theologians should see a socialist feminist approach as particularly useful and appropriate.

Yet feminists in pastoral theology are not alone in resisting labels, and many feminists do not fall neatly into one or the other category. Although they serve a useful analytic function, labels retain an artificiality that distorts the heterogeneous character of feminist thought. hooks's definition, which I have adopted and applied above, actually represents just such a blend of radical, socialist, and postmodern feminism. I have defined a type of pastoral theological feminism that builds on but slightly departs from the traditional liberal feminist emphasis on the logistical restraints that block women's entrance into the public sphere.

My working definition actually represents a broader shift in the feminist discussion. A simpler and theologically relevant schema for depicting the development of feminist theory in pastoral theology can be borrowed from a classification developed by philosopher Iris Young (1985). She identifies a movement in the late twentieth century from what she calls humanist to gynocentric feminism. Despite the blending from time to time of these two forms of feminism in the women's movements of the nineteenth and twentieth centuries, liberal or humanist feminism predominated in the United States from the 1960s to the late 1970s. Humanist feminism captured the public imagination and is often the position with which feminism is identified. Humanist feminism also has a decidedly White, North American bias, shaped by democratic ideals of equal participation and self-sufficiency. In the 1960s, early second-wave feminist theory evolved in response to the particular problems of the isolated and disempowered White, middle-class, college-educated housewife. In response to views of women as inherently inferior to men, humanist feminism defined "femininity as the primary vehicle of women's oppression, and called upon male dominated institutions to allow women the opportunity to participate fully in the public world-making activities" (Young, 1985, 173).

Several factors led to a shift from humanist to gynocentric feminism. Many women, especially women of color, working-class women, and mothers, felt disenfranchised by humanist feminist assumptions. African American women, for example, did not see men or confinement in the home as the source of their problems and depended on solidarity between women and men to resist racism and its related problems. They recognized the multiple and destructive ways in which White feminists who sought liberation acted in turn as participants in the belittlement and disenfranchisement of Black women and men, with little or no consciousness or concern. Women of color more generally did not aspire to the social status of the men they knew, who often did not have the same economic and social opportunities as the men of the dominant class. In addition, various injustices arose in treating women and men "alike" in the workplace or in divorce proceedings, for example, when reproductive and economic differences between men and women persisted and affected women's lives in distinct ways. In the late 1970s and 1980s, women began to recognize some of the goals of humanist feminists as male-defined ideals that involved the repression of the body and relationality—power over others, competition and triumph, individual self-sufficiency, and personal fulfillment. Gynocentric feminists located women's oppression not in femininity per se but in a masculinist culture's denial of the female body, nature, and other modes of relational knowing and deciding, including maternal thinking, and in broader structures of oppression. Feminists still wanted equality with men but began to talk about an equality that encompassed sexual and other differences.

The outcome of this shift in feminist theory for the academy is still unclear. In some respects, a gynocentric feminism is less critical or overtly angry and hence represents a less visible attack on traditional scholarship and practices. Gynocentric feminism can actually perpetuate stereotypes of women as essentially more caring, relational, and maternal. It can accommodate too easily to existing structures and underestimate both the danger of conventional definitions of femininity and the value of male-associated activities. Alone it is not a sufficient base for an adequate feminist pastoral theology. Humanist feminists are partly justified in their accusations that gynocentric feminists have forsaken radical feminist politics. Yet gynocentric feminism asks for more fundamental changes in basic assumptions about gender, sexual difference, and power in Western thought. Political action that subverts conventional practices becomes less tied to women's oppression, more tied to social oppressions as a whole, and hence more complex and difficult.

In general, feminists and womanists in the academy walk a tightrope between acquiring the necessary tools of the master's house to survive and creating new tools for genuinely transformative work. True, as Audre Lorde first argued, one cannot dismantle the master's house using the master's tools (1984, 110-113). One must break new ground and free oneself from portrayals of the world that obscure alternative realities. On the other hand, no one creates in a vacuum; dominant perceptions of the world must be confronted, and confrontation requires knowledge. Both moves, Black feminist Patricia Hill Collins suggests, are ultimately more necessary than Audre Lorde first supposed.[2]

Feminist Theory and Feminist Theology

Feminist theory did not emerge out of thin air, and Christian ideas about freedom and human worth appear at least implicitly in hooks's definition. Although the history of the relationship of Christianity and women is far from simple and unambiguous, Christianity has influenced feminism and womanism as much as the reverse. Anne Carr (1988), Elisabeth Schüssler Fiorenza (1984), Rosemary Radford Ruether (1983), and Delores Williams (1993), to mention only a few, have developed the thesis that Christianity has ideals internal to itself that are closely aligned with feminist and womanist ideals—justice, liberation of the oppressed, survival and well-being, radical mutuality, egalitarian community, the inherent worth of women. Christianity and feminism, Carr argues, are not only compatible. They "are, in fact, integrally and firmly connected in the truth of the Christian vision." Feminist critique has served to reveal the "transcendent truth" within the symbols and traditions (1988, 1-2).

Partially corresponding to developments in secular feminism, in theological circles feminist theory can be traced from (a) a humanist emphasis in early theological feminism to (b) a gynocentric religious feminism to (c) a nascent ecological religious feminism that combines elements of both. In the last two decades, feminist discussion has shifted from critical assessment of patriarchal traditions to inclusion of the history and knowledge of women and to new constructive projects in Scripture, ethics, and theology from a variety of diverse perspectives.

In contrast to both Tong's and Young's schema, however, feminist and womanist theologians are divided more along denominational or religious lines and according to conservative and progressive politics than as socialist, psychoanalytic, radical, humanist, or gynocentric (see Browning, Miller-McLemore et al., 1997, chap. 6). By and large, feminists in theology draw on more than one school of feminist theory and even subvert the divisions between schools.

Indeed, Ruether grounds her classic work *Sexism and God-Talk* (1983) in the very attempt to avoid the dichotomies between radical, social, and liberal feminism. Others, such as Judith Plaskow, suggest that a religious anthropology avoids the dualism between culture and nature typical of liberal and radical feminist theory. Plaskow observes, "Feminist theologians, perhaps because they have been forced to grapple with historical images of women, generally have not found rejection of women's body experience an attractive path," as in De Beauvoir or Shulamith Firestone (1981, 57). Nor have they indulged in exaltation of it. In general, feminist theorists in theology have not engaged in the bitter battles apparent among some secular feminists.

Powerful shared convictions among Jewish and Christian feminists lend at least a veneer of unity. Feminists and womanists of conservative and progressive religious backgrounds share the conviction that Christian and Jewish traditions are important sources of empowerment, despite their male-defined narratives and symbols. As part of this stance, religious thinkers share a list of theological affirmations. Feminist and womanist theologians emphasize the creation of women in the image of God and hence their inherent worth as partners and cocreators in life. They write about the imperative of egalitarian relationships of love, justice, and shared responsibility within families and society. The attempt to understand the religious and social grounds for radical mutuality is perhaps one of the most prominent common themes. They warn against the dangers and violence of patriarchy and racism, but contend that Judaism and Christianity when critically reinterpreted hold an array of antipatriarchal, antiracist values. They speak about the necessity of redefining religious doctrines of love, sexuality, sin, servanthood, and redemption. They seek a holistic view of creation and redemption that holds body and mind, material and spiritual needs in dialectical relation. Finally, they are sensitive to individuals and groups that have been relegated to the margins of social existence. These themes receive different interpretations, depending on the authority given to religious traditions and the extent of the critique of patriarchy, but their presence is pervasive among feminist and womanist theologians.

The Impact of Feminist Theory on Practical and Pastoral Theology

Given these definitions of feminist theory and feminist theology, three general observations about the impact of feminist theory on practical and pastoral theology can be made. First, not surprisingly, there is sometimes a greater unity of method between feminists in practical theology and feminists in systematic theology than among feminists in practical theology and other practical theologians. Feminists and womanists in the other fields of study in religion have themselves become more interdisciplinary and anthropological in their approaches. Understanding lived subjective experience becomes an important means of mapping the making and unmaking of culture in a variety of fields in religious studies.

Second, when feminist theory and women's studies become prominent dialogue partners for those in practical theology, the distinctions between different types of practical theology fade. For example, although the different chapters on religious education, pastoral theology, homiletics, and so forth in the edited collection *Arts of Ministry: Feminist-Womanist Approaches* (1996) represent different foci in practical theology, they are united by commonalities in feminist resources and orientation. Across the board, a praxis method attempts to privilege marginalized perspectives, deconstruct dominant texts, resist evil, and promote justice (Neuger, 1996, 201).

Third and related to my first point, sometimes the best pastoral and practical theology does not come from those who call themselves by such names. Church historian Roberta Bondi's work is a case in point. Her struggles with the repressive images of an authoritarian God in her confessional Baptist background and with the objective abstractions of higher education in religion led her to redefine "the primary stuff of theology." In contrast to theology as "abstract, logical, propositional, and systematic" and the "hierarchy of truth" that does not "waste its time addressing the personal and the 'subjective,' the everyday or the particular," theology is about the messy particularity of everyday lives examined with excruciating care and brought into conversation with the great doctrines of the Christian tradition (1995, 9, 17). While bell hooks would not identify herself as a pastoral theologian, when her efforts to address the sufferings and healing of African American women lead her to emphasize the wisdom of the elders, the movement of the spirit, and the resources of religious traditions and communities, then she comes close to qualifying (1993). Womanists in general and liberation theologians in Black, Hispanic, and Asian traditions almost always have a powerful pastoral intent and method behind their work in a variety of technically nonpastoral fields of study, such as Bible or ethics. Their work in particular cuts across and contests the traditional organization of the theological enterprise. This final observation raises two difficult questions: Is everyone who actually works as a practical theologian at the table in the formal academic discussion of practical theology? Is it even possible or realistic or wise to invite everyone?

Developments in Feminist Pastoral Theology

In contrast to progress made in other areas of systematic, biblical, and historical theology, explicit consideration of feminist and womanist theory in pastoral theology has taken longer to reach the table. There is a one-generational lag between the feminist and womanist publications in Bible, ethics, and systematic theology and those in pastoral theology. Unabashed feminist and womanist publications in practical theology are fairly recent (Ackermann & Bons-Storm, 1998; Bons-Storm, 1996a; DeMarinis, 1993; Hollies, 1991; Neuger, 1996). Many persons pursue feminist ideas and methods without candid or straightforward advocacy of a feminist position (Glaz & Stevenson-Moessner, 1991). Elsewhere I have speculated about one of the reasons (Miller-McLemore, 1996, 19). Proximity to the more conserving structures of congregations, designed to preserve traditions, makes the introduction of the politically and spiritually disruptive ideas and practices of feminism and womanism prohibitive and complicated. Perhaps, one might speculate, more conservative people are drawn to practical fields. Or on the other hand, when working with congregations, one temporarily suspends alien and disruptive notions until they can be well received. Or perhaps it is only that practical fields attract more "doers" than "theorizers."

Other reasons for delayed reflection on a feminist pastoral theology might be adduced. The precariousness of the field itself and the potentially increased liabilities of adding feminism and womanism preclude discussion. To be a feminist is "to be perpetually aware of [one's] marginality," remarks English professor Gail Griffin, "indeed, it means on some level to choose it, to resist full belonging" (1992, 26). Why would one choose further marginalization in a field that already suffers that plight? Adding feminist theory to pastoral theology renders its position even more precarious as a discipline peculiarly poised between practice, person, confessional religious congregations, and the academy. Feminist and womanist scholars work within a still largely masculinist academy only mildly disturbed by our invasion of the sacred grove of intellectual pursuits.

Another factor contributes to a relative absence of explicit feminist discussion in the field. Certain methods in pastoral and practical theology already resemble elements in a feminist approach. One does not need feminist theory, for example, to justify engaging personal and marginalized experience as a source of theological reflection or to see the value of critical correlation between theology and life or the use of the social sciences. Finally, more recently, scholars in pastoral theology have recognized the ambiguities and limits of liberal European American feminism. Early humanist feminism cannot speak for all women. In addition, humanist feminism tended to ignore commitments to nurture, care, and relationship that remain central to pastoral theology. Underrepresented perspectives, including womanist views, are partly jeopardized by the sheer fact of fewer numbers. Only recently have more women of color entered programs, received academic degrees, and acquired teaching positions in pastoral theology.

I am not alone in my concern about the need for explicit examination of feminist practical and pastoral theology. Riet Bons-Storm and Denise Ackermann open their introduction to an edited collection of feminist practical theologies by observing that "practical theology is probably the theological discipline least influenced by feminist voices" (1998, 1). In their effort to determine reasons, they go farther back and blame male scholarship itself. Practical theology remains "overwhelmingly a male-dominated discipline" (p. 4). This is most apparent on the international scene but true of the United States as well. As a result, three additional factors lead to the paucity of feminist reflection. First, the modern prominence of a male clerical paradigm excluded women as actors and subjects. Second, male clerics learned to practice "feminine" emotional skills and had even less need for female input. Third, related to my observation above, an obsession with the identity crises of the field and male insecurities about their own academic identity render the inclusion of the unfamiliar and the unexplored even more difficult and unsettling (pp. 1-3).

Prominent Characteristics of Feminist Pastoral Theology

The generational lag or dearth of explicit reflection on feminism in pastoral theology might be characterized differently, however. Over the past three decades, feminist pastoral theology has generated a significant body of literature with three kinds of projects in mind: implicit critique of patriarchy; explicit critique and advocacy for women and other marginalized populations; and topical reconstruction.

The first project of implicit critique and unrest appears in the largely unpublished but compelling activities of women in the field, perhaps best exemplified by the work of Peggy Way. Since the 1960s, Way has mentored women in the field and used public speaking engagements to disturb the status quo on subjects such as violence in the family. She contested the conventional boundaries dictated by systematic theologians and demanded that pastoral theology grapple with the particularities of suffering and the ecclesial context of care (Way, 1970a, 1980, 1990). Texts such as *Women in Travail and Transition* (Glaz & Stevenson-Moessner, 1991) and *Life Cycles: Women and Pastoral Care* (Graham & Halsey, 1993), also tend to focus on the experiences of women, assuming and promoting but not explicitly identifying, describing, and pursuing feminist theory or politics. The primary agenda is incorporating women's lives and voices into the traditions of reflection and practices of care, sometimes presuming that others have already completed the prior task of exposing androcentrism.

The second project of explicit critique of the classic texts and theories of pastoral theology has been more erratic. Articles on feminism and pastoral theology by Carrie Doehring (1992) and Christie Neuger (1992) and Valerie DeMarinis's *Critical Caring* (1993) suggest the importance of a hermeneutic of suspicion toward traditional scholarship and advocate active resistance to patriarchy as does the more recent book by Riet Bons-Storm on breaking the silences that render women invisible and powerless (1996). Even in this body of literature, however, the primary goal usually remains pastoral. As in the introduction to *Through the Eyes of Women*, the overarching intent is to give "hope to women in the midst of despair" (1996, 4). Feminist critique is secondary or rather important primarily in its relationship to this central pastoral goal. Sexism is seen as contributing to but not as the fundamental source of conditions for women's despair.

The third project of reconstruction in feminist pastoral theology involves extensive engagement with particular thematic practices or topics, placing them within a broader panorama of psychological, cultural, and theological critique and reformulation. Several book-length treatments of important themes pertaining to women but also relevant to men and the field as a whole have appeared in just the last decade—poverty (Couture, 1991), self-esteem (Saussy, 1991), anger (Saussy, 1995), depression (Dunlap, 1997), aggression (Greider, 1997), violence (Cooper-White, 1995), and work and family life (Miller-McLemore, 1994). These are paradigmatic texts that have not yet received adequate attention as a significant body of literature in feminist theory and theological practice. While diverse in specific focus, they establish a new example of pastoral theological research unified by at least five elements: revised correlational method; psychological and cultural sources; power analysis; feminist positioning; and pastoral intent.

Using Young's scheme, feminist pastoral theologians in all three projects have had a decidedly gynocentric, rather than humanist, flavor. Although concerned about rights and equality, they have focused on women-centered knowledge and relationships. This leaning toward a gynocentric approach accounts in part for the more oblique feminist critique.

Work in all three areas is also characterized by a threefold methodological emphasis on context, collaboration, and diversity. First, knowledge emerges within particular contexts and is defined by one's proximity to practices and not always along conventional academic lines. Clinical assessment involves social, contextual analysis. Psychological theory, though still important, plays a less commanding role. In using the social sciences, a feminist critique of the social and political biases of psychology is added as a second layer of analysis alongside moral and hermeneutical critiques of psychology. Other humanist and social sciences that contribute to understanding the broader cultural context, such as public policy, history, and sociology, have a place in pastoral analysis.

Second, adequate coverage of the issues requires a nonadversarial, even relational constructive interaction among colleagues. Several initial efforts to define a new pastoral care, including this text, have involved collaborative efforts and edited collections rather than work by a single author. Finally, acknowledging the limits of one's vantage point becomes a common refrain and an invitation for further conversation. At the end of my preface of *Also a Mother,* I express a prevalent sentiment: "I, for one, want to hear other voices, voices different from my own" (1994, 15). The work of feminist pastoral theology is necessarily as limited as the range of its participants. In the past several decades, the participants have most often been European American Protestants. Under hooks's definition, this remains cause for concern and inspiration for corrective action. How can a richer diversity of perspectives, particularly womanist, Asian, and Hispanic, begin to reshape fundamental presuppositions of pastoral theology?

New Developments in Pastoral and Practical Theology:
Wariness and Appreciation

In an attempt to define how one studies religion in the field of pastoral theology, I have argued that anyone who wants to do constructive theoretical work in pastoral and practical theology must address and in some fashion dispel the persistent identity crisis of the fields or at least situate one's work in relation to this crisis (1998, 179). David Tracy identifies three publics for which those in religion write: academy, society, and church. More than in any other area in the study of religion, those in pastoral and practical theology often attempt to speak and write for all three (1981, 5). This cross-public audience is not new. Historically, theologians who worked in ways analogous to the field of practical theology today also addressed multiple publics. A chief difference today is the striking divisions among these three publics in terms of language, standards of truth, practices and rituals, and norms.

In some contexts—including this chapter itself—*pastoral* and *practical* theology are used as interchangeable terms. The two fields do have a close relationship. Those within practical theology share three elements: a common history within the evolution of the academy of religion and the division into biblical, historical, systematic, and practical theology; a common correlational method bringing together theology, the human sciences, and religious experiences; and a common concern with specific religious and congregational disciplines and practices.

Practical theologians differ in the United States, particularly within Protestant circles, however, according to the particular science with which they are most conversant and the specific religious practices in which they have interest. Pastoral theology focuses on care of persons and finds personality theories, particularly within psychology, primary resources for the enhancement of this practice. Distinct from other areas of religious study, the object of study in pastoral theology is *"the study of living human documents rather than books"* (Boisen, 1950, cited by Gerkin, 1984, 37, emphasis in the text).

In the past decade, several feminist pastoral theologians have modified the individualistic leanings of Anton Boisen's metaphor by turning to an alternative, related image of the living web (see Couture, 1996; Gill-Austern, 1995; L. Graham, 1992; Miller-McLemore, 1993, 1996). The use of this metaphor, however, does not mean that the individual or the use of psychological sciences that provide insight into personal dynamics recedes in importance. It simply means that the individual is understood in inextricable relationship to the broader context. Psychology, as the primary cognate science for pastoral theology, is not inherently individualistic, having contributed to new understandings of connective selfhood in recent research (see Browning, Miller-McLemore et al., 1997, chap. 7). The metaphor of web also affirms the important role of other social sciences and holds potential for practical theology.

One might argue that to study religion in practical theology is to study the living webs of congregational and social practices. Pastoral care is practical religious, spiritual, and congregational care for the suffering, involving the rich resources of religious traditions and communities, contemporary understandings of the human person in the social sciences, and ultimately, the movement of God's love and hope in the lives of individuals and communities. Pastoral care from a liberation perspective is about breaking silences, urging prophetic action, and liberating the oppressed. Pastoral theology is the critical reflection on this activity. In this schema, pastoral theology is located within the wider umbrella of practical theology along with other disciplines that focus on other religious practices within the congregation, such as homiletics and religious education.

Yet in the mid-twentieth century, pastoral care and theology achieved a certain preeminence, however precarious and unstable, within the academic study of religion and in the congregation. This visibility resulted partly from the clarity that surrounded its disciplinary connections to psychology and theology. These connections established its place in the academy without negating its connection to congregational life. Prominent theologians such as Paul Tillich and Reinhold Niebuhr took developments in Freudian and Rogerian psychology seriously and, by extension, pastoral movements in the clinic and academy that engaged psychological theory. Pastoral theologians benefited from the popular acceptance, prominence, and rapid development of its primary secular science, psychology. And in contrast to religious education and homiletics, pastoral theology benefited from maintaining distinct connections to theology proper, even in the naming of its area of study itself as pastoral *theology*.

In the past several decades, those in the field of pastoral theology made notable contributions to the study of religion in the three areas of method, substance, and process in terms of (1) an emphasis on and exploration of a methodological focus on living persons rather than written doctrines or historical documents of the no-longer living (e.g., Boisen, 1936; Patton, 1990); (2) a substantive use and critical analysis of psychology to expand previous religious understandings of human anthropology to include intrapsychic dynamics, developmental and life cycle processes, and strategies of intersubjective communication (e.g., Browning, 1987; Capps, 1983; Gerkin, 1984; Hiltner, 1958); and (3) a dynamic commitment to healing or change or "therapeutics"—what Rodney Hunter calls the "master metaphor" of the pastoral tradition (1995, 17; e.g., Clinebell, 1984; Oates, 1962; Wise, 1966).

In addition, pastoral theology has not operated only within the sphere of practical theology. Pastoral theology is also one facet of a second arena often identified as "Religion and Personality" by several academic programs in the United States. Scholars of religion and personality can be roughly divided into three groups: those interested in pastoral theology, care, and counseling; those engaged in the critical correlation of religion and culture; and those involved in the empirical or hermeneutical social scientific study of religious experience. While some

European and United States scholars might legitimately see these three groups as subgroups of practical theology, secular scholars in religion and personality teaching in undergraduate programs in the United States would object to the classification of their research and teaching under the heading of theology.

The plethora of guilds in religion and personality and practical theology reflects both the richness of their manifold foci and the confusion over disciplinary boundaries. Some pastoral theologians, notably more of my women colleagues than men, for reasons worth considering, attempt to maintain an allegiance to several academic societies, however ambiguous and difficult. We might surmise that many women desire a more holistic approach to the study of religion, refuse conventional definitions of disciplinary boundaries, feel less bound by or less connected to ministry as it has been formally defined by men, and appreciate the freedom of thought and expression sometimes more characteristic of the academy and programs in religion and personality.

From the perspective of feminist pastoral theology, I am simultaneously wary and appreciative of new developments in practical theology. I am dedicated to a pastoral method that makes the immediate human experience of suffering and compassionate responses to it primary. In feminist pastoral theology, one studies religion at the point where human suffering evokes or calls for a religious response and sometimes at the point where a religious response is given and/or experienced. As bell hooks puts it, one dares "to create theory from the location of pain and struggle." Indeed, she expresses her gratitude to those who so risk, for "it is not easy to name our pain, to theorize from that location"; it takes courage to expose wounds and to lend one's experience as a "means to chart new theoretical journeys" (1994, 74). To a greater extent than other areas of religious studies, pastoral theology makes "limit situations," in Tracy's words, a central focus (1975, 93, 104-108). As I argue in another context, this requires a refusal of the pretense of pure objectivity, an invitation of face-to-face encounter, confrontation, and messiness, and a willingness to participate proactively in a revisionary project that changes the lives of the marginalized and of all the participants (Miller-McLemore, 1998, 186-196).

A great deal of literature in the field of practical theology can be rightly faulted as unnecessarily academic, obtuse, and abstract. In contrast to the practical intent and to other variations of practical theology around the globe, the primary audience and authors of practical theology in the United States mostly reside in the academy, not in the sanctuary or the kitchen (see E. Graham, 1998). At least two consequences emerge. First, some scholars in non-European American communities would not see their work included within the discipline as presently defined in the United States academy, even though they are engaged in important reflection in the midst of theological practices. Second, pressing questions are ignored. Discussions in practical theology and feminist theory remain far removed from faith practices. For example, most congregations have not considered inclusive language, much less the complex implications of new understandings of the Atonement and the Trinity for the words said at the Communion table, preached in the sermon, or sung in hymns.

Too often the problem with the "clerical paradigm" has been blamed on problems with conceptualizations in practical theology (Farley, 1983, 21-41). The focus on techniques of professional ministry as the main subject of modern practical theology is partially due to the limited horizons of the practical theological fields and the obsession with technical training in counseling skills. But the problem of the clerical paradigm is also a result of the movement of systematic and constructive theology away from the messiness of human suffering, the ambiguities and subjectivity of faith claims and spiritual experiences, and the complications of religious and ministerial practices of transformation. The complaints of Edward Farley and others about the clerical paradigm reflect an elitist academic failure to appreciate and to grapple with the work of ministry and the practice of Christian disciplines. Rather than grasping the pressing needs of those in the church and the reasons for the desirability of techniques and strategies, critics condescendingly portray the practical tasks necessary to maintain a local congregation as a healthy community and institution as nontheological or of little or no theological relevance. The final irony: the negative analysis of the clerical paradigm has resulted in a theological education even more abstract and removed from Christian life, faith, and ministerial practice than before the critique.

One goal behind the attempt to redefine practical theology in the past decade is the reclamation of its rightful place in the academy with clearer parameters, objectives, content, and foundations. On the one hand, one must wonder about the attempt to obtain scholarly validity by operating at a greater level of abstraction and theoretical generalization. In schemes in which the specific is less valued than the abstract, women, religious faith, and ministerial disciplines have more to lose since they are often associated with the private or personal and automatically perceived as substandard. Postmodern thought has revealed the culture-bound nature of this value judgment, even if scholars have difficulty letting go of abstraction as superior (see Sered, 1996, 22). Postmodernism suggests that those studying religion are seldom, if ever, able to extricate themselves from specific faith commitments of various kinds. All scholars, not just feminists, must assess the particular biases and advocacies that shape their understandings.

On the other hand, I am appreciative of new developments in practical theology as one means to retain a place in the academy. Practical theological reflection faces hard times in the current climate of university education. Even if it retains vitality within seminaries and congregations, the field will languish without university structures to sustain its theoretical development and refinement. Serious practical theology takes time, requires a rich variety of complex resources, and works best, despite the vast complications, with multiple authors (see Browning, Miller-McLemore et al., 1997). Even when this kind of practical engagement of particular subject matter becomes impractical, the discipline and theory of practical theology remain critical to the theological curriculum, less in and of themselves, than to suggest common methodologies shared by a variety of submovements in practical theology with different content and foci, such as pastoral care, religious education, and so forth. Of equal importance with the goal of academic integrity is the goal of recognizing the interconnections of the rich variety of specializations that have emerged in the practical arts of ministry of pastoral care, education, preaching, and so forth. In this respect, abstractions, generalizations, and metatheorizing about practical theology have an important place—but not at the cost of disdaining the contingent, immediate questions and contexts of suffering and responsive practices of feminist pastoral theology.

Examination of the impact of feminist theory on the development of feminist pastoral theology, as I attempted in this chapter, is important. Such codification partly goes against the grain of both a feminist method that prizes concrete, diverse experiences as the source of knowledge and a pastoral method that makes commitment to understanding suffering and compassionate response the primary focus. Reflection on developments of feminist and womanist pastoral theology is further complicated by the generational lag in feminist and womanist reflection in the field and the challenge of new problems of postmodernity. Scholars in other fields of systematic theology or theological ethics have already done some of the important work on pastoral issues. And other factors, besides the women's movement, will undoubtedly determine the future of pastoral theology.

Nonetheless, a sound grasp of the repercussions of new players in the pastoral theological discussion is absolutely critical to understanding developments in the conceptualization of pastoral care in theological education and in the ecclesiastical practice of caregiving. Following in the footsteps of those who have gone before them and yet making new paths, feminists and womanists in pastoral theology are hoping to prepare a way in the wilderness, making new highways for the entrance of God among us. Only ongoing reflective analysis will tell us when pastoral theologians have fallen far short of the hopes for transformation in justice and love and when we have genuinely made new possibilities happen.

Notes

[1] Partially based on Carroll Watkins Ali's informal remarks during a panel at the American Academy of Religion, November 1996, drawing on her dissertation work on womanist pastoral theology. See chapter 2.

[2] Patricia Hill Collins, public lecture, Vanderbilt University, November 1997.

5

A Method of Feminist
Pastoral Theology

Carrie Doehring

This chapter opens and ends with a recent pastoral conversation I had with an eighty-five-year-old woman. In the middle, I propose a method of feminist pastoral theology. I test the usefulness and relevance of this method by returning to my pastoral conversation. I want to see whether this method of feminist pastoral theology changes my practice of ministry.

This movement, from practice to reflection to practice, makes plain the contextual nature of feminist pastoral theology. The method proposed here is not meant to be ahistorical and universal. I construct a particular method of feminist pastoral theology that draws primarily upon recent discussions of liberal pastoral theology and poststructuralist feminism and ultimately relates these discussions to the practice of a particular ministry. We need many feminist pastoral theologies so that we can fully utilize the myriad of feminist and theological perspectives and fully reflect upon the many forms of ministry we practice.

A Recent Pastoral Experience

I conduct worship and provide pastoral care in a small United Church of Christ congregation in a middle-class suburb of Boston that is predominantly Catholic. This congregation is comprised of a small number of Caucasian elderly members, many of whom have become frail in the past six months. Church members are increasingly aware that this year it is harder for many of them to get out to church, attend meetings, and manage the church school and coffee hour. Amid the personal losses of decreased physical functioning, they are aware of the approaching loss of their church since there is no younger generation to assume congregational responsibilities.

Within this congregational context, I recently had a series of pastoral conversations with several women in the church about an incident that took place on a Sunday morning in the kitchen, prior to worship. One of our few middle-aged members, Susan, was preparing the coffee hour. Mary, one of our frail elderly members, was also in the kitchen, and she gave Susan some unwelcome directions about the best way to make coffee. Susan lost her temper and became angry with Mary for interfering. Susan proceeded to vent her anger.

Later, I talked with Susan, who was feeling overwhelmed with a sense of responsibility for both the future of the congregation and her elderly parents, both members of the church. Susan's eighty-year-old mother is terminally ill with cancer. Many church members are fond of and concerned about Susan's mother.

I was not sure whether Mary was aware of the reverberations from her advice about how to make coffee. A few days later Mary called and wanted to talk with me. She had had several sleepless nights and had drafted an apologetic note to Susan, which she wanted me to hear. We talked about this conflict and touched upon the layers of loss in which it was embedded. Mary is sad about the likelihood that the church will close. She is worried about how Susan is coping with her mother's terminal cancer. Mary herself struggles with loneliness and a lifelong anxiety disorder. She really misses her husband, who died eight years ago. All of these layers of loss shaped her distress and made her urgently want to reconnect with Susan. She had used her religious faith to help her reconnect by praying for guidance.

While the pastoral care conversations I had with Susan and Mary originated in a thoroughly insignificant matter (how to make coffee), they were fueled by ongoing issues dealing with gender, aging, and religious faith that were important to understand. I want to use my conversations with Mary as a starting place for feminist pastoral theology. I want to build a bridge between this experience of ministry and the many specialized perspectives on gender, aging, and pastoral theology.

Bridges Between Theory and Practice

Such two-way bridges are a tradition in Protestant liberal pastoral theology. In the 1920s Anton Boisen's student chaplains began theological reflection with a verbatim of a pastoral care conversation. Use of the verbatim as a primary tool for learning continues in clinical pastoral education to this day. In the 1950s Seward Hiltner proposed that pastoral care encounters could be a source of revelation to persons assuming a pastoral perspective (Hiltner, 1958).

The purpose of this chapter is to follow in the pastoral theological tradition of Boisen and Hiltner in constructing a method of feminist pastoral theology that is grounded in pastoral care practice. The bridges I will describe in this feminist pastoral theology will have to be able to bear the weight of traffic in a postmodern, pluralistic context. These bridges require a different kind of engineering and construction from the bridges of Boisen and Hiltner, constructed in modern contexts where a Christian religious tradition was dominant and Western intellectual traditions were thought to yield universal, absolute truth claims.

Outlining a Method of Feminist Pastoral Theology

The method of feminist pastoral theology presented in this chapter draws upon current feminist, pastoral theology, and practical theology studies and develops the following four criteria. I will introduce each criterion briefly as a prelude to a fuller discussion of this method of feminist pastoral theology.

First, to be *pastoral theological*, this construction of feminist pastoral theology is based upon ongoing conversations about methodology in pastoral theology. The discipline of pastoral theology proposes methods for relating cross-disciplinary perspectives (such as theology, psychology, and gender studies) to practice (for example, pastoral care to people in the midst of gender-related crises and transitions, like the women in the opening illustration). People who are concerned with both feminist and religious issues may intuitively use feminist pastoral theology as a way of traversing a gender-related crisis such as consoling women experiencing aging and loss. Such caregivers may not be aware of what their methodology is. Using a method without understanding it can be likened to simply crossing a bridge without being aware of how the bridge is constructed and what might be other ways of building a bridge. When we become methodologists, we can appreciate and evaluate all the ways there are to build a bridge. Using what we evaluate to be the best current methods, we can build bridges capable of bearing the weight of twenty-first-century traffic that moves both across disciplines and between theory and practice. When someone is moving through the gender-related crisis as the women in the opening illustration were doing, this sort of bridge building is necessary for fully practicing faith in the midst of transitions.

Second, to be *feminist*, this construction of feminist pastoral theology will use a feminist perspective that is poststructuralist, contextual, and pragmatic. By *poststructural*, I mean an assumption that there are no "core" meanings or deep structures to life experiences (for example, to do with gender and aging) that are singularly, absolutely, or universally true. Rather, there are always multiple meanings to life experiences. These meanings have to do not only with what it means to be a woman, but also with what it means to be a woman like Mary, for example, who is also heterosexual, middle-class, European American, in her eighties, and a lifelong member of the United Church of Christ. A poststructuralist perspective pays close attention to the ways in which meanings are often created through value-laden oppositions. Whatever is deemed "other" is often hidden and/or devalued. So, for example, Mary's gender and age may lead us to devalue or even not see her experiences. Being elderly and being a woman may leave her out of the picture.

In a poststructural feminist perspective, meanings are always *contextual* or shaped by the particularities of our life experience, and they are also *political*, that is, seen or unseen depending upon the status conferred or deferred by aspects of one's identity in terms of age, gender, sexual orientation, and race. The political aspects of the meaning systems in relation to Mary's gender and age prompt me as a feminist and a Christian to take action. My actions have to do with ministry. Thus, this poststructuralist feminism is ultimately *pragmatic*. Whatever meanings emerge from my reflections on Mary, these meanings need to shape my practice of ministry to her.

The third criterion for the feminist pastoral theology described in this chapter has to do with our accountability as pastoral theologians and practitioners. I can be explicit about my accountability by naming the sources and norms of authority I use in constructing feminist pastoral theology. Such sources and norms become the basis for how I identify myself. I would like to describe my accountability at the outset of this chapter so that readers can understand the allegiances and loyalties that shape my writing. My first allegiance is to my religious faith, tradition, and community, which is Christian and reformed (both Presbyterian and Congregationalist). My second allegiance is to a feminist theological perspective that is poststructural, contextual, and pragmatic. My third allegiance is to a psychodynamic understanding of human beings. These allegiances are highly colored by the particularities of my life; for example, my gender, social class (upper-middle class), racial identity (European American), academic profession, and religious identity. By being accountable at the outset of this chapter, I am assuming that any feminist pastoral theology is a value-laden construction that arises out of the various commitments we have as people of faith, scholars, and practitioners.

The fourth criterion for the feminist pastoral theology described in this chapter arises out of the allegiances described above and has to do with the ultimate purpose of feminist pastoral theology. This ultimate purpose depends upon how we prioritize our norms and sources of authority. In this chapter, I draw upon Christian theologies as an ultimate source and norm. The ultimate purpose of my construction of feminist pastoral theology is to use my Christian tradition to transform structures (intrapsychic, familial, and cultural) that marginalize people based on interacting contextual factors (such as gender, race, class, or sexual orientation).

Having introduced this chapter by sketching a blueprint of my construction of feminist pastoral theology, I will continue by elaborating each of the four criteria.

1. To be pastoral theological, my construction of feminist pastoral theology will
be based upon ongoing conversations about methodology in pastoral theology.

To understand this criterion, one needs a historical overview of the discipline of liberal pastoral theology (although I include liberal Catholic, Protestant, and progressively evangelical religious traditions, I will not attempt to describe the particularities of how these various religious traditions shape pastoral theology). The term *pastoral theology* was first used in the mid-eighteenth century (see Farley, 1990, 934; E. Graham, 1996b, 56; Mills, 1990, 865) among Protestants to refer to the pastoral care functions of ministry (preaching, education, worship, etc.). The term did not initially refer to pastoral theology as a discipline that was an "ongoing, corporate inquiry with more or less agreed upon topics of investigation and principles of research" (Hunter, 1980).

In the 1920s and 1930s, a discipline began to emerge in which psychodynamic psychologies (i.e., Freud and Jung) were used to understand religious experiences and pastoral care of persons. Advanced studies offered in this discipline had various names: psychology of religion, pastoral psychology, pastoral theology, pastoral counseling. Scholars of this young discipline, such as Seward Hiltner and Wayne Oates, articulated its theological nature. Among many practitioners and theorists, a therapeutic paradigm predominated (as Holifield, 1983; Hunter, 1995; Hunter and Patton, 1995; Patton, 1993; Stokes, 1985 have noted), especially in the 1960s and 1970s, when therapeutic techniques often became the basis for models of care, in what Gerkin (1997, 84) has called a toolbox approach.

In the 1980s a shift occurred, such that the discipline of pastoral theology began to define itself more in terms of practical theology and less in terms of therapeutic practice. This shift occurred in part because of a growing awareness of the contextual nature of pastoral care and the extent to which the therapeutic paradigm arose out of a middle-class Western context. Wimberly's (1979) *Pastoral Care in the Black Church* is an early example of contextual pastoral theology. An awareness of this contextual nature pushed pastoral theologians to move from second-order reflection on practice to third-order reflection on methodologies for relating psychology and theology. In using the term *third-order reflections*, I am borrowing distinctions made by Jennings (1990, 862-864) to describe pastoral theology. First-order language is the description of the practice of pastoral care and counseling. Second-order language uses various disciplines such as theological and psychological studies to reflect theoretically on practices. In cross disciplines such as pastoral theology, third-order reflections concern methodologies that relate psychology and theology (for examples of third-order discussions, see Farley, 1990; E. Graham, 1996b; Holifield, 1983; Jennings, 1990; Loder, 1990; Miller-McLemore, 1996; Pattison, 1994; Schlauch, 1996).

An addendum to this brief history concerns the term *pastoral psychology*, which was rarely defined (as Schlauch [1996] notes). Often the term implicitly referred to a form of psychological studies that was interested in the ways religious beliefs and practices functioned in people's lives. In the 1980s, as theological reflection became a more integral part of pastoral psychology, the term *pastoral theology* became "the appropriate, comprehensive term for the discipline [of pastoral psychology]" (Burck & Hunter, 1990, 867-868). Schlauch defines pastoral psychology as a bridge discipline that brings together theological studies, psychological studies, and a practical-clinical enterprise in a way that is ultimately theological (Schlauch, 1996, 239).

Feminist pastoral theologians such as Elaine Graham (1996b) and Bonnie Miller-McLemore (1996) engage in third-order reflections upon methodology and thus identify themselves as pastoral theologians. In the past, feminist pastoral theologians have often engaged in second-order and not third-order reflections on the practices of pastoral care, counseling, and psychotherapy. They have drawn primarily upon theological *or* psychological literature. They have not made explicit their methodologies and have not engaged in ongoing methodological discussions in the discipline of pastoral theology.

In setting forth the criterion that this construction of feminist *pastoral theology* will engage in third-order reflections on methodological issues in pastoral theology, I am encouraging feminist pastoral theologians to be explicit about being pioneers by considering how their methodologies may be pushing the discipline into new directions (see Elaine Graham [1996b] for a pioneering example).

2. To be feminist, my construction of feminist pastoral theology will use a feminist perspective that is poststructuralist, contextual, and pragmatic.

The second criterion concerns the definitions of feminism used by feminist pastoral theologians. Over the years, feminism has been concerned with femaleness (a matter of biology), femininity ("a set of culturally defined characteristics"), and feminism ("the struggle against patriarchy and sexism") (Moi, 1989, 152). Kristeva (1979, 33-34) describes three positions of feminism:

1. demanding equal access by addressing issues of gender equality and gender oppression;
2. rejecting patriarchal structures, naming women's experience as different from men's, reforming and constructing systems by using women's experience;
3. rejecting any meaning system (patriarchal, racist, classist, heterosexist) that has universalized and made metaphysical any binary categories (i.e., masculine/feminine, white/black, straight/gay) that place people in privileged and marginalized positions. Miller-McLemore (1996, 16) defines this position as follows: "A feminist perspective demands an analysis of structures and ideologies that rank people as inferior or superior according to various traits of human nature, whether gender, sexual orientation, color, age, physical ability, and so forth."

The third definition is a poststructuralist approach to understanding gender in that gender is seen as having multiple meanings that are generated by various interacting meaning systems (for example, the meanings that our families, our communities, and our cultures attribute to being a woman and being a man). Poststructuralist feminists have highlighted the foundationalist binary approach that looks for "core" opposite traits that are common to all women or all men; for example, men are rational, women are emotional (see E. Graham, 1996a, 1996b; Nicholson, 1997; Weedon, 1997).

A poststructuralist approach can be further described by highlighting the difference between Kristeva's second and third positions of feminism. In the second position, feminists who value traits and roles traditionally associated with women may unwittingly continue the patriarchal practice of defining women according to some essence and/or prescribing femininity. Moi drily comments:

> Gratifying though it is to be told that women really are strong, integrated, peace-loving, nurturing and creative beings, this plethora of new virtues is no less essentialist than the old ones, and no less oppressive to all women who do not want to play the role of Earth Mother. (Moi, 1989, 123-124)

My construction of feminist pastoral theology uses a poststructuralist approach that defines gender as positional, relational, contextual, and political.

101

I want to consider several contextual factors at the same time (for example, Mary's age, ethnicity, and gender). Because gender is not isolated from other contextual factors, all women can no longer be described as the same regardless of their different social identities as related to sexual orientation, class, and race. A contextual approach becomes a feminist approach when feminist/gender studies are used correlationally with other disciplinary perspectives in a way that allows the androcentrism of any disciplinary perspective to be critiqued.

A pragmatic approach takes into account the ways in which language, in spite of its endless meanings, is used as if its meanings were singular. Consider, for example, the ways in which a singular experience of one's self is held in the foreground, while a multiple experience of self is held in the background. Pragmatically speaking, people experience their subjectivity as singular in order to function in the daily life of most cultural systems. Similarly, it is much easier to act based on singular rather than multiple meanings of events. Combining poststructural and pragmatic perspectives brings into view the tensions between the multiplicity of meanings (which tends to be less conscious) and the pragmatism of having to operate with a sense of singularity (which tends to be more part of conscious experience).

When using a poststructuralist, pragmatic feminist approach, I find it important to continually remember the *provisional* nature of the truth claims that become the basis for my actions. As someone educated in Western philosophical traditions, I have been acculturated to assume that truth claims are ahistorical and universal. Thus, the criteria I set forth in this method of feminist pastoral theology may sound like absolute criteria for an ahistorical, universal method of feminist pastoral theology, but they are intended as provisional criteria that describe a particular highly contextual method. Using adjectives that continually identify my authorship reminds me that these criteria are provisional and contextual.

> *3. To be accountable, my construction of feminist pastoral theology will be explicit about the sources and norms that shape our identities.*

Describing my accountability makes plain the communal, even covenantal nature of pastoral theology, which is undertaken by people like me who have implicit and explicit commitments that create a web of promises. Accountability includes acknowledgment of my context and the power afforded by my position. The importance of such self-reflexivity is part of feminist perspectives that emphasize both the situatedness of knowledge (Chopp, 1995, 181) and the interrelatedness of the knower and what is known (E. Graham, 1996b, 162).

Also included in accountability are beliefs that shape my perspective. These beliefs can be articulated in terms of my sources and norms of authority (see E. Graham, 1996b; Young, 1990). Sources of authority can include data from

- the Bible (historically, a primary source for Protestants);
- experience (i.e., of women and those who are marginalized);
- social scientific data (i.e., on biological and gender differences);
- denominational sources such as creeds, rulings from the magisterium in the Roman Catholic tradition, or denominational constitutions;
- gender and feminist studies.

Norms are the criteria by which source material is evaluated. Norms can include

- methods of interpreting the Bible (literalism and/or inerrancy, a range of historical-critical methods including feminist biblical studies);
- feminist norms (creating gender equality, restructuring patriarchal structures using women's experience and the experiences of the marginalized);
- social scientific norms for undertaking and evaluating research;
- denominational standards (i.e., norms of appropriateness);
- theological norms (i.e., liberation theology's norm of liberation).

Given that no source material can be used without interpretation, sources are always paired with norms for how such material is used.

Accountability is part of a feminist poststructural approach for two reasons. First, if knowledge is socially constructed, that is, based upon the ways in which people put together understandings of themselves, God, and the world, then knowledge is very much shaped by who we are. Given that what we see depends upon where we are standing, then we need to name not only what we see; we also need to name where we are standing. Second, where we stand may either confer authority upon what we see or take away authority. For example, I am a university professor, and this social location confers authority upon what I say. If I were a social activist without any institutional accreditation, what I say might not be given as much credence; indeed, it might be suspect. Because of my explicit statements about my social location and my norms and sources of authority, readers can appreciate the perspectival truth of the claims I make, and assess the relevance of such claims to their own social location and norms and sources of authority.

Many contemporary pastoral theologians describe in their writings their accountability to particular traditions and communities. For example, Poling (1995) describes how his work on abuse and oppression is shaped inevitably by the values of academic institutions and organizations in contrast to the values represented by feminist and practical theologians who work in other contexts, such as Africa, Central America, and Asia. In undertaking qualitative research on care received by lesbian and gay persons, L. K. Graham (1997) describes his primary accountability to the narratives of the persons he interviewed. By contrast, in his case study of a homosexual man (Browning, 1983), Browning states his preunderstanding of homosexuality at the outset of his case study: that the church will uphold heterosexual marriage as normative for human sexuality. Browning's statement comes across as an absolute truth claim, not a truth claim based upon his sources and norms of authority.

> *4. In my construction of feminist pastoral theology, the overarching method of feminist practical theology that bridges gender studies, social science studies, and theological studies will have as its ultimate purpose the transformation of structures (intrapsychic, familial, and cultural) that create power differentials based on interacting contextual factors (such as gender, race, class, or sexual orientation).*

The fourth criterion concerns how sources and norms are ranked in relation to each other. Poling and Miller's (1985) typology of practical theology is helpful in describing such ranking. For example, conservative evangelical feminist pastoral theologians give priority to the norms of their evangelical tradition (i.e., personal piety and salvation through confessing Jesus as Lord and Savior). Under these norms, they may use women's experience as a source for elaborating (but not radically reconstructing) their religious tradition. They describe themselves as feminists in that they value women's experience and they may seek to revise women's sex roles within their tradition. They practice what Poling and Miller (1985) call a confessional method of practical theology in which norms concerning their evangelical identity take precedence over norms concerning the relevance of their theology to women's experience. Their primary source is Scripture, and they may or may not use literal or biblical critical methods for interpreting Scripture. Whether or not they practice a *critical* confessional method depends on whether they are willing to revise their methods and presuppositions (Poling and Miller, 1985, 32).

The confessional method of evangelical feminist pastoral theologians can be compared with the scientific and feminist methods of liberal feminist pastoral theologians who have used a therapeutic paradigm in their pastoral theology. These feminists tend to draw upon women's experience and social scientific data as their sources, and use norms from psychological and feminist studies in their pastoral theologies. Sources and norms from religious traditions play a secondary role in this method.

Contemporary feminist pastoral theology utilizes, for the most part, a critical correlational method of relating feminist/gender studies, social scientific studies, and theological studies. Poling and Miller locate the critical correlational method between the critical scientific method and the critical confessional method (Poling and Miller, 1985). Within this critical correlational method can be found three subtypes of liberal Protestant pastoral theology, which I will call, borrowing from Chopp's typology (1995, 79-84), hermeneutical, emancipatory praxis, and a hybrid of the two.

The hermeneutical method exemplified by pastoral theologians such as Gerkin (1984, 1986), Browning (1991), and Schlauch (1995) relies heavily upon philosophical sources and norms in addition to social scientific and theological sources and norms. In Browning's method, ethical and social scientific sources and norms are used first to develop multidimensional descriptions of practice. These thick descriptions of practice are then brought into dialogue with sources and norms from historical theology in order to construct systematic theologies that can become the basis for multidimensional strategies for practice.

In the emancipatory praxis method, exemplified by Poling (1991, 1996) and E. Graham (1996b), hermeneutics is part of the greater process of emancipatory praxis (Chopp, 1995, 82). A praxis method locates sources and norms less within the past (and its academic and ecclesial traditions among dominant groups in Western culture) and more within the present and future (and the living out of religious traditions in communal and individual faith practices).

These two correlational methods (hermeneutical and emancipatory praxis) can be contrasted by looking at E. Graham's (1996b) critique of Browning's hermeneutical method. She describes Browning's method of practical theology as being too theoretically determined by Western philosophical sources and norms of authority. In using these sources and norms, Browning does not consider the extent to which interacting contextual factors (e.g., gender, ethnicity, sexual orientation, and social class) can privilege some voices and marginalize others.

Many recent contextual pastoral theologies combine hermeneutical and emancipatory praxis methods. Miller-McLemore describes the shift in pastoral theology: "This emphasis on confronting systems of domination has been instrumental in creating the shift in pastoral theology from care narrowly defined as counseling to care understood as part of a wide cultural, social, and religious context" (Miller-McLemore, 1996, 16). Her examples (James Poling's [1991] *The Abuse of Power;* Pamela Couture's [1991] *Blessed Are the Poor?;* Larry Graham's [1992] *Care of Persons, Care of Worlds;* and Miller-McLemore's [1994] *Also a Mother*) can be described as utilizing both a hermeneutical method and an emancipatory praxis method.

A Concluding Illustration

I would like to illustrate how to use the four criteria I have proposed by returning to the pastoral care conversations I had with Mary. These conversations can be the starting point for feminist pastoral theological reflection that uses the criteria described above to construct a theology of faithful aging, a term used by Saussy (1998) in her practical insights on aging.

Denominational Sources and Norms

Mary and I are in a relationship in which there is a power differential because of my role as her minister. This role is based upon promises made when

105

I was ordained and also upon ongoing denominational standards for care, spelled out in United Church of Christ sources and norms, such as the "Ordained Minister's Code" in the *United Church of Christ Manual on Ministry* (1986). Mary also has made promises, at her baptism and confirmation, and she is part of a congregation that has articulated a covenantal relationship among its members and with sister congregations. These promises and standards create the web of promises within which these pastoral conversations occur. The image of a web of promises describes the interrelatedness of all life (see Keller, 1986; Miller-McLemore, 1996).

In reflecting further upon my pastoral conversations with Mary, I can also draw upon the United Church of Christ Statement of Faith, revised in 1981, and in particular what it says about Christian life:

> You call us into your church
> to accept the cost and joy of discipleship,
> to be your servants in the service to others,
> to proclaim your gospel to all the world
> and resist the powers of evil. (Shinn, 1990, xi)

I am going to begin constructing a feminist pastoral theological understanding of Mary with this statement on Christian living. In some ways, I am testing the relevance of this denominational source and seeing the extent to which I need to reconstruct its theological meanings.

The norm of congregational polity gives our local church the responsibility for defining doctrine, using "our common creeds and confessions as 'testimonies' rather than 'tests'" (Fackre, 1992, 8) and as doxologies celebrating the Great Story (Shinn, 1990). Mary and I are responsible for interpreting the theological meanings of the statement on Christian living. In bringing this statement on Christian living and the congregational norms of openness, diversity, and the primacy of congregational polity to our pastoral conversation, Mary and I can see her distress over the incident at church in theological terms, as part of her ongoing struggle for Christian living. These congregational norms give Mary and me room to reconstruct the meanings of discipleship and servanthood by using a third term, *faithful aging* (coined by Saussy [1998]), to describe Mary's struggles as an aging woman. This term does not carry the historical meanings of discipleship and servanthood, but gives a more neutral term to reconsider the viability of terms such as *discipleship* and *servanthood*.

Mary and I are also part of the more dominant Congregationalist-Christian subculture, and not the German Reformed Church and Evangelical Church subculture (see Schroeder [1995] and Sheares [1990] for a description of subcultures in the United Church of Christ). We can draw upon our commonalities to construct theological meanings of faithful aging, which may be quite different from theologies constructed by other subcultures of our church. One source Mary and I draw upon in constructing our theology is the new hymnal (*The New Century Hymnal,* 1995). For example, we can use a Communion hymn that we regularly sing:

> I come with Christians far and near to find, as all are fed,
> The new community of love in Christ's communion bread. . . .
> As Christ breaks bread, and bids us share, each proud division ends.
> The love that made us, makes us one, and strangers now are friends.
> (Wren, 1968)

The immediacy of the sacramental imagery of Wren's hymn urges us to make connections between faithful aging and the sacrament of Communion. The living bread broken and shared in the circle of faith becomes Mary's bread for the journey of aging.

A Theological Framework for Faithful Aging

Patriarchal Christian paradigms have been used for centuries to interpret the implication of theological concepts such as discipleship and servanthood. Asserting that "women were created second, sinned first, and are to keep silence in church, to be saved by subordination and childbearing" (Ruether, 1998, 2), such patriarchal paradigms would see discipleship and servanthood as having to do with subordination and childbearing. Such paradigms would associate "the cost . . . of discipleship" with passive suffering and being a "servant in the service to others" with the sex roles of wife, mother, and dutiful daughter who maintain the home and relational ties with the family and the church. For many frail elderly women in Mary's generation, not being able to serve others through homemaking can be profoundly troubling. Finding a term like *faithful aging* can allow me to be true to the life-giving meanings of the statement on Christian living without carrying forward as much of the patriarchal, ageist meanings associated with concepts such as servanthood.

Current sociological literature on aging can help me think more fully about the extent to which my understanding of aging is socially constructed, shaped by both the media and the social scientific attitudes toward aging. Much attention has been given in the media and the social sciences to the negative stereotypes we have of older persons. A social constructivist approach has been used to critique the meanings we give to aging and also to construct more life-giving meanings, in particular notions that older persons can be vibrant and active. In many ways I want to affirm these notions and see Mary as someone who is actively engaged in living out her faith as she ages. I need to stop and reflect, though, upon the extent to which these images of active aging have been utilized in marketing strategies targeted at elderly men and women who have disposable incomes (see Featherstone and Hepworth, 1995). To what extent are these images of active aging a denial of some of the realities of aging, particularly the experience of becoming frail, and also the very real financial limitations of many elderly women (Arber and Ginn, 1991)? For Mary, increasing frailness is very much part of her life (although financial hardship is not).

In his pastoral reflections on aging, L. Brynoff Lyon (1985) draws upon historical theology to reconstruct a theological paradigm for aging as moral becoming. Lyon sees aging as involving religio-ethical witnessing, which is continuous with the witnessing in all of one's previous years. He describes this witness as moral becoming.

Lyon's uncritical use of historical theology is problematic in that he does not assess how these historical meaning systems carry with them assumptions about gender. As feminist theologians such as Ruether (1998) have documented, many of our historical sources for theological reflection rely on patriarchal norms when describing women. It is problematic to use Lyon's description of moral becoming for several reasons. First, I am liable to equate moral becoming with traditionally Western models of rationality. If I then turn to feminist psychological descriptions of women's ethic of care and women's ways of knowing, I may generate essentialized meanings of moral becoming, supposedly true for all women everywhere. These reflections on Lyon's theological concept of moral becoming lead me to return to the concept of faithful aging as a valuable theological framework for understanding Mary's experience. This concept does not carry forward the polarized meanings of moral becoming.

In the process of elaborating a theological framework of faithful aging, I have thus far drawn upon denominational sources and norms to depart from their text concerning servanthood and discipleship. I have proposed an alternate theological concept: that of faithful aging. I have used feminist perspectives to become more fully aware of the patriarchal paradigms inherent in the historical theological sources that Lyon uses to develop his understanding of aging as moral becoming. I have used cultural studies to be suspicious of adopting both the social scientific attitudes concerning active aging and the marketing strategies that capitalize on attitudes about active aging. My theological concept of faithful aging, if it simply incorporates these attitudes toward active aging, will ultimately dehumanize Mary because I will not fully see her increasing frailty. I will not see certain polarities (the young body, the frail elderly body; the active elderly with disposable income, the elderly who are poor). These polarities overvalue some aspects of an elderly person's life (a disposable income, a "youthful" appearance that belies the aging process) while devaluing other aspects (limited, fixed income, a frail elderly appearance that masks the humanity within).

A Thick Description of Mary's Experience

Having established a theological framework of faithful aging that includes the frail elderly and those with limited financial means, I will proceed to elaborate a thick description of Mary's experience. Rather than beginning with theoretical perspectives, I want to look at Mary's practices. Mary enacts faithful aging by acknowledging wrongdoing, praying, and writing a penitential letter that seeks reconciliation. In the midst of these practices, Mary is constructing meanings of faithful aging that are particular to her (her religion, gender, age, social class, family background, and communal memberships). Her religious identity is most influential in this experience. Mary's socialization as a woman makes her sensitive to the negative effects of conflict and motivates her to reconnect with Susan. Her age identity makes her feel less inhibited about speaking out and taking action than she used to, and she is aware that life is too short to leave important tasks undone. Because of her social class, Mary is able to maintain a sense of agency in part because she can afford to stay in her own home. This enhances a sense of dignity and self-reliance, which she draws upon in taking action to make amends.

Feminist pastoral theologian Saussy (1991) uses object relations theory in a psychosystemic approach that looks at how patriarchy affects women's self-esteem and how pastoral caregivers can attend to the ways in which perfectionism affects women's self-esteem. Mary's perfectionism shapes her spontaneous instructions to Susan on how to make coffee and also the harsh judgment she levies on herself. Her lifelong tendency toward perfectionism can exacerbate her frustration with her aging body on her "down" days. Feminist pastoral theologians' writings on depression are helpful (Dunlap, 1997; Neuger, 1991) in reflecting upon Mary's experience of down days. Dunlap uses a post-structuralist feminist approach to consider the social construction of gender and its relation to depression. Following her lead, I can continue to listen for how Mary's social location as a woman, her sense of self, her relationships, and her sense of her aging female body can predispose her to depressed moods. These depressed moods can be reinforced by the cultural meanings of having a frail elderly body. She lives in a culture that highly values certain youthful appearances of the body. She also lives in a culture in which it is all right to be elderly if you are active and maintain as youthful an appearance as you can. On her down days, when she is frustrated with herself, she may be more likely to focus her anger upon her aging body because of cultural meanings to do with aging.

Mary's initial criticism of Susan is distorted aggression, directed at someone in her vicinity who is also a caregiver and not someone in authority. Mary feels highly remorseful about this aggression. Some of Mary's remorse is typical of a woman socialized to view her aggression as dangerous, especially when it leads to public, and not private, expressions. Mary's faithful aging depends upon the vigor that comes from constructive aggression (Greider, 1997). For example, when Mary sends her letter, this action can be seen as a constructive act of aggression in that Mary "intrudes" upon Susan and is not going to let sleeping dogs lie. By taking action, Mary becomes a vigorous eighty-five-year-old woman engaged in faithful aging.

It is helpful to put Greider's thoughts on the interrelationship of vigor and aggression in an elderly woman like Mary alongside Saussy's (1998) strategies for faithful aging. Saussy's first strategy is to face death, and the denial of death, head-on. Mary is someone who wants a peaceful death, and who also wants to hold onto a vital, positive life in whatever ways she can. Her aggression can help her do this. In reflecting upon the role of vigor and aggression in Mary's faithful aging, I want to be wary of enforcing activity as a way of denying the frail aging process and death.

This thick description of Mary's faithful aging could be further elaborated by social scientific literature on aging. The feminist pastoral theological literature that I have used is especially helpful in considering someone with Mary's ethnic, economic, and religious identities. However, if Mary were not Christian, middle class, and European American, this literature would not help me elaborate the meanings of her experience of faithful aging. I would need to utilize the extensive ethnographic literature on aging, and sociological literature on gender, income, and aging (such as Arber and Ginn, 1991).

Strategies for Transforming Meaning Systems

The community of faith can be instrumental in constructing life-giving meanings of faithful aging for Mary (Larsen, 1995). As Elaine Graham notes:

> If the "causes" of gender [and age] are constituted in, and enacted through, material, embodied and symbolic praxis, then the role of religious practices and ideologies in the creation and maintenance of gendered [and ageist] systems becomes a crucial area of study. How do religious practices, institutions and symbolic practices serve to reflect, reinforce and create particular dynamics of gender [and age] identity, gender [and age] roles and representations [of gender and age]? (Graham, 1996a, 227)

In this closing section of the case study, I will outline multidimensional pastoral strategies for practicing faithful aging.

Focusing on Mary first, I want to offer her ongoing supportive pastoral care in the form of regular conversations that span both the up days and the down days. I want to be more explicit about how as a frail elderly woman, she is in a process of faithful aging. I can use my pastoral theological reflections on her anxiety, perfectionism, vigor, aggression, and acknowledgment of death to deepen our conversations on faithful aging.

I can encourage life-giving faithful aging, not only in my conversations with Mary but in my prayers, sermons, and Bible discussions. We can acknowledge that we all have good days and bad days, and that on bad days it can seem as if our problems are wholly due to particular aspects of our lives: our aging bodies, our gender, our marital status, our psychological vulnerabilities (such as anxiety or depression). At moments our age differences can make us become strangers to each other. We can consider the limited and often negative images we see of elderly women in the media. We can also be suspicious of the images of active aging that we see in the media: images that may deny the experience of becoming frail. We can be aware of the attention on youthful physical appearance so dominant in the media.

Scriptural resources need to be used carefully with an understanding of the social context in which they were written and the various ways scriptural stories can be interpreted. A careful study of the book of Ruth, for example, can help church members appreciate the gender roles in biblical times, the courage of women and men who, in covenant with God, could live faithful lives that often challenged the limitations of their age and sex roles.

These life-giving meanings of faithful aging can be fully realized only when they bear fruit in our actions, and part of the strategy for both Mary and the congregation will be considering how these meanings change what we do. For example, a constructive theology of faithful aging for these elderly members can become the basis for how they approach the ending of their congregational life. Such a theology can help them discern when the time to let go has come, and how they can be an active part of deciding the future of their church building. The trustful rather than legal relationships we have with other congregational churches can allow Mary and the members of her congregation to decide when and how to end the life of their congregation.

The strategies of care described above are local. In order for meaning systems to change, strategies must involve the wider culture. In our teaching and publications, constructing feminist pastoral theologies on aging and gender is an important strategy for transformation. Pastoral theologies using feminist poststructuralist psychological and sociological perspectives can prompt further work in the area of aging and gender.

Conclusion

This closing case study illustrates how feminist pastoral theologians can use the methods of pastoral theology (specifically a correlational method of emancipatory praxis) to build bridges. These bridges connect the operational theologies we use in our practice of pastoral care of the aged with poststructural feminism, social scientific understandings of aging, denominational theologies, and theological understandings of aging. The method I have constructed allows me to reflect on an experience of ministry that is shaped by various contextual factors (namely, Mary's and my ethnic, gender, age, class, and religious identities). My method and reflections could be useful in similar ministries. It is obvious that a ministry to someone of a different racial, class, and religious identity would have to use more relevant theological, feminist, and social scientific perspectives. The more such pastoral theologies can begin with the particularities of pastoral conversations, then the more relevant, and also diverse, will be the feminist pastoral theologies built upon these conversations.

6

Women and Relationality

Christie Cozad Neuger

Jenny Jensen, a twenty-seven-year-old, European American, married woman, has come to a pastoral counselor at her church. As they sit down together to talk about the concerns that have motivated Jenny to get counseling, the following issues emerge.

Jenny is feeling unsure of herself and worried about what people at her new job think about her. She has tried to be friendly and to be a "team player," but she also has seen that the workplace is competitive and that there is hardly enough time to get the necessary reports done, much less do some of the extra research that seems to be expected. However, she recently overheard a conversation in which one of her coworkers (male) said, "That new 'girl' certainly seems stuck-up." Jenny has always gotten along well with people and has several good friends, but this is her first real job after graduate school, and she wants to be a success. She also has noticed that her mostly male coworkers pretty much stick to their desks and work demands.

Jenny has also come to the counselor because she is having some rough spots in her marriage. She has been married for six years and has a three-year-old child. While she was in graduate school, she and her husband, Jim, coparented well, in part because she had a flexible schedule. Now they have decided to put their daughter in day care for five days a week, and Jenny feels a great deal of guilt for "abandoning" her child to "outsiders." The little girl appears to enjoy the daycare experience, but Jenny still has a nagging sense of failure, which Jim cannot understand.

What Jim does feel is that Jenny seems to have withdrawn from him emotionally, and he misses "his old Jenny," who would get him to talk about his day and would share her insights and experiences, especially about their daughter. Jenny reports that Jim feels like she's giving everything to work. Jenny feels a bit detached from Jim and feels guilty about not being as attentive to him, but she also resents that he does not understand her work dilemmas.

When Jenny has talked her concerns over with her two best friends, they have been very supportive. Each has come over to her work and taken her out for lunch and listening. They, and three other friends, still have their "women's night out" once a month, and these friends have been a real lifesaver for Jenny. She worries, though, that she's been "taking too much and giving too little" with her friends, which may jeopardize their relationships. This was one of the primary motivators in seeking counseling.

Finally, Jenny says that she isn't happy with her spiritual life. She has felt that God was leading her toward the vocation for which she has prepared and now embraced, but somehow she feels more off-center than ever. She feels that she's failing everyone, even God, and this makes her very unhappy and agitated. She used to teach church school and do other church activities, like Bible study, but she feels that family claims on that time need to take priority. Yet that choice makes her feel somewhat cut off from God.

*She has come to the pastoral counselor, hoping for a warm and caring rela-
tionship that will help her look at all of these complicated and interactive
dynamics without making her feel worse about herself. She wants to build a
healing relationship with the counselor and feels that's more likely because of
the pastoral connection.*

Introduction

This chapter is about women and relationality. I use the term *relationality*,
rather than *relationships*, because I want to focus through a gender lens on the
origin, function, nature, and role of relationships and relating in women's lives.
As this brief case study (to which we will return later in the chapter) indicates,
many issues that emerge in women's lives are understood relationally. Carol
Gilligan's early work demonstrated, almost paradigmatically, that many
women make decisions primarily through assessing their relational implications. From that time forward, relationality has been a focus in feminist theory
building.

Thus, relationality has become an organizing concept for talking about
women's psychology, feminist ethics, and feminist theology. As Margaret Farley states, "There may be no more central concept and concern in feminist theological ethics than relationship. It has appeared in one form or another at the
heart of feminist theory in general as well as in feminist theology, psychology,
sociology, and political theory" (Farley, 1996, 238). Yet the concept of relationality in feminist theory is not without its debates. As feminist theorists began to
reframe male-based evaluations of women's deviance and weaknesses, one of
the areas of women's experience to be reclaimed has been that of relationality.
For example, women's unique tendencies toward and skills in building and
maintaining relationships now can be seen as morally valuable and familially
necessary, rather than being grounded in a lower developmental level than a
more male-linked autonomy.

This focus on women's ability and tendency to be committed to cooperation,
care, and the nurture of relationships has been an important reclaiming for the
valuing of women's lives and culturally given roles. However, reclaiming
women's behaviors and roles as strengths can also get in the way of analyzing
their sources and risks. Women often get caught in what Ellyn Kaschak calls
"compulsive and compulsory relationality," feeling responsible and being held
responsible for maintaining family and cultural harmony (Kaschak, 1992, 124).
Skilled relationality may be as much a gender-trained service for a patriarchal
culture (with its significant costs for women and for men) as it is a valuable orientation in women's lives. Bonnie Miller-McLemore has said, "How does one
appreciate women's relational proclivities without essentializing them?" (or
exploiting them, I would add). This debate is the focus for this chapter.

Relationality in Pastoral Theology

Concerns about relationships and relationality are not just concerns in feminist theory building. The notion of relationality, its source and purpose as well as its power to heal, has always been a central focus for pastoral theology and pastoral care. Larry Graham, in his discussion about the centrality of relationship in pastoral theology, has written that the image of God in which humanity is created is fundamentally grounded in the ability to be in relationship with one another. He writes, "Most of all, to be in the image of God is to be relational, in diverse fellowship characterized by the kind of love that creates new and more adequate forms of human community, including the interactions between human environments and the natural order. . . . Understood in this way, to be in the image of God is to be embodied relationally" (L. Graham, 1996, 23).

Not only is the human understood to be essentially relational in pastoral theology, but that which heals in pastoral care has traditionally been understood to be fundamentally grounded in the quality of the pastoral relationship. The healing power of pastoral ministry has been understood in the deep care for the other mediated through an honest, empathic pastoral relationship.

Consequently, the study of relationality—its source, its developmental dynamics, its function and purpose—is essential to ongoing theory building in pastoral theology. Who we are as relational beings, how we got that way, what it means for us as women and men—these are all important questions for understanding the nature of therapeutic relationships in pastoral care. Since relationality is a core concept in feminist theory, exploring the debates and dynamics in feminist thought will enhance the conversation about relationality in pastoral theology. In addition, much of the contemporary pastoral theology literature reflects differing positions within these debates about gender and relationality.

Relationality in Feminist Thought

Relationality has many layers in feminist thought. Probably in contemporary feminist pastoral theology, the first focus is on relationality as a valuable and unique dimension of women's lives. This is not to say that men are not relational but that women, for varieties of (debated) reasons, have a relational orientation that seems to be more central to their functioning than it is in men's lives. Much of the important theory building in feminist psychology has focused on data indicating that women seem to develop in the context of a more continuous relationship with their mothers then do men. Gender identification and cultural affirmations of close connections for girls more than for boys contribute to engendered relationality. The consequence of this unbroken and same-gender connection through the early developmental processes, these authors suggest, is that girls develop the capacity and the motivation to orient themselves toward the maintenance of key relationships in their lives as essential to both self-esteem and self-knowledge.[1] Since most developmental psychology has traditionally focused on the growth of self as a movement from dependency in relationship to mother (rarely is father considered in these developmental schema) through a generally conflictual process toward a more separate and autonomous way of being, these feminist approaches to women's development have provided a counter paradigm. Because women have traditionally been seen in these developmental theories as less capable of true maturity due to their tendency to stay "dependent"/interde-pendent/ relationally connected, these counter paradigms offer a more positive and woman-centered way to understand women's personalities. Women no longer have to fit into a paradigm oriented around men's experience where women have been seen as "the other" and generally found deviant in some form. Considerable agreement exists among feminists that methodology that pays attention to women's experience for its own sake, rather than seeing it as deriva-tive of or deviant from men's experience, is of central importance. Yet consider-able debate occurs around what it means to talk about "women" as a group and about a trait or quality of women that defines them as a group. We will return to the debate about this dimension of relationality later in the chapter.

A second way that relationality has served as a focus for feminist theory is through the lens of ethics. The way that relationships have been ordered in the culture and have served as vehicles for oppression and for empowerment is an important dimension of this lens. This look at relationality has most often grounded itself in a critique of dualism or the binary assignment of supposed opposites, and their resulting valuing. Dualism takes dualities (a recognition of difference without a value judgment) and assigns dominant and subordinate sta-tus to the differences. Realities that could be seen as unities, or as equally valu-able parts of a whole, are separated and given differing value. These dualistic splits between things like mind and body, spirit and matter, thinking and feeling, autonomy and dependency, male and female have been given theological signif-icance in their valuing. The first of each of these pairs has been seen as more valuable, closer to God, and associated with men. The second of each pair has been associated with nature and with women and has been devalued. A corre-sponding hierarchy based on this dualistic starting place and descending from the most male to the least male has been used to structure society. God, who has been seen to be at the top of this hierarchy, has also been understood to be the authority of the hierarchy/natural order. So, a "sacred circle" has been established consisting of a God who is named, defined, and empowered through patriarchal assumptions and who in turn, through human-created symbols and structures, names, defines, and empowers (some) males. Women (and other peo-ple and things more closely associated with nature) become defined as "other." Men (at least those who follow patriarchal rules for maleness) become defined as closer to God and as responsible for creating and maintaining systems of meaning. The culture defines in this way a system of hierarchical power rela-tionships.

Feminist theory across disciplines takes on these dualistic assignments and challenges the relational ordering of power based on these assignments. One focus of relationality has been oriented toward identifying and deconstructing these unjust power arrangements between people. Originally, feminist theory focused on the unjust relationships organized by a patriarchal and dualistic culture between women and men, and this focus continues. These relationships, whether in the workplace, in the family, or between strangers, still tend to be arranged out of preferred valuing of males over females. They continue to need analysis, deconstruction, and reinvention in mutually enhancing ways. However, it has become evident that if women's voices, in general, have been suppressed through the disordering of relationships with men, so have the voices of other groups who have been marginalized via the value hierarchy of patriarchy (or kyriarchy according to Elisabeth Schüssler Fiorenza). The experiences of the poor, the uneducated, people of color, people with disabling conditions, gay men and lesbians, and others have been and continue to be excluded from the meaning-making processes of the culture. Consequently, issues of justice and the ordering of relationships have become expanded beyond women's concerns. The enormity of the conceptual error of patriarchy has begun to be understood.

This lens of power and ethics continues to be a central focus in feminist theory and theology. Much of feminist pastoral theology has relied on this work of deconstructing the unjust ordering of relationships as central in developing strategies of pastoral care and counseling that help people live in right relationship with one another. One can see this work very clearly in writings by pastoral theologians Pamela Couture (*Blessed Are the Poor?* [1991]); Bonnie Miller-McLemore (*Also a Mother* [1994]); and Riet Bons-Storm (*The Incredible Woman* [1996]).

And this leads us to a third dimension, and that is the notion of relationality in feminist theology. Feminist theology has consistently operated within a relational paradigm as well as offered a sophisticated analysis of relational hierarchies and issues of justice. Maybe the area where these elements of relationality are most apparent in feminist theology is that of eco-theology. Various feminist theologians have taken up the work of understanding the deep relationality of all creation as God's intended web of life. Bonnie Miller-McLemore has shifted a key metaphor in pastoral theology from exploring the "living human document" to a "living human web" out of a commitment to the interrelationships within all of creation (Miller-McLemore, 1996).

Much of early feminist theology worked to deconstruct the patriarchal order, which subsumed women under men. However, as feminist theology has matured, it has taken on the rest of this hierarchical order, understanding that children, animals, and creation itself have been generally treated as objects to be used for the benefit of those higher up the pyramid of power. Ecofeminism continues to work for the reordering of relationships between men and women as it relates that work to the reordering of all relationships within the living web. Ivone Gebara captures this when she writes, "Ecofeminist theology is an effort for some to rethink Christian traditions in order to recover values, experiences, and commitments in an understanding of the way human beings are connected to the ecosystem. This new understanding invites us to welcome the Mystery that is everywhere and in everyone without reducing it to a masculine entity" (Gebara, 1996, 79).

Feminist theology has also been about the work of deconstructing and reconstructing theologies that describe and define the relationship between the Divine and humanity. Various feminist theologians have discovered new ways for the Divine-human relationship to be expressed that would empower women (as well as men) to see themselves more clearly as both created in and able to reflect the image of God. Sallie McFague's work in *Metaphorical Theology* (1982) was one of several important theological reconstructions that worked to break down language and image barriers that, using McFague's language, were both idolatrous and irrelevant (McFague, 1982). McFague and several other feminist theologians working on images of God and the meaning of our religious traditions have attempted to deconstruct the Christian tradition, to reclaim women's voices and the voices of other marginalized groups that had been left out of the public witness of those traditions, and to reconstruct theologies that reflect the full participation of all in the divine intentions for creation.

These three foci for relationality in feminist theories and theologies—(1) women's relationality as uniquely gendered; (2) the just and mutually enhancing ordering of relationships; and (3) theological understandings of relationship in the web of creation—are important as they inform key dimensions of feminist pastoral theology. The rest of this chapter will focus on these dimensions of relationality as they have been debated in feminist theory. Since relationality has been a foundational context in both pastoral theology and feminist theory, these three dimensions of relationality have often provided significant points of debate between those who hold a more essentialist starting point and those who start in constructivist assumptions. It is to those debates we now turn.

The Essentialist/Constructivist Debates

The essentialist/constructivist debates have run through all three of these dimensions of relationality in feminist theory, especially in the first. Before we look at the nature of those debates, it is important to define these two terms and the way these positions have functioned in feminist theory building.

Essentialism

Essentialism is a philosophical position that either implicitly or explicitly claims that certain traits, abilities, behaviors, or "vocations" belong universally to a certain group and, as such, become defining qualities for that group. There are a variety of ways to ground essentialist claims. The place of earliest, and maybe most persistent, debate has come out of essentialist claims grounded in biology. Since biological essentialism has been used to explain female "otherness" at the very least and, more often, "deviance" or "inferiority," considerable anxiety has arisen in much feminist scholarship about the use of biological essentialism—a fear about a new biology as destiny. And yet there is concern by some feminists that if we give up our right to name experiences that are mediated through the realities of living in a female body, we may also lose the right to claim women's bodily experience as normative and valuable, reclaiming it from the "deviance" paradigms. Exploring issues such as menarche, childbirth, menopause, and sexual expression, this more essentialist perspective claims, is key to reclaiming women's experience as central in defining psychological, spiritual, relational, and intellectual norms. This group of feminist theorists argues that when women's embodied experience is not seen as different and unique from men's, a dualism results, again splitting off spirit from matter and mind from body. The roots of patriarchal oppression of women are thus not adequately critiqued.

Another place where essentialism is grounded has been in looking at "women's" experience as potentially universal. In other words, the tendency has been to look at some women's experience (usually women of some privilege—white, educated, middle class, heterosexual) and conclude from that experience that it fits most or all women. Much of feminist research began with this set of essentialist assumptions. As women discovered that a male perspective and power dominated the formation and maintenance of culture, the reclaiming of women's voices and experiences, as both unique and generally unheard, became a central focus. This focus on women's experience allowed for a body of knowledge to be built that was extensive enough to stand as significant critique to male-based knowledge and to reveal it to be partial and nongeneric. To be able to reveal the false generic in language was a very important movement in feminist theory building. However, over time these more privileged perspectives were challenged by those women whose experiences were not represented by the claims of women's lives. Women of color and lesbian women, especially, began to develop research that revealed different kinds of experiences, and the essentialism of "all women's experience" began to be appropriately deconstructed. Yet to abandon this philosophical and methodological position is to risk relativizing women's experiences by focusing entirely on particularity, thus diminishing or potentially eliminating the solidarity (or at least critical mass of solidarity) that has made possible political and societal change.

Constructivism

The counter position to essentialism is the philosophical claim of constructivism. Constructivism posits that traits, abilities, behaviors, or "vocations" do not belong to a group in any universal way and that cultural notions like gender are constructed and socialized in people according to the rules of the culture. A constructivist might say, for example, that relationality is not an inherent or universal trait in women, but that relationality as a valued orientation is deliberately fostered in girls and women so that they might better fulfill the role that culture has defined for them.

In addition, a constructivist position would also suggest that the experiences that seem to belong in a universal way to a particular group are often challenged when that group is analyzed via different cultural classifications. So, what looks universal in women, a deep concern for and orientation around the formation and maintenance of relationships, for example, might well be contradicted or challenged by looking at women of different races, different classes, different ages, different sexual orientations, different physical abilities, and different ethnicities. A constructivist starting point would assume particularity and difference as it examined the different layers of social construction around any specific quality or behavior. Constructivism is generally understood to be a part of a postmodernist perspective on reality.

Linell Elizabeth Cady, in an article on identity in feminist theory and theology, succinctly captures some key issues in this debate. She writes:

> The recognition of the depth of [women's] exclusion contributed to the turn to a distinctively female nature and experience. The articulation of women as a distinct class, oppressed in a particular way by virtue of membership in that class, was an important plank in the development of a distinctive feminist movement and politics. . . . The categories of woman and experience have served ever since as the fundamental and defining categories of feminist theory, generating many of the theoretical riddles with which it has struggled. [However], feminist theory, as [Judith] Grant notes, "was becoming captured by the patriarchal ideas it sought to oppose. . . . It had created a stereotypical Woman, a monolithic, abstract being defined only by her source of oppression." (Cady, 1997, 20-21)

The answer of a postmodern or constructivist perspective to the problems of essentialism was to address this monolithic abstraction called "Woman" by acknowledging the deep and fundamental particularity of each life experience. With this emphasis, each person's story is seen in its uniqueness and within its own particular context. Generalizations are avoided; the power that any one story (or cultural narrative) can have over another is limited. In this way, the power to oppress any one group by another is reduced. However, in a similar fashion, any chance for a shared narrative within a group and the resultant possibility for solidarity is also limited. As Cady says about this postmodern position, "Identity is subject to fragmentation, and the political and normative voice is muted as the individual loses a sense of location from which to speak" (Cady, 1997, 23).

Multiple Layers of Feminist Method

One way to think about negotiating between the essentialist and the constructivist positions is to look at how they may belong together in a multilayered feminist method. Rita Nakashima Brock has offered such a paradigm through which to look at the history of feminist theory and theology (Brock, 1995, 8-19). She suggests that each of the five strategies of resistance and change is and has been important in building a feminist consciousness and an extensive body of knowledge. These five approaches have occurred in a chronological order. Each has been important, and each needs the others for correctives and applications. And each strategy has emerged out of the strategy before it. Brock also suggests that this paradigm appropriately conveys the process of feminist methods for a large group of women but not for all women within the culture. Many women of color, for example, saw the interweaving of forms of oppression from the beginning as did other women from multiply marginalized perspectives. Her paradigm is partial (especially in terms of its chronological assumptions) but useful for trying to understand how essentialist and constructivist views of relationality may actually inform each other rather than exist in polarized contradiction. Using Brock's five strategies, we can examine relationality as it operates in the lives of women and informs the work of pastoral theology and pastoral care.[2] So, let me name Brock's five strategies and how they are applicable to various approaches to relationality.

Brock suggests that women in the late 1960s and early 1970s pursued college education in record numbers. With that education, there was a sense that women could be "just like men." The strategy for women, then, was to model themselves after the dominant (male) styles in the workplace and attempt to succeed by minimizing any behavior that would be seen as too "feminine" to qualify them for that work. However, over time many women began to realize that, in order to succeed in the workplace, they had to hide their greatest gifts as well as much of their identity and that they were not playing on "an equal playing field."

The "just like men" strategy is relevant in looking at some of the pressures on women's relational preferences when they attempt to enter a world that has been organized around a male-based value system. Women who enter this world with hopes to be accepted and to succeed often find themselves attempting to model themselves, despite their gender training and self-image, on the workplace models already operating. In this scenario, women tend to compartmentalize their lives, putting the more highly valued independent working style into play in the environments where that is expected, and fragmenting off their relational commitments and needs to be used in other contexts or ignored altogether. This strategy is reflected in much of the media about women being "tougher managers or bosses than men" or women who point out to other women that "they didn't need a feminist movement to get ahead—they pulled themselves up by their own bootstraps," and so forth.

122

We see some of this "just like men" strategy operating in the case study from the beginning of this chapter. Jenny is aware that the work expectations are modeled on a kind of single-mindedness about the nature of the work and the workplace. There is a great deal of work to be done that does not allow time or ethos for relationship building. And yet, at the same time, Jenny experiences some pressure (as evidenced by the overheard comment by her coworker) that she should behave in ways consistent with gender stereotype expectations—an attentiveness to relationships and a general friendliness and nurturance that go with being female in this culture. This tension, and the ambivalence Jenny feels within herself about the need to succeed at her work (by the standards and methods of that culture) and the need to be herself (relational and caring), creates an agitation and unhappiness that Jenny does not know how to resolve.

Brock's second strategy, "add women and stir," seems to emerge out of these kinds of tensions within women and out of an understanding of women's hunger to join other women in trying to understand who they are in the midst of these cultural changes. Women begin to meet together and to research together the legacies that have been left to them from women who have gone before and whose lives have not been entered in the public records of the culture. Brock writes:

> Adding women into the recipe of history and restirring the pot has created a whole new cuisine and a much richer mix. . . . There was a problem, however, that emerged as this phase of active research on women flourished. No matter how hard we searched and no matter how far we looked, there were not enough women to balance the male-dominated picture. . . . If we believed we were made in the divine image, we had to figure out what went wrong, and it was clear something was wrong; something worked against women. (Brock, 1995, 12)

In terms of applying this strategy to the study of women's relationality, "add women and stir" seems to imply two possibilities. On the one hand, there are women who recognize that they are inclined to do things somewhat differently from the stereotypical "male environment." In this environment, women often begin to recognize that, in order to achieve, they are expected to behave and work in ways that go against their own preferences and experience. Yet there is also the message that women should act "like women" (stereotypically). If the message of "adding women" suggests that women will succeed best if they behave "like women," then there may be a tendency to behave in relationally stereotypical ways. This then generates a "compulsive and compulsory" relationality that builds a pathway to achievement based on "being liked and needed." There are multiple risks to this kind of response. Focusing on the needs of the other in order to protect or advance the self is a dangerous strategy. It is dangerous because it is not reliable in the traditional value systems of the culture and it assumes a mutuality that does not usually exist.

The Stone Center writings suggest that women have trouble with relatedness to the self in such a way that they often are unable to identify their own stake in or make claims on relationships with others that reflect their own goals and hopes (Jordan, 1991). There are times when women need to learn how to put their own needs first rather than pay attention to the maintenance of relationships, especially when that maintenance appears to be primarily or solely located in the woman's motivation and responsibility. If ignoring relationships became a primary goal for women's (or men's) lives, of course, then it would become clear that an important dimension of self was being ignored or denied. However, women generally get into trouble not because they are ignoring relationships, but because relationship maintenance becomes so one-sided that it consumes enormous amounts of time and energy and thus puts women at a significant disadvantage in the various public and private contexts of life. Recognizing this reality often helps women move to a desire to explore how other women are trying to balance relational needs with needs and hopes that are more grounded in the self.

The other possible response to the "add women and stir" strategy is to compartmentalize oneself in such a way that relationality is understood to have its place, but not where building relationships will jeopardize the values of that particular context. In this case, there is a tendency to follow the rules of the workplace but with a sense of rebellion and resistance. Women, trying to live full lives in a cultural context that prefers a model of gender complementarity, often need to gather together to figure out what it means to try to break through the gender stereotypes and cultural limits. One of the primary strategies for resistance to and change in an oppressive culture is solidarity that gives women support and generates new strategic options. Women can be supported in trying to live in contexts that are hostile or diminishing without losing themselves or their relationships. Relationality, especially with other women, emerges as a necessary adjunct to living in a culture that demands stereotypical relational support (supporting men and children especially) while not valuing it in the public domain.

Again, one can see the relevance of this strategy to the case with which we began this chapter. Jenny seems to have used a strategy in her various contexts that focuses on being attentive to and caring for those around her. Whether this has been at home, at work, or with her friends, Jenny seems to have the tendency to either deny or be unaware of her own needs. Her spontaneous assessment of problems in her various relational contexts is to locate the blame in herself and to attempt to do it all without challenging the context and its "rules." Jenny needs to be able to be in relationship with others who are able to give each other permission for paying attention to their own needs in such a way that this permission becomes a part of Jenny's core narrative. It seems as though her friends have been able to function for her in this way, as have her marriage and her educational contexts to a certain extent, but there is ongoing need for her to stand back and question her assumptions about responsibility to and for others.

What is generally missing in this strategy for Jenny and in this theory building method is the cultural analysis that calls for fundamental changes in the social arrangements. There tends to be both an adjustment orientation and a "trying to do it all" mentality inherent in this strategy.

Consequently, a third strategy, which Brock calls "women as victims," is needed. In this strategy of research and resistance, the focus is on the male-dominated systems of oppression that discriminate against and harm women. Much is discovered about patriarchal systems, and the more discoveries that are made, the more outrage and energy are generated. This energy works to motivate women to challenge unjust practices and to create protective structures for women harmed by these systems.

This third strategy explores relationality from the perspective of its purpose and function within a patriarchal, women-devaluing culture. The first strategy generated understandings of what happens when women enter a public world, especially when they enter expecting equality, and what kinds of responses are most adaptive and helpful. The second strategy generated an awareness of the importance of women's experience and the centrality of relationships with other women who were experiencing similar forms of discrimination and devaluing. However, it is in this third strategy, where analysis of cultural factors is central, that awareness of how women's compulsory and compulsive relationality is built into cultural gender expectation becomes clear.

As women gain clarity about the cultural factors that shape the way that relationality is to be understood, enough energy and anger are often generated for both theory building and cultural change. Women begin to develop theories that challenge the things that have seemed unquestionable and to shape new possibilities for themselves and for their relationships. Much of the work of this strategy, though, is deconstructive. An awareness of what is wrong and the energy to maintain this critical perspective in the face of enormous pressures to conform to cultural definitions are the primary orientations of this dimension.

Many of our best feminist theorists operate primarily through this strategy. Ellyn Kaschak's work, *Engendered Lives* (1992), is one example, as would be the work of Miriam Greenspan, Laura Brown, Carol Tavris, Joanne Brown, Carole Bohn, and many others. When talking about relationality in a patriarchal culture, for example, Kaschak writes:

> It is clear that women are actively directed and guided toward a life of relatedness and caring, and not only as a result of being mothered in a nuclear family. Women in this society are driven to relatedness by the messages of the culture, which include the demand to be unconscious of the masculine context and of the danger and derision it affords women. The particulars of any woman's situation are intertwined with her racial and class membership, as well as with individual experiences and meanings, but I would argue that sensing the presence of danger is ubiquitous. (Kaschak, 1992, 124-25)

Another example of this kind of work could be found in Phyllis Trible's work *Texts of Terror* (1984) and in Brown and Bohn's *Christianity, Patriarchy and Abuse* (1989), where the focus is on deconstructing what has stood as religious truth and tradition by bringing an awareness of cultural patriarchy as the analytical lens.

For a pastoral counselor working with Jenny, strategy three would be an important starting place. This is the place where Jenny, preferably in some sort of consciousness-raising environment, could begin to question the social arrangements that have, to some extent, continued to appear normative to her even though they disadvantaged her as a woman. She needs to learn to do cultural analysis that not only uses her own experience but also moves beyond her own story to an appreciation of gender arrangements and their function in a patriarchal world. The hope is that this will not devalue a relational orientation but help her to question when her relational foci work against both her and her primary relationships and when it is choiceful and helpful. As she learns to challenge the compulsory nature of relational care, she will be able to make choices that take her own wholeness as seriously as they do the needs of others.

This strategy, in counseling and in theory building, allows women's relationality to be examined and deconstructed, thereby questioning its sources, its inevitability, and it potential shape. Those theorists and theologians who operate out of this feminist method focus on the rules and assumptions of the culture(s) in which women live, and use that analysis to create the critical space for new paradigms to be built.

The work of this strategy continues to be important, but feminists have realized that there is more to women than the systems that oppress them, so there is a fourth strategy that Brock names "women-centered."

The focus of "women-centered" methods has been on women's strengths and creativity. The research examines the aspects of women's lives that have often been seen as inferior or deviant because they have been measured against male norms. In this category, one would put the work of the Stone Center research on women's identity development, Carol Gilligan's research on women's moral development, and Mary Belenky et al.'s work on women's ways of knowing. This approach is constructive and begins in women's experience, attempting to draw at least tentative conclusions from those experiences.

This, again, has been a very creative arena for feminist theory building around issues of relationality. Much of the work on relationality that starts in this strategy tends to find ways to reframe and rebuild theory by focusing on women's strengths and by looking at women's experience for its own sake rather than as compared to men's experience as normative. As Janet Surrey writes,

> The notion of the self-in-relation involves an important shift in emphasis from separation to relationship as the basis for self-experience and development. Further relationship is seen as the basic goal of development: that is, the

126

deepening capacity for relationship and relational competence. The self-in-relation model assumes that other aspects of the self (e.g., creativity, autonomy, assertion) develop within this primary context. (Surrey, 1991, 40-41)

Relationality, from these perspectives, is seen as a positive orientation that women are able to model and through which changes in our cultural norms and developmental theories might be made.

This fourth strategy risks the essentialist problems named earlier in that it assumes that relationality is inherent in some form in women's lives and it assumes that "women" as a group can be named and common experience explored. The importance of finding platforms of shared analysis—and thus, potential solidarity in bringing about liberating changes—should not be underestimated even while we recognize that once these conclusions are drawn, it becomes hard to adapt them when exceptions to that "common" experience are identified.

In pastoral counseling work, this fourth strategy will help Jenny to begin to explore her own experience and her own strengths. She will have worked to identify the problematic contexts of her life, to build relationships of solidarity, and to begin the process of cultural analysis around norms of justice and equality. Then having some distance on her gender training and the patriarchal norms she has internalized, she will better be able to assess her strengths, goals, and possibilities. She will learn to trust her judgment, rely on her embodied experiences, and express her needs.

This building of confidence in her perceptions and strengths, combined with appropriate cultural analysis, will help her to join in mutual partnership with her husband and child as they make decisions about their family that benefit all members. It will help her to make decisions about her work that allow her to be herself while still accomplishing her vocational tasks. And it will help her to explore her spirituality in ways that maximize the image of God within her and others. The pastoral counseling work will need to continue to hold strategies two, three, and four together as they mutually inform and correct the caregiving process. They will help her continue to recognize the need for solidarity, for cultural analysis, and for relying on her own experience, even though these three may sometimes seem to provide contradictory data.

This fourth method has many strengths, including a major reframing of many of the theories and theologies that had previously shaped pastoral theology. However, its limits have to do with how we define *woman* and how universally we correlate these theories of behaviors and being with the biological reality of being in female bodies. Out of these limits there has come a fifth strategy of feminist research that Brock names as "include everyone."

This fifth strategy suggests that feminist research needs to explore categories of "women" within groups who are usually not represented in this research. This would include lesbians, women of color, working-class women, women with disabilities, and so on. Including the women who are usually excluded changes both the questions and the answers of the previous research in ways that allow conclusions to be more tentative and less universalizing. This strategy begins to reveal how we can talk about "women" only when we do so by identifying their contexts because it is in the midst of the contexts that various components of identity can be seen together. The risk here is, of course, the fragmentation of postmodernism and constructivism.

However, Linell Cady offers a way to shape this last category that allows for the category of woman to serve as an important signifier even in the midst of multiple contexts. She names this perspective the historicist alternative.

In this philosophical method, the individual exists with her or his own history and context, but the social context in which this person can be seen also exists and contributes to that individual identity. In that way, the social context can be understood to be both enduring (and thus offering structure to those within its boundaries) and dynamically changing over time.

Cady summarizes this by saying,

> A historicist construal of identity rejects the abstract, unified subject of modernism [and of essentialism]. But it does so without embracing its mirror opposite. It recognizes that identity is multiple, fluid, and shifting, but for all that, it is not fictitious, ephemeral, or limitless. Identity is still bounded, constituted over against that which is different. . . . Identity is constituted by the subject's creative, agential negotiation of the intersecting currents and competing loyalties that run through her.

In other words, we draw our identities through our own particular experiences in the midst of the social contexts in which we are embedded and which we have chosen to claim as our narrative frameworks.

This historicist alternative offers a way to talk about women's lives, but women's lives within particular contexts and circumstances. It allows a shared narrative that may lead to shared meanings, identities, and political analyses, but it does so recognizing that the shared narrative is partial and evolving over time.

This fifth strategy of including all, with a historicist corrective, is useful in exploring relationality. It insists upon research from groups not fully represented in the "women-centered" work and, thus, tests out the claims of that work. It also includes work that begins by identifying experiences thought to be common to groups of women identified by other marginalized contexts, which may or may not be related to the work generated by more culturally dominant women.

Relationality as a construct seems to be open enough to allow for diverse ways of describing its function in varieties of constructs. For example, Clevone Turner speaks from an African American woman's perspective and describes the importance of relationality within a particular culture in order to have the strength of self-in-relation to function biculturally. She suggests that without these intracultural connections, the oppressive dynamics around race and gender of the larger culture close down a healthy development of self (Turner, 1997, 74).

Beverly Daniel Tatum, also writing from an African American woman's standpoint, similarly suggests that the dominant culture "almost guarantees empathic failures, experiences of disconnection," for African American women (Tatum, 1997, 92). The strong negative messages about African American women can be countered only by strong empathic relationships within one's own racial group. Only then are intercultural mutual relationships possible.

Although both writers are willing to start with the more essentialist assumptions about the importance of and orientation toward relationships in the lives of women, these starting assumptions are modified by describing the types of relationships that offer the most positive potential and the relationships where harm is most likely to be done. In these ways, the developmental perspectives on relationality are joined by ethical analysis on the nature of mutuality and health in relationships.

This aspect of feminist method provides an ethical component for pastoral counseling as well. Using this strategy, Jenny will begin to recognize that, even as she identifies the ways in which she has been oppressed and needs to resist ongoing forms of oppression, she also, as a white, heterosexual, educated woman, often stands in the place of oppressor in a culture that advantages her race, economics, and sexuality. She will learn to pay attention, not to just what her own experience tells her, but to where it may also mislead her given her place in a hierarchical culture. Jenny will learn that she needs to allow adequate room for difference from herself in the lives of other women even as she, sometimes desperately, seeks similarities.

The hope is that the pastoral counselor will help her to engage her spirituality in this movement toward greater personal and cultural health. She will recognize that her ability to be in relationship is a reflection of the image of God in her and in all of creation but that relationality requires the deep appreciation of the particularity of the other. God's enormous diversity of creation sustains this conclusion. True relationality seeks out difference in order to celebrate it rather than look for one's self in the other. This is a hard balance for people who have experienced the isolation and devaluation of cultural oppression—to trust the self and its inclinations at the same time one trusts the differing experience of the marginalized other. Maintaining relationships with those who have much in common and with those whose experiences and contexts are different is crucial to maintaining this balance.

A look at relationality using Brock's five strategies of feminist resistance and knowledge building suggests that each method offers insight into the nature of relationality in women's lives. Holding the five in tension seems not to create necessary contradictions, but to allow mutual critique and enhancement.

Strategies three and five ("focusing on the harm cultural oppression does to women" and "including other voices") stand as important sources of critique to the potential essentialism of strategy four ("women-focused"). The cultural focus of method three insists that political analysis and cultural critique are at the heart of any analysis of women's experience. Without that political analysis and its implications for shaping, reinforcing, and enforcing the experiences in women's lives, including the nature of relationality, there is the risk of creating a new set of norms for women that reproduce patriarchal strategies even though they seem to be "in a different voice." The inclusive perspective of method five insists that to create a monolithic abstraction called "woman" (which is a risk for women-centered methods) again reproduces oppressive dynamics within the category of woman. This strategy requires many voices, diverse voices, in the study of women's experience. The inclusion of these perspectives at the heart of developing categories that will help bring an end to oppressive relationships between people and between groups allows for a greater likelihood that damaging power dynamics will be identified and held accountable more easily.

The women-focused method four also holds cultural critique and inclusivity methods accountable. It challenges the cultural focus method in its tendency to do only deconstructive critical analysis and in its tendency to frame women as victims and, thus, relatively powerless. Women-focused methods focus on women's strengths and encourage agency and construction of theory, even if that theory must be closely examined for false generalizations. Method four also challenges method five in its tendency to fragmentation. A women-focused strategy claims that there must be a way for at least tentative conclusions so that just and empowering strategies may be developed. It allows for theoretical constructs out of which solidarity may be developed, even if that solidarity needs to be dismantled so that new alliances may be built.

This dynamic theoretical movement between strategies that have tended to be polarizing is fluid enough so that monolithic structures do not get built and stable enough so that fragmentation does not destroy all hope of taking theoretical constructs into existing, male-centered bodies of knowledge as critique and challenge. Without that much solidarity, social structures cannot be changed. Whereas the polarizing nature of the debates tended to deplete some of the strength of feminist theory building around issues of relationality in women's development, in ethics, and in theology, a method that allows for mutual informing and accountability will help move feminist theory building into a more effective status.

Implications for Pastoral Practice

It seems to me that at least four primary implications for pastoral practice emerge out of this methodological discussion.

The first has to do with the importance of methodological clarity in creating strategies for ministry practice. It seems clear that where we start as pastoral practitioners in terms of the focus of our method has considerable impact on what we conclude about fundamental issues of health, wholeness, justice, vocation, and so on. Without knowing our methodological options and without allowing critique and accountability to flow between these options, we are not able to make well-informed decisions about pastoral assessment and therapeutic directions. It is especially problematic for those of us who have found one of Brock's strategies particularly helpful for our own growth as women not to recognize that other ways of interpreting and analyzing experience are both possible and necessary.

A second implication for pastoral practice around issues of relationality has to do with how we help women explore their experiences in pastoral counseling work. Various theories about women's relationality seem to indicate that women need relationships with one another, particularly within intracultural groups, in order to be able to develop mutually enhancing relationships in a variety of contexts. In addition, women need to develop different kinds of relationships that ground them in the various contexts that make up their identities. These relational groundings help women then to make decisions about the nature and form and limits of other relationships in which they are engaged. The intracultural women's relationships help women with their analyses of power within relationships and ways to seek mutuality and justice. Intercultural women's groups then become necessary in order to generate new questions and counter false generalizations about women that may emerge in the intracultural groups.

Third, even as women find satisfaction in and motivation toward relationality in all dimensions of their lives, it is important for them to be able to engage in appropriate cultural analysis that may frequently reveal a persistent socialization of women's relationality at the cost of a woman's self-development and of knowing her own "voice." Kaschak's discussion of compulsive and compulsory relationality as foundational to women's gender training is significant. Women may well feel guilty or selfish if they sometimes choose to disconnect from relationships that are damaging to them without recognizing that this "guilt" is a culturally induced motivator for keeping women in supportive relationships with men and children. Cultural analysis of patriarchy alongside the recognition that relationality may well be deeply satisfying and life giving is a tension to be maintained in the work of pastoral counseling.

Finally, pastoral caregivers need to develop a theology of relationality that takes seriously the positive gains in feminist theory building. Feminist theology, which has learned how to make careful connections between the tendency to subordinate and devalue women and the tendency to misuse other elements of creation, offers real possibilities for understanding the potential for healing relationships throughout the web of life. These powerful interconnections, however, must be tempered by recognizing the importance of context in the shaping of theology. In other words, theology is always a product of the immediate relationships and their contexts, and it is only within those concrete and particular realities that the nature of the human-divine relationship can be understood. Each relational moment, in its immediacy and in its specific context, nonetheless contributes to the total potential for relational wholeness within the entire living web. Relationships are indeed a core construct in pastoral theology. As we seek to understand the divine-human-creation matrix of life, the nature of our relationships becomes the building blocks for good and for ill of that matrix.

Notes

[1] For more extended discussion of these issues, see Nancy Chodorow, *The Reproduction of Mothering* (Berkeley: University of California Press, 1978), and Judith Jordan et al., *Women's Growth in Connection* (New York: Guilford Press, 1991).

[2] Many of the articles in *Setting the Table* have chosen a multilayered approach in exploring various issues such as women's approaches to the Bible and issues of language and liturgy. I am indebted to their modeling of this method and to Brock's paradigm for some ideas in this chapter.

7

Discourse Theory and Pastoral Theology

Susan J. Dunlap

For some time now, our field has been engaged in the process of reinterpreting traditional pastoral care practices in the light of greater concern for the corporate context of both human problems and pastoral responses. Larry Kent Graham (1992), James Poling (1991, 1996, 1997), Christie Neuger (1991, 1996, 1997), Bonnie Miller-McLemore (1994, 1996), and Pamela Couture (1991, 1995) are among those who have been instrumental in leading the field toward greater awareness of the social and cultural contexts of care. John Patton has called this a shift to a "communal-contextual" paradigm in which attention is given to the impact of corporate structures, both ecclesial and cultural (Patton, 1993). Recently, two theologians, continuing in this vein, have introduced to pastoral theology an important theoretical base for this enterprise, discourse theory.

Riet Bons-Storm has used discourse theory to explain why women are "incredible," or not believed, in traditional pastoral counseling settings (Bons-Storm, 1996). She uses feminist post-structuralist Luce Irigaray to criticize unitary, and therefore hegemonic, notions of truth that have excluded women's voices, or women's truth. Elaine Graham, in a rigorous defense of the social construction of gender, has made rich use of discourse theory (Graham, 1995). Although hers is not a book specifically about practices of care, she addresses topics of concern to pastoral theology, such as the epistemological status of the social sciences, ways that theology functions to create persons, the impact of social structures on selfhood, and theoretical assumptions regarding the body. I would like to continue in the direction begun by these two theologians and add my own brief argument for the usefulness of discourse theory for pastoral theology.

What is discourse theory? In the tradition of the "linguistic turn" inaugurated by Wittgenstein and continued through Saussure's structuralism and on to Foucault's poststructuralism, discourse theory holds that language is not an inert representation or reflection of what is "out there." Language is not the label given to preexisting human experiences or perceptions. Rather, language constitutes things. Language creates: "It is not as though we have meanings, or experiences, which we then proceed to cloak with words; we can only have the meanings and experiences in the first place because we have a language to have them in" (Eagleton, 1983, 60).

Some in pastoral theology have recognized that language creates "worlds," either for the individual psyche to dwell in or for the individual-in-community.[1] However, discourse theory casts the net wider and views language as enmeshed with other entities, such as social structures, institutions, truth claims, "scientific" knowledge, power dynamics, the body, and the psyche. The notion of discourse links such seemingly disparate realms as the knowledge produced in the academy with the inner world of the individual and with the very construction of human bodies. Discourse is never simply language; it is always linked with concrete, social, cultural, historical realities, including psyches and bodies.

Why is this important for pastoral theology? Because I believe an important way to understand pastoral praxis is the activity of bearing discourse. The pastor, then, is a "bearer of discourse."[2] Pastors bring discourse to multiple settings. The most apparent site is the pulpit. The weekly Sunday sermon is the occasion of bringing Christian discourse to bear on global, congregational, and personal concerns. The pastor also takes discourse to the hospital, the nursing home, the inpatient treatment center. The pastor speaks Christian discourse in testimony before state legislatures and city councils. The pastor prays at football games, the U.S. Congress, business prayer breakfasts, fox hunts, graduations, military ceremonies, and around countless dinner tables. Regardless of how we might judge the appropriateness of these as sites for a pastoral role, many pastors find themselves as bearers of Christian discourse in many places in the world. Theories of discourse will be helpful in articulating the broad implications of this role. Because pastors use language in many sites, and because language is linked broadly to myriad entities, discourse theory offers a way to understand the broad implications of the pastoral use of language. It offers a way to say that something much more is going on than a neutral representation of things in the pastoral uses of language. Pastors are participating in language's creative, constructive, constitutive capacities in their role as bearers of discourse.

Discourse theory, particularly feminist versions, challenges pastoral theology in at least three concrete ways. One, we are pushed to move from speaking of "selves" to speaking of "subjects," a shift that highlights the power of political and cultural context in the social construction of those for whom we care. Two, its treatment of the body reminds us that care for others as fully corporeal beings has always been part of pastoral praxis, and discourse theory invites us to link the body to power dynamics in the sociocultural arena. Three, we are challenged to view our own field as discourse, as connected to institutional forms and movements of power that may or may not enhance human flourishing. These three challenges will be explored in this chapter.

Discourse and Subjectivity

Discourse theory can make a critical contribution to feminist pastoral theology through its understanding of subjectivity and the socially constructed subject. Chris Weedon, a feminist using discourse theory, defines *subjectivity* as "the conscious and unconscious thoughts and emotions of the individual, her sense of herself and her ways of understanding her relation to the world" (Weedon, 1997, 32). The attentiveness to the inner world described here is also a central concern of pastoral theology and provides a link between our field and discourse theory. Because discourse theory establishes the connection of subjectivity to the play of discourses in the larger field of practices of power, the discursive understanding of the inner world offers a critical contribution to a pastoral theology that seeks to situate the individual and her internal processes in a larger social, cultural sphere. Traditionally, the private thoughts and emotions of an individual, her longings, griefs, pleasures, and intuitions, have been separated from the movements of power at a macro level. Discourse theory links innerness with sociocultural power dynamics. For example, the inner experience of depression has traditionally been viewed as an individual matter, having to do with psychic structures, though possibly connected to family of origin (Dunlap, 1997; Neuger, 1991). Discourse theory can be used to theorize the interior experience of depression as very much linked to patriarchal discourse regarding woman as madonna/prostitute played out in disempowering images in the media, institutions that alternately romanticize and despise women, and women's bodies commodified either for reproduction or for male sexual fantasy. Pastoral theology's traditional concern with the inner is expanded by the way discourse analysis theorizes the connection between the inner world and the sociocultural world.

While we are accustomed to referring to the "self" in our field, the notion of "subjectivity" is preferable because it places the individual in social context. In discourse theory, the individual is more of a "subject position" that is made possible by the interplay of discourses rather than a prelinguistic "substance" called "self." Positionality suggests location, situatedness, a view or stance from some finite place. In the past, pastoral theology has viewed the care receiver in modernist terms as a self that is a separate, autonomous, freely choosing being, disconnected from community, context, tradition, power relations, and constitution by language. Such a view ignored the influence of social location, and the power of race, class, gender, to construct who we are. Discourse theory's notion of subjectivity, with the full force of positionality that it implies, enables us to more adequately theorize social location in the care for souls. The soul, and its desires, rages, passions, and instincts, is always a product of place and position in the world. To use subjectivity language in our theorizing conditions us to remember this.

French philosopher Michel Foucault, a primary source for discourse theory, views the individual, or subject position, as the site of continually competing discourses (Foucault, 1980). Subjectivity is fluid because it is constantly being constituted and reconstituted by discourses at battle. The sources of competing discourses are many: church, family, journalism, popular media, psychiatry, advertising, medicine, social welfare, and liberal feminism, for example, each linked to institutions and languages and authority structures. Each discourse functions with different strategies and mechanisms of power. As we listen to those to whom we give care, we can listen for the competing discourses in their words and in their actions. In one moment we may hear Christian discourse regarding love of neighbor and welcoming the stranger, at another we may hear strains of capitalist ideology that more-is-better, or we may hear pop psychological language of codependency or Mars/Venus talk. These discourses, invested with varying and changing amounts of power, each linked with habits, subcultures, authority structures, mechanisms for determining the true, offer competing subject positions. We would do well for the moment, to hear which discourses emerge as definitive, and to enable choices about positions to occupy. For example, in one woman we may hear competing strains of the cosmo woman, the liberal Protestant clergywoman, the virtuous churchwoman, and the nineties' supermom. Each of these kinds of women, or subject positions, is linked to discourses, and this woman is the site of their competition. As caregivers, we can empower women to choose where they will stand.

The question of agency arises: If we are wholly constituted by discourses, are we nothing but their passive creatures? Can we make choices about what constitutes us? Is it possible to choose to identify with a discourse, or are we mute products of discursive competitions? Weedon clearly believes it is possible to speak of the discursively constructed subject and still maintain that subject's agency:

> In the battle for subjectivity and the supremacy of particular versions of which it is a part, the individual is not merely the passive site of discursive struggle. The individual who has a memory and an already discursively constituted sense of identity may resist particular interpellation or produce new versions of meaning from the conflicts and contradictions between existing discourses. Knowledge of more than one discourse and the recognition that meaning is plural allows for a measure of choice on the part of the individual and even where choice is not available, resistance is still possible. (Weedon, 1987, 106)

For Weedon, choice is possible because subjects have a "memory" and a "knowledge of more than one discourse" and see that "meaning is plural." Agency is possible for the one who draws on memory and alternative sources of knowledge, and for the one who has the eyes to see that more than one meaning is possible. Caregivers can increase agency by actively invoking alternative discourses that may lie dormant in a person's memory, by nurturing new sources of knowledge, and by empowering care receivers to make choices for creative and life-giving discourses. Feminist theologians have demonstrated that Christian Scripture and tradition have functioned ambiguously, as both life giving and death dealing. Therefore, we must cultivate the awareness that meaning is plural, that more than one "take" on things is legitimate. Weedon reminds us:

> Although the subject in poststructuralism is socially constructed in discursive practices, she nonetheless exists as a thinking, feeling subject and social agent, capable of resistance and innovations produced out of the clash between contradictory subject positions and practices. She is also a subject able to reflect upon the discursive relations which constitute her

and the society in which she lives, and able to choose from the options available. (Weedon, 1987, 106)

This understanding of subjectivity engenders hope because it is contested. Subject positions are not fixed. There is no one, eternally correct way to be woman, Christian, citizen, or mother in the world. Battles are under way over ways to be these things, and the various contestants are invested with varying amounts of power. For example, in most social contexts traditional Christian discourse regarding women is invested with greater power than radical lesbian discourse regarding women. Capitalist discourse, which offers the subject position of "passive consumer," is more powerful than community-organizing discourses of the subject as a "member of a community that creates political options." The relative power of discourses may account for one difficulty of making life changes through pastoral counseling: what is called client resistance in psychotherapeutic language may be the persistence of a powerful discourse. And yet the very presence of the contest, the battle, is hopeful. Nothing is set in stone. Identities and subject positions are fluid, contested, and in motion. It is precisely the contested, unfixed nature of subjectivity that means options for those who thought they had none. For those of us who seek to free others from restricted, dead-end lives, this is a hopeful realization.

To move away from "self" to notions of "subject" risks erasing the unique souls who come to us for care and compassion. To conceive of these souls as "nodes of intersecting and competing discourses" hardly inspires the gentleness and radical commitment to the other that our work requires. Julia Kristeva, philosopher and psychoanalyst, speaks of the "subject in process" (Kristeva, 1987, 9) and the subject as a "work in progress" (Moi, 1986, 13-14). She calls our attention to the fact that we are constantly being made and remade, shaped and reshaped, by the constellation of interpersonal and social influences. Such a notion provides a useful way of conceiving those to whom we give care. We can understand "who they are" as fluid yet recognizable. We can name the multiple power dynamics, social forces, economic pressures that are continually forming, reforming, or deforming persons while holding in view a persistent identity. This is preferable to the implication that the individual as "subject position" is somehow an empty space.

An additional advantage of the notion of the subject in process, or as a work in progress, is that we can see the future as more open, loose. We are enabled to see that no one is completely bound, irreversibly fixed, by the current arrangement of things. A recognition that each of us is constructed by social context invites us to play a role in shaping these contexts or choosing the ones with which to affiliate. As caregivers, we can influence these choices. As *pastoral* caregivers, we act as bearers of Christian discourse, always attentive to how a particular interpretation will function in a particular context.

The inner, personal worlds of emotion, consciousness, and the unconscious are constituted by discourses in the larger arena. When we as pastoral caregivers recognize the enmeshment of even the most private emotion in larger structures, even power structures, we locate care receivers in a political, cultural, and social matrix. Cultural forces continue to seduce caregivers to reduce human pain to individual psychopathology, personal maladjustment, and interpersonal discord. When pastoral theology neglects to see individuals as situated in the context of power relations, with unequal access to political and economic resources, our care is not only ineffective, but it subtly "blames the victim" for her pain rather than names the power structures that are involved.

Discourse and the Body

Because so many of our caring practices address the body, it is critical for us to be aware of how our words, behaviors, uses and practices of Scripture and tradition, participate in constructing the body. A quick review of the introductory course I teach reminded me of how embodiment is implicated in most areas of care: death and dying involve the body's mortality; alcoholism involves the body's physical dependencies and cravings; battering involves the body's damage; sexual violence involves the body's violation; aging involves the body's limits; illness involves the body's fragility; the genesis, treatment, and symptoms of depression involve the body. The body must be discussed in order to adequately address care in these cases. Foucault describes discourse as not simply having effects on the experience of the body, but as actually constructing the body: "The body manifests the stigmata of past experience. . . . The body is the inscribed surface of events (traced by language and dissolved by ideas) . . . [the] task is to expose a body totally imprinted by history" (Foucault, 1984, 83). The body is shaped by multiple regimes as well as the site of resistance: "The body is molded by a great many distinct regimes; it is broken down by the rhythms of work, rest, and holidays; it is poisoned by food or values, through eating habits or moral laws; it constructs resistances" (Foucault, 1983, 87). For Foucault, the body is the site of power struggles; "the body itself is invested by power relations" (Foucault, 1979, 24). "The body is also directly involved in a political field; power relations have an immediate hold upon it; they invest it, mark it, train it, torture it, force it to carry out tasks, to perform ceremonies, to emit signs" (Foucault, 1979, 30).

Susan Bordo appropriates Foucault to explain the prevalence of eating disorders among women as the inscription of patriarchal concepts and practices on women's bodies (Bordo, 1988, 1989). Culturally mediated messages and behaviors create in women not only the desire to be small, to take minimum amounts of space, but also the thrust to eliminate the body altogether. According to Bordo, the Western heritage of dualism dating back as far as Plato and continuing through Augustine and Descartes fosters notions that the body is an unfortunate constraint on the mind and spirit, something whose passions and desires and appetites should be stringently controlled, if not destroyed. The desire to control one's bodily appetites has particular impact on women who have a sense of personal and social powerlessness. At some level they reason that, though power is lacking, they can at least have mastery over their bodies. Of course, the mastery is tragic because it can result in starvation and death. Bordo's argument supports the claim that Western discourse on the body becomes imprinted on the emaciated bodies of anorexic women, that they bear the stigmata of this dualistic heritage.

Bordo uses Foucault to distinguish between the "intelligible body" and the "useful body":

> The intelligible body includes our scientific, philosophic, and aesthetic representations of the body—our cultural *conceptions* of the body, norms of beauty, models of health, and so forth. But the same representations may also be seen as forming a set of *practical* rules and regulations through which the living body is "trained, shaped, obeys, responds," becoming, in short, a socially adapted and "useful body." (Bordo, 1989, 25-26)

The official and legible language regarding the body is what is "intelligible," while the "useful," or in terms preferable to Bordo, the "practical," body is the concrete physical being produced by the implicit ordering of the official and legible.

This discussion of the body brings an extremely important contribution to our field. We must be able to hear the "practical rules and regulations" that may render bodies, and thus body-selves, thwarted, damaged, stunted. All sorts of discourses produce such rules: the practice of medicine, images of beauty, definitions of gender, norms of sexual practice. Our inherited conceptions and practices of the body in Christian tradition and pastoral practice should also not escape scrutiny. Pastors as bearers of discourse "inscribe" the surface of bodies with words, practices, and institutions. In our prayers at the hospital bedside we must avoid subtly referring to the body that is ill as a machine to be fixed, or something to be loathed for its weakness, or to be disciplined for being out of control.[3] In sermons and teaching, when referring to a woman, we must stringently avoid the habit of lifting up a woman's appearance, contributing to the cultural forces that would create her body as a surface to be decorated and a currency to buy love, acceptance, success. Consciousness of the power of our discourse to inscribe might raise questions as to how such liturgical recitations of words like "Christ's body broken for you" might glorify bodily victimization.[4]

It is appropriate that we as caregivers focus on internal feelings of grief or guilt, on interpersonal discord or alienation, on personal or professional decision making, and on spiritual or emotional sustenance. Discourse theory beckons us to see how these are internal processes of fully embodied human beings.

Pastoral Theology as Discourse

Discourse theory also raises the intriguing question, How is our field, our body of literature, discourse? What subject positions do we create as the field of pastoral theology? What institutional forms are we linked with? How are our ideas connected with practices in the churches? Feminist Nancy Fraser's work raises an important question for our field when we consider it as discourse (Fraser, 1989).

Fraser raises the question, What gets included in the public debate? She makes a distinction between the political, the economic, and the domestic. If a matter is considered political, it is included in public debate. A matter is politicized when it is "contested across a range of different discursive arenas and among a range of different discourse publics" (Fraser, 1989, 167). On the other hand, matters from either the economic realm or the domestic realm are lifted from the debate, and one view tends to be established as orthodox. The economic and domestic "enclaves" have the power to depoliticize issues relegated to their realm, the power to "shield such matters from general contestation . . . and, as a result, both entrench as authoritative certain specific interpretations of needs" (Fraser, 1989, 168). What is interesting in Fraser's analysis is her description of how the shielded realms of the economic and the domestic are in fact "leaky," or "permeable," and certain "runaway" needs break out of the confines of the personal and the economic and join the ranks of the political. For example, for years the issue of battered women had been considered a part of the domestic realm and therefore a private problem, not a matter of public concern. However, because the domestic enclave is leaky, the problem of battered women became politicized and a matter of public debate and therefore able to be addressed through systems of justice and not simply in the private sphere of counseling or confession.

Once a need has become politicized, it is contested in three kinds of discourses: oppositional, reprivatization, and expert. *Oppositional* discourses emerge when needs become deprivatized by groups who begin to contest the orthodox need interpretations attributed to them. For example, battered women became organized and contested the claim that their need is to learn to adjust gracefully to a bad situation for the sake of Christian marriage, and they began to name their need for safety. This move challenges the boundaries between the political and the economic or domestic. The emergence of oppositional discourses marks "a moment in the self constitution of new collective agents of social movements" (Fraser, 1989, 171). To create discourses that challenge the orthodox view is to simultaneously claim the power to shape sociocultural arrangements. For example, naming "sexual harassment" in the workplace marked the emergence of women able to interpret their needs at work and broke this issue out of the economic into the political realm. Oppositional discourse arises as groups begin to politicize what was enclaved in either the domestic or the economic sphere, offering needs interpretations that compete with conventional ones.

Reprivatization discourses aim to keep issues enclaved in the uncontested realms of the domestic and the economic. "They seek to contain forms of needs talk that threaten to spill across a wide range of discourse publics" (Fraser, 1989, 172). These discourses would maintain that domestic violence is a family or religious affair. They would view a factory closing as apolitical, having to do with impersonal market forces, and not a matter to be publicly debated. These discourses seek to return runaway needs to the uncontested realm of domestic or economic.

Expert discourses arise out of both university and state institutions where public policy is created and debated. Experts tend to objectify those whose needs are debated, who can be "rendered passive, positioned as potential recipients of predefined services rather than as agents involved in interpreting their needs and shaping their life conditions" (Fraser, 1989, 174). Experts tend to "stigmatize" what is considered "deviant" (Fraser, 1989, 174). The "welfare mother" and "psychiatric patient" and "homeless person" have been topics of expert discourse, defined as outside the bounds of "normal," and therefore silenced.

Fraser's challenge to pastoral theology is to become aware of our status as oppositional, reprivatizing, or expert discourse. Certainly, pastoral theology is highly vulnerable to functioning in a reprivatizing mode. The traditional stance of pastoral theology has been to focus on the private realm of the personal and domestic, and has been most comfortable treating problems as belonging to that sphere. As a field, we sequestered the inner world to the apolitical, uncontested realm of the private until recently. While a focus on care and counseling of the most private, confidential, soul-baring issues is at times appropriate, what is most private is always connected to social and cultural processes. The field of pastoral theology implicitly supports reprivatizing cultural forces when it refuses to place the private in a social and political context.

We are also capable of operating as expert discourse, one that functions as disempowering, patient-making language. Pastoral counseling centers can be institutional forms that create passive patients rather than social change agents actively engaged in addressing oppressive structures. Our field functions as expert discourse in churches when it marginalizes the "deviant" rather than enables the embrace of the stranger as one who belongs, is one of us. Such "deviants" might be the chronically unhappy woman, the man on antipsychotic medication, the pregnant teenager, or those whose life issues are unfamiliar to middle-class, white people. Our field as expert discourse can make patients of such parishioners rather than establish them as equal members of the body of Christ.

Is it possible for pastoral theology to self-consciously choose to function as an oppositional discourse, one that challenges narrow interpretations of the normal and the deviant, the just and the good, the healthy and the pathological? Is it possible to be accountable to oppositional voices from both ecclesial and countercultural communities? When writers in pastoral theology name our location in political and social matrices and are self-critical about power ends that are served by our intellectual claims, we are able to make choices about whether our work will function in a reprivatizing, expert, or oppositional mode. Cultural critique, resistance literature, and social movement analysis become resources for pastoral theology.[5] Theological grounding for our claims would be scrutinized for such systemic evils as sexism, racism, anti-Semitism, and classism. Only when we are also able to function in an oppositional mode can we promote good care for all God's children. Pastoral theology, as a form of discourse, will inevitably serve the power ends of some groups and not of others. Because we are highly vulnerable to implicitly making alliances with both reprivatizing and expert discourses, we must intentionally choose to function as oppositional as well.

Implications for Teaching Pastoral Theology

Having presented some of the feminist contributions of discourse theory to the field of pastoral theology, moving from self to subject, linking the body to discourse, and viewing our own field as discourse, I wish to turn to a consideration of how discourse theory might affect the way in which we teach our courses.

The Limits of Empathy

First, discourse theory makes it clear that students need more than skills in empathic listening. Empathy has been defined as having a cognitive component and an affective component. *Empathy* is "the ability to identify with and experience another person's experiences . . . by (as much as possible) suspending one's own frame of reference in order to enter the perceptual and emotional world of the other" (Hunter, 1990, 354). As caregivers, we know the importance of this kind of connection for validating the other. It is a powerful way to establish a caring attitude toward the private, inner world of another. Many have never spoken the truth of their lives, feelings, rages, pleasures, desires, longings in an accepting environment. To do so is an extraordinary experience of authorization: to be authorized to claim the legitimacy of their existence *just as they are* in the world.[6]

But empathy has its limits. What happens when the cognitive framework, the perceptual world, is distorted or based on falsehoods? Many are shackled by falsehoods wrought by psychopathology, by cultural lies about women and racial and ethnic minorities, by family messages of humiliation and shame. No one can dispute the importance of empathy as a critical first step in establishing

143

connection, but in many cases cognitive structures need restructuring because they bring depression, anxiety, disrupted relationships, self-hatred. Another way to state the issue is, What happens when a person occupies a subject position that is harmful, when discourse damages?

The "perceptual framework" or "cognitive structures" of the psyche can be described in terms of discourse: they are products of discourse in all the fullness of what discourse implies—a web of ideas, institutions, bodies, subjectivity, practices. Discourse theory teaches us that a "cognitive structure" is never divorced from its social context, and therefore never out of the field of power relations. For example, depression is linked to such cognitive beliefs of self as incompetent, ugly, and helpless. Clearly, these beliefs are parallel to cultural attitudes toward women, borne out in powerlessness in institutions, in practices that are violent, humiliating, and disempowering to women. Not surprisingly, depression afflicts women at twice the rate it does men. These discourses do not just change with empathy. Empathy alone leaves discourse or cognitive structures intact that are harmful, and is therefore not an adequate form of care. Therefore, we must include some techniques beyond empathic listening in our introductory courses. Simple psychotherapeutic techniques from cognitive therapy, brief therapy, and rational-emotive therapy can be a place to begin disrupting problematic discourse.[7] Behavioral techniques can take the form of encouraging countercultural behaviors that subvert hegemonic power arrangements, such as assertiveness in a woman. A simple introduction to teaching skills in assertiveness, communication, and negotiation can begin to redress power imbalances in marriages. Our course work alone cannot produce skilled pastoral counselors, but it can initiate the beginner into simple counseling techniques that address discursive hegemony.[8]

The Importance of the Social/Cultural Context

Second, discourse theory reminds us as teachers to nurture in our students the habit of placing the various forms of human distress in cultural context. We are constantly tempted to perceive human problems as individual in origin and solution. Students, to say nothing of their teachers, need the discipline that develops the habit of asking the contextual questions.

Discourse theory pushes us to see the interconnectedness of an individual problem with ideas, institutional forms, power matrices, and cultural patterns of interacting. We teach this habit by consistently referring to the larger social forces at work in particular issues. For example, when speaking of the pastoral care of sick persons, the effects of class on health care delivery can be discussed; when speaking of care for unemployed persons, the dynamics of a global economy can be explained; when speaking of care for alcoholic persons, the social isolation and ennui of the middle class can be explored; when dealing with family matters, gender issues must always be considered. Caregivers must be trained to instinctively ask the contextual questions, to ask the questions regarding the relative power accorded by virtue of social location. We can model that skill in the way we discuss care in our courses.

The instinct to ask the contextual questions is helpful in diagnosing the problem, bringing to awareness the complexity of the issues involved, and identifying resources. A contextual problem will have a contextual solution; a problem involving power dynamics calls for rearranging power relationships. When resources are found in social context, sources of hope multiply, including not only ecclesial resources, but also private and public social services and support groups of many sorts. Although some might criticize the individualistic, "therapeutic" language of some of these groups and services, it can nevertheless be stated that these imperfect, secular entities have been sources of healing and power for wounded and disenfranchised persons. To discount them because of the inadequacy of their rhetoric when they in fact function in healing ways is irresponsible.

The Importance of Embodiment

Our courses can name the problematic form that a spirit/body dualism can take in our care. Our caring words and practices will lend power to discourse inscribed on bodies, for good or ill. The body as enemy, machine, unclean, commodity can find its way insidiously in our care, as discussed earlier.

In addition, our courses can lift up the body as a site of resistance and hope. As teachers, we can highlight the importance of the body as a starting point for spiritual growth in at least four ways. We can teach pastors to nurture the body as a source of the holy. First, through bodies there can be extraordinary *communion* with others. Through the joy of dance with others, through healing touch, through intimate sexual relations, bodies can be the starting point for connection with others, and thus the arena for connection with God.

Second, the body is a source of *pleasure,* not only sexual ecstasy, but also enjoyment of such delights as massage, hot tubs, and the flavors and presentations of food. Though it is spare, Christian tradition does not obliterate a celebration of the sensual, the goodness of touch, smell, taste. "O taste and see that God is good."

Third, our bodies continually remind us of our *mortality* and of our limits as physical beings. A deep appreciation of our fragility as creatures opens the awareness that each breath is by the grace of God. We are reminded that we are all equals in our vulnerability and the inevitability of death.

Finally, our bodies can be sources of *solidarity* with the suffering. The bodies of the faithful have been put at risk in situations of political repression, in care for those with infectious diseases, in sheltering the victims of battering. The body at risk is a profound point of connection with the powerless of the earth.

Through these forms of spirituality, the body can be the site of resistance to oppressive discourses, deconstructing their damaging power. Pastoral theology courses can function to bring to awareness the implication of the body in many of the situations we address as caregivers, as well as guide students to an understanding of the body as a crucial source of spiritual growth.

Scripture and Tradition as Discourse

It is clear that Scripture is no one thing: not in itself or in the way it functions in various contexts.[9] Multiple and conflicting messages about the good, the true, the redemptive, and the person and work of Jesus Christ are heard from the Bible. The matter is further complicated by the context in which Scripture is read. The affirmation that Jesus is Lord functions differently in a small inner-city storefront church, a wealthy suburban church, a church in rural China, and a feminist house church. We can raise the question: What is the difference in the function of Christian discourse at a country club debutante ball, a midwestern Pentecostal holiness church, Mother Teresa's funeral in Calcutta, Diana Spencer's funeral in Westminster Abbey, or a hospital room with a television evangelist blaring? How is power distributed in a particular context, and how will discourse function to reinforce or disrupt oppressive arrangements? Students who are aware of the power of context to shape meaning, who have developed the habit of asking how discourse functions, will provide more faithful care. As we all were as beginners, students tend to want to apply the correct, orthodox, fresh-from-seminary theological truths to particular situations without recognizing that a "true statement" in one setting may not function in the same way in another. Liberationist commitments may require a different language in Appalachia from that required at Princeton Theological Seminary. The caregiver who is attentive to the power dynamics will be a more capable caregiver and a bearer of discourse that functions to heal, not to wound.

Conclusion

Many of the ideas in this chapter are not new. I am thankful that many thinkers in pastoral theology are raising questions of context and power, the adequacy of Western formulations of selfhood, how Scripture and tradition can function in damaging ways, and so forth. Feminist versions of discourse theory provide a rich base for pushing farther some of these questions. By considering some of the pressing issues of our field in the context of an intellectual apparatus as developed as discourse theory, we can add rigor to our thinking as well as discover pathways not yet considered.

Notes

[1] Donald Capps (1984, 29) uses Ricoeur to speak of metaphorical language as "world-disclosive." For Charles Gerkin (1986, 47), narrative theology provides a theological base for describing pastoral care as the process of helping others to dwell in the Christian narrative, to "come to see and be formed by the images and themes, metaphors and stories, that shape a Christian vision." Edward Wimberly (1991, 1994) skillfully discusses the contributions of narrative to pastoral care and counseling using such concepts as "re-authoring" (1994, 11) to speak of the change process.

[2] While "bearer of discourse" may at first sound as though the autonomous, socially disconnected subject freely picks and chooses among infinite discursive options and speaks/writes what she will, it will become clear in the following argument that this "bearer" is constructed herself by discourse, and therefore constrained by discourse. The bearer of discourse is also the product of discourse. This raises questions about the possibility of agency for this bearer. Again, as will become clear below, my reading of discourse theory does not erase all capacities for choice and agency. While the discursive options may be limited, pastors may nevertheless choose between those that are better and those that are worse.

[3] See Arthur Frank (1995).

[4] See Brown and Bohn (1989).

[5] James Poling (1992, 1996) has incorporated such voices. In *The Abuse of Power* he has taken seriously not only the voices of survivors of abuse, but also those of perpetrators of abuse. Carrie Doehring (1995) uses case studies from literature, thereby expanding sources for our field. Donald Capps (1993) has made creative use of poetry for the theory and practice of pastoral care.

[6] See the *Journal of Pastoral Theology* (1993) for further discussion of the importance of empathy.

[7] See the work of Donald Capps (1990), Brian Childs (1990), Charles Taylor (1991), James Lapsley (1992), Howard Stone (1994), and Susan Dunlap (1997) for more on brief therapies and cognitive therapies.

[8] Bonnie Miller-McLemore (1996, 19) adds to this discussion of empathy.

[9] Feminist theologians Sharon Welch (1985, 1990), Rebecca Chopp (1989), and Mary McClintock Fulkerson (1994) have used versions of discourse theory in their work.

8

Pedagogy Under the Influence of Feminism and Womanism

Brita L. Gill-Austern

A wise pedagogue once said, "The substance of what we know may change us, but changing how we know can revolutionize us." As one long interested in processes of transformation and how pedagogy can facilitate transformation, feminist pedagogy has captivated my interest for several years. I have engaged in extensive conversations with feminist pedagogues out of a passion for the art of teaching and its transformative possibilities and out of a desire to understand how feminism shapes who we are and what we do as teachers. These conversations, my own teaching in a seminary context for ten years, related reading, leading workshops on teaching at the Society of Pastoral Theology, questions to colleagues, and the gathering of syllabi from many women provide the substance for the reflection of this chapter.

As a feminist pastoral theologian, I am committed to discovering those ways of being and doing in teaching that increase the love of God, neighbor, self, and all being and that help mend our broken creation.[1] Love grows through knowledge and understanding. Therefore to increase the love of God, neighbor, self, and all being through the educational process, there must be self-discovery, discovery of the other, discovery of God and the world in which we all participate. Such discovery leads to the possibility of new creation. But discovery that results in a transformation of consciousness and commitment depends not only on the acquisition of secondhand knowledge, but also on firsthand experience that confirms and anchors intellectual knowing. To foster spiritual maturity and the formation of whole persons for the ministry of care (lay or ordained) requires a pedagogy and a relationship that foster both.

Feminist and womanist pastoral theology, in its method and content, focuses on the deep relationality that strengthens life-giving and healing connection in persons' lives.[2] Teaching then becomes less about techniques and methods, and more a way of being in relationship. Central to any feminist pedagogy must be attention to how our practice of teaching deepens authentic, just, and life-giving connection in all spheres of life and what detracts from or threatens such connection. Our teaching is pastoral care. Mutuality in relation is of the highest value for many feminists; therefore, the learning process itself needs to be one of cocreation, where two subjects are involved in the act of constructing knowledge together. Pedagogy under the influence of feminism and womanism, as English professor Gail Griffin accurately states, is more a dynamic, "mundane, practical and personal; a way of living more than a school of thought; a process more than a product; a tool more than a solution" (Griffin, 1992, x).

Feminist and womanist Christian pastoral theologians are committed to teaching that can transform the life of the church into a more responsive and faithful witness of the gospel in the twenty-first century. Only a church that addresses the profound suffering of our times, particularly the suffering caused by structures, rules, and ways of being that use difference (be it gender, race,

> yearned was the one who would help them articulate and expand their latent knowledge—a midwife teacher. Midwife teachers are the opposite of bank teachers. While the bankers deposit something in the learner's head, the midwives draw it out. . . . One who would help them matriculate—that is, one who provides a voice; one who speaks for them and with them in order that they might speak for themselves, learn what they know, bring forth what is in them, achieve a voice. (Belenky et al., 1987, 217)

The midwife, like an obstetrician, is a skilled professional, very conscious of her particular role and task in relation to another. "The midwife teacher is no security blanket—usually quite the contrary. She is an authority. She too has an open mouth. But she gives information as food, to be digested as fuel. And she speaks with a mind to the dynamics of voice" (Griffin, 1992, 168).

2. Feminist Pedagogues as Voice Coaches

Midwife teachers also know that for women and persons who have lived under structures of inequality, domination, and control, the experience of feeling silenced is a common phenomenon. Midwife teachers know the transformative power of "hearing another into speech" (Morton, 1985, 207). The theme of voice is one heard incessantly in feminist writings. When one is denied the opportunity to name and interpret one's experience, it is not surprising that a central metaphor for describing women's experience and development is the one of voice. In the research into the educational lives of more than one hundred women, the authors of *Women's Ways of Knowing* discovered that when describing their lives, women commonly talked about voice and silence:

> "Speaking up," "speaking out," "being silenced," "not being heard," "really listening," "really talking," "words as weapons," "feeling deaf and dumb," "having no words," "saying what you mean," "listening to be heard," and so on in an endless variety of connotations all having to do with a sense of mind, self-worth and feelings of isolation from or connection to others. We found that women repeatedly used the metaphor of voice to depict their intellectual and ethical development; and that development of a sense of voice, mind and self were intricately intertwined. (Belenky et al., 1987, 18)

When women cannot voice their own needs, experiences, and feelings, the heart and mind become constricted. Only through speaking and listening do we develop the capacity to talk and think things through (Belenky et al., 1987, 163). Research studies show a connection between a greater incidence of clinical depression and learned helplessness among women and the curtailment of voice (Belenky, 1987; Jack, 1991; Seligman, 1987).

Loss of voice is also about a loss of subjectivity and the loss of the "authentic I" that can be brought to relationships. In adolescence, as Carol Gilligan and her colleagues at the Harvard School of Education have discovered in their longitudinal studies of hundreds of adolescent girls, girls come to believe that to stay in relationship, they must take their authentic selves out of relationship (Brown and Gilligan, 1992, 2). In an effort to conform to images of the "good girl" whom everyone will promote, value, and want to be with, girls silence the voice they fear others do not want to hear. Many women carry this pattern of silencing the voice into adulthood. The loss of voice is intimately tied to a woman's loss of subjectivity and therefore her capacity to love with her all (Gill-Austern, 1997).

Poet Marge Piercy in her poem "Unlearning to not speak" names what must happen for subjectivity to develop:

> She must learn again to speak
> starting with I
> starting with We
> starting as the infant does
> with her own true hunger
> and pleasure
> and rage.
> (Piercy, 1982)

When women are denied the authority of their own perceptions and experiences, powerlessness, helplessness, and the structures of inequality are reinforced. The possibility of genuine mutual relation, which allows the possibility of cocreation in the learning process, is subverted. Paulo Friere (1970), an educator who has in many respects modeled emancipatory praxis, reminds us that the practice of freedom begins with naming and interpreting one's own reality. Without calling women out of silence and empowering them toward greater subjectivity, women are made more vulnerable to being made someone else's object and thereby less able to challenge race, gender, and class oppression. "Oppressed people resist by identifying themselves as subjects, by defining their reality, shaping their new identity, naming their history, telling their story" (hooks, 1994, 43). Voice coaches further emancipatory praxis by creating a space in which persons can speak their truth and name their own reality.

The metaphor of voice coach guides me powerfully, particularly in working with women doctoral students. I find repeatedly that helping women to speak from the "authentic I," to find their own true voice in conceiving a doctoral project, is critical to its successful completion. For clarity to emerge, one has to listen carefully to the passion and embryonic beginnings of an intellectual quest so that it can find shape and form. Good voice coaches know that when we are learning to speak a new language or sing a new song, our initial attempts may be rough, imprecise, and missing a clarity of expression. Voice coaches know how to begin with where people are and lead them gently into depth conversation that calls forth ever clearer articulation.

154

3. Feminist Pedagogues as Storytellers and Evokers of Stories

Rebecca Chopp names narrativity as one of the three most central feminist pedagogical practices. She reminds us, "If we cannot write new stories that imagine a new future for women and men, we will die still holding to old narratives that do not liberate, but bind. In writing we create and recreate ourselves" (Chopp, 1995, 22). Critical to feminist pedagogy is helping women rewrite their lives in ways that speak the truth of their existence, their dreams, and their hopes. Narrativity is central to feminist pedagogy because it is one central means by which we are enabled to resist oppression and definition by others (Chopp, 1995, 32). When we tell women's tales and are able to evoke women's own stories through classroom discussions and assignments, women's subjectivity and agency are increased. So much of women's experience has not been the subject for theological reflection. Without evoking the specific experience of women we lose a capacity to see and name some of our richest experiences as spiritual. Experiences that accompany women's biological rhythms,[4] such as menstruation, pregnancy, lactation, and menopause, as well as experiences such as sexual abuse (rape, incest), the centrality of female friendships, and community, are rich resources for theological reflection.

The practice of narrativity, of telling one's story and evoking the stories of others, is enhanced by a rich use of novels, poetry, video, and drama in the classroom. These depict in full color the texture, feel, and mood of women's experiences and help call forth women's own narratives. I have found that a rich exercise that deepens the practice of narrativity is having students write "Dialogues for Connected Knowing"—an assignment that invites students to bring their own experiences into dialogue with the reading and material of the course. Doing this requires an intentional integration of the subjective, imaginative, and intuitive with the analytical, critical, and objective. Students also exchange and comment on each other's dialogues as part of the requirement for class. This facilitates a rich sharing of diverse narratives that deepens the connections between persons in a class. As they see their own narratives within a rich tapestry of themes, they are enabled to imagine new story lines and plots for their lives, replacing those that have limited their freedom and capacity to love with all their being.

Last year one of my students, a director of a children's theater, shared with me how the class Psychology and Spirituality of Women encouraged her to make some feminist revisions in the play *Cinderella* she was directing with some preadolescent girls. The changes she made evoked stories from the young actresses of feeling freed up, empowered, and feeling more of themselves.

4. Feminist Pedagogues as Contemplative Artists

Feminist and womanist teaching at its best maintains the attitude of a contemplative artist. The teaching task begins with an awareness of the subject before one. Contemplative artists acquaint themselves with the subject before them, before they try to bring their craft to bear. A sculptor studies the stone, a wood-carver the grain of wood, the artist the setting of the painting. Feminist and womanist teaching places primacy on relationships and connections and therefore must begin with the subject of education, the persons before us. Whom we teach precedes what we teach. The teaching of pastoral theology and care is not first about technique, but begins with contemplative attention to the subject before one. Abraham Heschel once said, "All things are holy, but the human being is God's holy of holies." The subjects of our teaching are indeed God's holy of holies and therefore deserving of not only our respect, but also reverence for the mystery of their person—a mystery we can enter into relation to, but never fully grasp or know. Yet a beginning knowledge of who is in the classroom becomes the first act of care in teaching.

Contemplative artists are those fully awake to the possibilities of the moment, having what teachers of Zen call a "beginner's mind," meaning a willingness to come to things fresh. Academia is dangerous terrain for the discipline of cultivating the beginner's mind because mastery, expertise, and specialization are honored more than receptive openness to the other. The beginner's mind requires a kenosis of self-sufficient expertise and knowing, a radical opening to what or who is before us that deepens perceptions. When this happens, there is a transformation of relationship. When one dwells with what one is contemplating, one begins to see in a new way, and the possibility of self-transcendence emerges. Barbara McClintock, the Nobel prize–winning geneticist, offers this description: "Well, you know when I look at a cell I get down in that cell and look around" (cited in Fox Keller, 67). "As you look at these things under the microscope they become part of you. And you forget yourself. The main thing about it is that you forget yourself" (p. 118).

One winter day I was given an unusual teaching moment to awaken the contemplative artist in my students. I awoke one morning to see the world around me transformed. Overnight an ice storm had transfigured a barren winter landscape into a scene of surreal, startling, excruciating beauty. As I arrived on campus people were out with cameras, walking with mouths open and hearts undone, eyes misty with tears, ears hearing sounds never heard before, and with gratitude exploding for this most unexpected gift. All were married to amazement and embraced by wonder. It felt like blasphemy to the Holy Spirit to require students to sit in a windowless classroom for three hours when nature was lavishing its extraordinary power to transform sight, hearing, and perception. Seizing the moment, I assigned students a forty-five-minute walk to contemplate the fragility and beauty of the world around them and to listen to what this walk through nature's paradise of beauty and treacherous terrain had to teach them about pastoral care. The metaphors that emerged from that walk about care and the stories that it evoked transformed the class into one of my most memorable.

Contemplative artists and feminist pedagogues are also mindful of physical space and its impact on the learning environment. How are chairs and desks arranged? Where does the class meet? Where is the focus in the room? Teaching well requires creating environments where the aesthetics of teaching matter and where the whole person is invited into the learning process. The contemplative artist knows how to open up the borders of the possible, where the environment grows in richness and diversity, where there is more room, not less, for persons to bring their fullness and wholeness as persons. Beauty, ritual, timing, process, and mutuality create the kind of environment where persons can grow into their own fullness. Contemplative artists know the power of ritual to sanctify space and community. Feminist teachers might begin class with the lighting of a candle to remind students that the classroom is no less sacred a space than a sanctuary. One might close classes with rituals in order to hold and empower the community gathered to go forth. Ritualization becomes a way of embodying what we know and sanctifying space and time by helping people dwell fully in the present.

Poets and artists cannot do their work without imagination, without a sense of play. And yet, when we cross the boundary into the world of imagination and to methodologies that deviate substantially from the traditional lecture, discussion, or seminar, we may feel we are inhabiting a foreign land where we may be called alien or, worst of all, not serious enough, not scholarly enough. The pressures to stay within the boundaries to maintain legitimacy and respect press in upon us with the seduction of conformity.

5. Feminist Pedagogues as Reticent Outlaws in the Classroom

Many women pastoral theologians, when you speak to them privately, harbor fears that they are outlaws in a world where the rules and laws of the academy have been carved out by different visions of what constitutes education. A secret fear is that we are a bit "deviant" according to the standards of the academy. These rules and practices have tended to honor and value the rational over the emotive, analysis over synthesis, the objective over the subjective, the hard over the soft, the linear over the circular, the empirical over the imaginative, argument over empathy, head over heart, compartmentalization over integration, specialization over generalization, product over process.

Women pastoral theologians carry the fear of being doubly marginalized. We are often perceived by colleagues as being in a "soft" field, not the "hard" (classical) disciplines. The use of nontraditional methodologies that draw from the other side of binary oppositions risks greater vulnerability for not being taken as seriously by colleagues, even while students flock to feminists' classes with a hunger for what we have to offer.

Women who incorporate the use of the arts and nontraditional methodologies in classes may feel that we are doing it on the sly. We grin sheepishly as we are "caught" bringing clay into class for an exercise, and the voice inside says, "They do not think I'm doing serious teaching." We sit in silence in a class of prayer and wonder if we will be found out for not filling the time with more academic material. We take students on field trips to a play or an art exhibit, and we fear others consider it a form of playing hooky. A fear of exposure may haunt us, believing that "if they really knew what I was doing, I wouldn't have a chance for tenure or promotion." We fear and dread male disapproval because of the power that often accompanies it. Although most of us want to believe we are far past this, "the power of a whisper of male disapproval to unbalance us" lurks in our psyches (Griffin, 1992, 110).

I remember well that for the first seven years I taught a course called Spiritual Resources for Healing, I was very reluctant to share what I was doing in this class with others. I felt I was on the outer reaches of the boundary of the academy and was fearful of being found to be illegitimate—even though student after student would tell me that this class had a major transformative impact on her life and prayer. Why my hesitancy? We began the class by spending an hour in silence, in prayer and meditation. The ethos was a combination of retreat and classroom, church and academy, and the resources for healing being explored took us into the interior landscape of our souls.

Some of us may feel captive to some unwritten rules and assumptions in which we had no hand, but are expected to implement and obey. Yet many of us who are feminist and womanist pedagogues perceive ourselves, more often than not, tuned in to another frequency, where we are listening for different voices and sounds from those found on the conventional channel of the academy. Transformation often comes at moments when we are willing to step out of the usual mode of things, when we are willing to risk unconventionality and being considered outrageous. Transformative teachers are risk takers.

Women in our field experience themselves as outlaws when they deviate from usual ways of evaluating performance. The use of a process where students are coparticipants in the evaluative procedures and therefore codeterminers of final evaluation flies in the face of traditional expectations of the teacher as the sole evaluator. When women use appropriate forms of self-disclosure, they often feel they are crossing a forbidden boundary. When women risk writing on feminist methodologies in a university context that evaluates scholarship along traditional male standards, they may experience themselves as outlaws and vulnerable. When women name God using feminine appellations, they experience themselves again and again as being outlaws where the rules of patriarchy still dictate.

To be a feminist, in most places, means to choose the fact that you will always reside somewhat on the margins of the institution. This can be a place of creative tension, but also at times a lonely place and a place of discomfort. Women academics tend to ask ourselves, "What am I doing here?" "Who am I to be teaching this?" When we deviate from the tried and true norms around us, we wonder, "Will they sniff me out and find out the truth—I'm not the real thing?" Such questions lead women to feel like impostors and frauds. And when we feel like impostors and frauds, we want to hide and cover up what we know and what we do as somehow subversive or deviant. Yet we must risk exposure if our praxis is going to help transform the academy and the church into more life-giving and liberating environments. When we give up our power to make ourselves and our work in the classroom known, we also give up the power to shape theological education toward emancipatory praxis and thereby abdicate our power to also influence transformative practices in the church.

Less than full belonging may simply be an essential component to our work. Patricia Collins rightly states that "marginality provides a distinctive angle of vision" (Collins, 1991, 12). African American women know in a particularly painful way what it means to be outsiders in academic discourse and social and political thought. Many black women have had "the outsider-within" experience that is part of being embedded in a white culture, but not fully belonging to it. And yet from this place they have an indispensable angle of vision to offer to feminist thought. Alice Walker describes well the impact that an outsider-within stance had on her own thinking: "I believe . . . that it was from this period— from my solitary, lonely position, the position of an outcast, that I began to see people and things, really to notice relationships" (Walker, 1983, 244).

Finding out how to be at home on the margin is part of feminists' work in the academy. Simultaneously we need to recognize that our deepest longing is that the concerns we hold central become part of the mainstream so that real change and transformation may take place. Many of us feel conflicted, besieged, frustrated, exhausted, and often lonely, but simultaneously challenged, enlivened, and with a convicted sense that even though we live on the margin, this is precisely where we are supposed to be. These five metaphors I have named give us courage and imagination to carry out some of the essential practices of a feminist and womanist pedagogy.

How We Teach—Seven Practices of Feminist and Womanist Pedagogy

The remainder of this chapter focuses on the question of how we teach through an exploration of seven practices in feminist teaching that further emancipatory praxis. Pastoral theology as a discipline helps persons develop the relational and analytical skills to care for others intelligently and sensitively by attending to what constitutes loving and just relationships in the realm of the interpersonal, in the context of the church, and in the systemic contexts of our society. Feminist and womanist pastoral theology focuses a sharp eye on understanding sin and evil as the obliteration of loving and just relationships and expanding the context of care beyond the personal and therapeutic to the social, economic, cultural, and religious. Given these concerns, our classrooms become arenas where we identify pervasive patterns or logic that may be used to keep persons and creation in their defined place so that loving and life-giving relationships cannot and will not be formed (Chopp, 1995, 60). When teaching is seen in this light, it also becomes a political act and an agent of justice. Seven practices become central to energize emancipatory praxis: speaking in the mother tongue and the father tongue, owning our subject positions, engaging in systemic thinking and analysis, building an inclusive and safe community for learning, becoming partners in resistance, evoking imagination, and teaching through embodiment.

1. Speaking in the Mother Tongue as Well as the Father Tongue

Until very recently, the texts, the ethos, the structures, the methods, and the evaluation procedures of theological education and our discipline of pastoral theology have not been significantly influenced by women. This is certainly beginning to change. Yet we live in a world where the language of the academy has been primarily dominated by the father tongue. The father tongue excels in reasoning, in abstract, logical, and systemic analysis, which tends to set subject and object apart. Ursula Le Guin names the essential gesture of the father tongue "one of distancing, making a gap, a space between the subject or self and the object or other. Enormous energy is generated by that rending, that forcing of a gap between man and the world. . . . The father tongue is spoken from above. It goes one way. No answer is expected or heard. In short it is professorial" (cited in Griffin, 1992, 168). The father and professorial tongue puts priority on speaking about a subject, professing the truth, declaring publicly. The mother tongue puts priority on speaking with and to someone. Griffin identifies a tension many women experience in the classroom between the pulls of being a professor (more authority, legitimacy, and status) and being a teacher (more of our vocational identity, strength, and desire), but notes that the latter is not valued as highly (Griffin, 1992, 169).

Within this world of pedagogy modeled in the father tongue are demons that threaten continually the emergence of feminist and womanist pedagogy—a pedagogy oriented toward cocreation with the subjects. Being held captive and accountable to some of the traditional methods and idols of academia can undercut the creativity and imagination of feminist pedagogues.

Griffin describes well the experiences of many feminist pedagogues:

> As often as I speak the mother tongue in class, I hear the father tongue, so deeply embedded in me that I often think it is my own. It calls, it analyzes, it takes exception. "All the time I wrote the book," says Susan Griffith in *Woman and Nature*, "the patriarchal voice was in me, whispering to me that I had no proof for any of my writing, that I was wildly in error, that the vision I had was absurd." To speak on, listening intently to your own voice despite the persistent drone of that other voice, is truly to cry out of the

160

wilderness and to cry from and for the wilderness. To attend to your vocation. (Griffin, 1992, 169)

"Methodolatry" as Mary Daly (1973) has named it, making an idol of method, is one way persons are held captive to forms of the father tongue that may impede education as cocreation. An emphasis on left-brain, analytical, critical thinking to the exclusion of right-brain, integrative, and intuitive thinking and feeling may lead to an overvaluing of abstraction and intellectual aridity. Critical thinking when overemphasized can shut down creativity. An overemphasis on the distance between teacher and student in academic hierarchy can undermine collaborative forms of learning and further attitudes of arrogance where the teacher is seen as the sole authority. Evaluation procedures that do not include students in the design and process may disempower persons in relation to setting appropriate learning goals for themselves and infantilize adult students. But without a capacity to speak in the father tongue, we are disabled in our capacity to enter into public discourse and to bring the sharp tools of analysis to bear on critiquing systemic injustice.

Yet feminist pedagogues seek to learn and speak the language of the mother tongue in order to bring some neglected elements into the teaching arena. "The mother tongue, spoken or written, expects an answer. It is conversation, a word the root of which means turning together. The mother tongue is language not as mere communication, but as relationship. It connects. Its power is not in dividing, but in binding, not in distancing, but in uniting" (Griffin, 1992, 168). The mother tongue excels in synthesis and integration.

Pastoral theology's central focus has always been on understanding accurately and responding appropriately to the suffering in people's lives. The suffering of our time is largely characterized by pervasive and persistent patterns of disconnections throughout all levels of our society and between persons. Such suffering calls particularly for the voice of the mother to be sounded in pastoral theological education. Many men in the field of pastoral theology are also fluent in and incorporate this language of connection and care in their doing and being. Our field has been abundantly blessed with many men who have been bilingual for a long time. Teaching in the mother tongue requires resisting the temptations of arrogance that so often accompany being in the academy and that has such a powerful way of disempowering others.

The devaluation and discomfort of some in the academy with the "nurturant" dimensions of our pedagogical role are related in part, I believe, to a fear that what is considered nurturing will be equated with a lack of substance and a lack of rigor. One question on the student faculty evaluation forms where I teach asks, "Is the professor appropriately tough minded?" a question that can strike terror into the heart of a nurturer. The bias is evident—there is no corresponding question, "Is the professor appropriately nurturing?"

Emancipatory praxis addresses the whole person, which means teaching in both the mother tongue and the father tongue. In the creative tension between the two the possibility of reaching fuller truth and deeper transformation emerges. Because the father tongue has been dominant for so long, we need to give particular attention to teaching in and listening for the mother tongue.

2. Owning Our Subject Positions

The emancipatory praxis of teaching begins with the acknowledgment that where we stand as subjects conditions what we see. What we see is largely determined by the context in which we are embedded, what discourse theory refers to as subject positions. Before dialogue can begin or community can be built, we must be explicit about how our gender, class, social location, ethnicity, race, sexual orientation, and personal experience greatly influence what we see and how we make meaning. Because meaning and perception shift according to our embeddedness, knowing where we stand and where others stand radically impacts our care and teaching.

I begin my introductory class of pastoral care with an assignment that helps make students conscious of where they stand and how it impacts what they see. This assignment is used as a part of our being introduced to each other and creating a community in which diversity becomes safe.

The extent of our own position of power or powerlessness has a profound impact on what we see. At the heart of feminist pedagogy lies a commitment to a careful analysis of power relations in the contexts of personal, cultural, political, and economic lives. Identifying how the dynamics of power contribute to the exploitation of others and interfere with developing an ethic of care and justice for all persons grounds our work. The focus in feminist pastoral theology on the personal, ecclesial, and public dimensions of the ministry of care makes this a critical commitment.

Because feminists and womanists have had, and continue to have, different subject positions within our culture, maintaining the distinctiveness of these experiences enables us to view reality from different lenses that contribute to depth seeing. Early in the feminist movement white middle-class feminists were experiencing the limitations and strictures of a life cut off from the public world of work and defined primarily around husband and family. They tackled early on issues of gender roles, equality of rights, and meaningful employment. Early feminist analysis grew out of the particularity of white middle-class women living mainly in suburbia. Yet the vast majority of African American women have worked outside the home since the days of slavery. Toni Morrison has observed that this difference lies at the heart of difference between the writing of white women and black women: "Black women seem able to combine the nest and the adventure. They don't see conflicts in certain areas as do white women. They are both safe harbor and ship; they are both inn and trail" (Morrison, 1983, 117-131). Knowing our subject positions allows more respectful dialogue and listening.

3. Engaging in Systemic Thinking and Analysis

As feminists and womanists expand the understanding of the contexts of care beyond the interpersonal to the social, cultural, and economic contexts in which we are embedded, we know we cannot survive without practicing systemic thinking and analysis. Systemic thinking allows one to see oppressive structures and practices that one might otherwise miss. Think about a bird cage. If you look carefully at one wire, you do not see the other wires. Each wire looked at individually presents no real threat to the bird's flight or freedom. Only when you stop looking at the wires microscopically and see the whole cage and the systemically related barriers do you see that by their relation to one another, they are as confining as solid walls of a dungeon (Frye cited in Anderson and Collins, 1995, 39). Systemic thinking and analysis lead to interdisciplinary dialogue and to what Katie Cannon calls trialogues. Katie Cannon describes her pedagogy as

> a three level wheel of discourse of metalogues like Ezekiel's wheels in the middle of wheels way up in the middle of the air. These wheels include three distinctive discourses or trialogues: 1) the intellectual predisposition of traditional male thinkers, usually dead and of European ancestry, who persist in binary opposition; 2) the specificity of Afro-Christian culture, systemic accounts of the history and achievements, perspectives and experiences of members of the Black church community; and 3) the experiential dimensions of women's texts and interpretations. Listening to the African Diaspora speaking our mothers' tongues as we refine and critique our realities across time and space through the written word. (Cannon, 1995, 138)

To generate the energy to activate this three-level discourse, Cannon invites students to actively seek and name the cognitive dissonance they experience in their belief systems, lifestyles, and/or behavior. The intent of such pedagogy awakens self-consciousness in seminarians and confronts them with the contestability of life's contradictions (Cannon, 1995, 139). Cannon's method of metalogues is a way of carrying on a triple conversation that engages the intellectual tradition handed down to us, largely by white males, the specificity of one's own culture, and the particular experience of women as seen through their interpretations and texts. This threefold conversation invites systemic thinking and analysis.

Without analysis one cannot see how the structures of power in any given context or relationship influence or impede the dynamics of care. Depth analysis belongs to emancipatory praxis because it forces the questions regarding root or systemic causes and clarity about who or what benefits from a given relational arrangement. Christian educator Maria Harris reminds us that analysis can be a part of the imaginative and prophetic process because it helps move us toward new envisioning (Harris, 1987, 107).

When we engage in systemic analysis, we may come into conflict with another or others. This is a vulnerable moment, especially for women pedagogues and our women students. Conflict threatens our sense of community and connection and risks upsetting the relationships that have been built over time. Until our self-understanding as selves-in-relation includes the reality of conflict, we shall always be unduly threatened by its existence. Women teachers are particularly vulnerable to unintentionally reducing women's analytical and critical capacities if we become too nurturing. Students may feel a sort of loyalty, somewhat like many experience toward their mothers, that may hinder their ability to express anger or be critical of us (Parks, 1986, 118).

Transformative emancipatory teaching often entails some conflict. New insights and life emerge out of places where initially we may squirm with discomfort. Conflict occurs in the moments when we become aware that something does not fit. "Previous assumptions we held tight, a discomfort with the ways things are, interpersonal conflict, intellectual dissonance or a moment when we are thrown off balance," are all such moments (Parks, 1986, 118). Pastoral theologian Sharon Parks, drawing on the work of James Loder's grammar of transformation, names three things required in the moment of conscious conflict if transformation is to take place: the conflict must be felt, allowed, and made conscious; the conflict must be clarified; and the conflict must be suffered with the expectation of a solution. Precisely at such moments, a community must be in place that can tolerate, sustain, and even nurture conscious conflict (Parks, 1986, 118).

4. Building Safe and Inclusive Community

Feminist and womanist teachers know we do not learn in isolation. Solitude may be required, but not isolation. Women students, in particular, report again and again that they learn best in community. Feminist pedagogues insist in being grounded in the present community to which we belong, but with a concern to always be expanding the circle of who belongs to that community. When we remember that we belong also to those who came before us, we know, in the words of Alice Walker, "We are not the first to suffer, rebel, fight, love and die. The grace by which we embrace life in spite of the pain, the sorrows, is always a measure of what has gone before" (Walker, 1986, 1). The community to which we belong also includes future generations. Whatever we teach must promote greater well-being for future generations. Our interactions with each other in the present become part of the learning, and thus, the community in which learning takes place becomes vital to the task.

A feminist/womanist emancipatory praxis gives particular attention to the organization and structure of class sessions, as well as to the content of discourse in terms of issues of inclusivity. Pastoral theology's concern for those suffering requires attention to those who may be particularly vulnerable to suffering from oppressive structures and environments in theological education. Katie Cannon speaks of black women pursuing advanced theological degrees in a predominantly male setting and experiencing alienation, isolation, and marginalization as part of their daily fare. She writes, "Even with the requisite credentials for matriculation in hand, we were constantly barraged with arrogance and insults, suspicion and insensitivity, backhand compliments and tongue in cheek naivete" (Cannon, 1995, 136-137).

Feminist/womanist pastoral theology is committed to bringing into substantive dialogue those who have been perceived as being on the margins. Typical orienting questions for feminist and womanist pedagogues attentive to issues of inclusive and safe community might be: Are voices from the margins included in the conversation and allowed space where they do not have to shout to be heard? How seriously are all voices engaged, and what ensures that this happens? What structures have we set in place to make it safe enough for all voices to be heard? The traditional syllabus becomes one key to discerning whether the course is structured toward an emancipatory praxis that is genuinely inclusive. Sharon Parks calls the syllabus "a confession of faith" (1986, 174), an excellent description of how the syllabus functions.

5. Becoming Partners in Resistance

Analysis and a safe and inclusive community of learning strengthen a person's capacity to resist. Womanist pedagogy, according to ethicist Katie Cannon, emerges out of the experience of black women challenging conventional and outmoded dominant theological resources and deconstructing ideologies that lead black women into complicity with their own oppression (Cannon, 1995, 137). Such practices lead to what Cannon calls "a mindful activism," which can resist domination and helps one live more faithfully the radicality of the gospel (Cannon, 1995, 138).

Becoming partners in resistance is one way emancipatory praxis is furthered. Resistance supports the work of truth telling when a group refuses to allow the power of a dominant group to suppress the knowledge that belongs to a subordinate group. The well-known African American intellectual Maria Steward advised, "Turn your attention to knowledge and improvement; for knowledge is power" (quoted in Collins, 1991, 4). Black women's intellectual work has fostered black women's resistance and activism. Black feminist Patricia Collins writes, "Educated black women traditionally were brought up to see their education as something gained not just for their own development, but for the purpose of race uplift. The feeling was so strong that the women founding the National Association of Colored Women's Clubs chose as their motto, 'Lifting as We Climb' " (Collins, 1991, 149). Becoming partners in resistance furthers the common welfare of one's people, not simply personal well-being.

This was brought home to me in a Psychology and Spirituality of Women class I taught where a small minority of African American and Hispanic women resisted powerfully full participation in a class where they did not feel the lives of African American and Hispanic women were adequately represented in the readings or analysis. Their resistance gave me the courage to let a very popular class be retired for a year until I could radically reshape it in design so that it more accurately reflected our shared commitment of creating a more just and inclusive community of learning.

6. Evoking Imagination

Imagination is the fire of emancipatory praxis. Imagination sets hearts, minds, and wills on fire on the playground of the possible. Emancipatory praxis begins with imagining what has not been, and dreaming it toward reality. It is not by direct appeal to the will that people become motivated to move into new ways of being and doing. Life-giving images lure us into a new future. When we can imagine a reality, we take a first step toward creating it.

Imagination is nurtured by the use of the arts in pedagogical approaches. Art has a prophetic role in its capacity to envision other realities and in its capacity to confront the idolatries of a culture. Art transposes us into our world in such a fashion that we are enabled to see it anew. The arts become indispensable to feminist emancipatory praxis in part because they encourage fuller and more holistic ways of knowing, tapping the unconscious, the intuitive and spontaneous as well as the conscious, rational, and more linear modes of knowing. I work particularly hard in finding ways to ignite students' imaginations through creative assignments inside and outside class that force them to make new and deeper connections with the material and their own ministries. I often find that some students' best work comes when their imaginations are given permission to play.

Healthy imagination requires inclusive communities where there is a vision of a common life and a common good. Coleridge spoke of "evil imagination as being isolated imagination, divided from the unity of the 'One Life' and therefore cut off from its Source" (cited by Parks, 1986, 128). Without healthy communities to ignite the fire of imagination toward life-giving imagination, our transformative capacities are disabled.

7. Teaching Through Embodiment

Without embodiment feminist/womanist teaching does not exist. Incarnational, embodied, sensual teaching treads where others fear to step. It does not bypass the analytical, but passionately seeks out other forms of knowing so that the whole person is addressed and able to respond in the fullness of his or her being. Beverly Harrison reminds us that all knowledge is body-mediated knowledge so that our feelings become part of how we know (Harrison, 1986). Given how the mind/body dualism has contributed to the oppression of women and the earth, embodied teaching becomes nothing less than a moral virtue (Chopp, 1995, 41). The affective life becomes a part of the learning process and is woven into the classroom and assignments by giving it space in which to be. Dispassionate knowing is not the only way to pursue truth.

I remember taking a course on the spirituality of prayer with a well-known professor from Germany while I was a student at Harvard Divinity School. During the course of a whole semester, not one prayer was uttered in class nor was one assignment related to a praxis of prayer or any discussion of our own prayer lives. I am chagrined to say that I do not remember anything from that class about prayer that has been transformative for my life. Nine years ago when I began to teach the course Spiritual Resources for Healing, I knew that if students were to learn the power of spiritual resources for healing, they would have to experience the transformative effect in their own lives. I asked myself, "How can you teach a course on forms of prayer without taking substantive time to pray together?" We began each three-hour class with forty-five minutes of semistructured meditation and prayer.

When planning to teach the course A Practical Theology of Embodiment, I knew that I would need to bring the body as an experience and source of knowledge into the class with the help of someone who could help us integrate bodily experience with intellectual knowing. I was blessed to have a friend who was both a graduate of a seminary and a superb yoga teacher to coteach the course. Pastoral theology has excelled in its methodology in embodied knowing. This sparks both envy in the academy of our developed skills in this area and unfortunately, devaluation—the flip side of envy.

Embodied knowing is not just about how the professor teaches, but who she or he is in and out of the classroom. I know that the most important things I have learned about pastoral care and theology were mostly a matter of "catching it" by seeing it lived concretely in the life of another. I remember the acts, gestures, facial expressions, engagement, and relational brilliance of my teachers Peggy Way, Bessie Chambers, William Rodgers, James Fowler, Robert Leslie, and Archie Smith more than the specifics of the content. I caught pastoral care as much as I was taught it. The great teachers in my life have been very different from one another, but in each and every one of them, the person incarnated in some way the material and subject he or she wanted to reveal to us. We knew through knowing them. We learned by studying them as much as the material at hand.

Embodiment is the content of what we teach. We cannot teach without being what we teach. But because of women's traditional roles as caretakers, women pastoral theologians bear a double burden of embodying the meaning of care in their teaching and being, while simultaneously taking on the burden of being more sought out, precisely because women are most often perceived as the nurturing presences on campus. Again and again I see students coming to women professors because they trust they will be listened to, they will be given the precious commodity of another's time and the opportunity to engage in an in-depth conversation that goes beyond question and answer.

Because women are often perceived as being among the most relational of professors, their time is often interrupted far more than men's time. Thus, many women find it harder to balance students' needs with their own need for solitude for scholarly work. Women professors are vulnerable, as most women are, to falling into equating love and care with patterns of self-sacrifice and self-denial (Gill-Austern, 1995). These realities make women more vulnerable to being exploited and used. Women's time, i.e., mothers' time, has always been interrupted time, giving people permission to interrupt women's time more than men's. Thus, embodied teaching also means we carry less mystique, for mystique is fed by distance. Gail Griffin names the experience of many women professors when she writes, "We are beloved of our students and denied the respect we watch them lay at the feet of our bearded colleagues" (Griffin, 1992, 26).

These seven practices, like the five metaphors I have named, are not exhaustive, but suggestive of what is primary in pedagogy practiced under the influence of feminism and womanism. When held consciously, they enable us to empower those we teach to shape an identity and share practices that hold transformative power for mending our broken creation and increasing the love of God, neighbor, self, and all being.

Notes

[1] Following in the steps of H. Richard Niebuhr (1965), I also understand this to be the purpose of the church and theological education. Within a feminist and womanist framework, love must include the notion of freedom and justice. The word *love* is used with this meaning throughout this chapter.

[2] See Christie Neuger's chapter "Women and Relationality" for an in-depth discussion of this theme.

[3] I use the word *patriarchy* with caution in referring to the structures of domination and control because, as Delores Williams reminds us, the word *patriarchy* cannot capture all that we mean when we speak of forces of oppression, for it omits too much. "It is silent about class-privileged women oppressing women without class privilege. It is silent about white men and women working together to maintain white supremacy and white privilege" (Williams, 1993, 185).

[4] Bonnie Miller-McLemore's *Also a Mother* (1994) is an excellent example of a pastoral theological reflection on mothering and the rhythms of women's lives.

9

Pastoral Theology as Art

Pamela D. Couture

We had not really intended this trip to be an "outward bound" experience.

Several years ago five other women and I planned a six-day canoe trip in the Boundary Waters Canoe Area (BWCA) in northern Minnesota, from Snowbank Lake near Ely to Lake Saganaga at the end of the Gunflint Trail. Previously, none of us had paddled in an intergenerational group of all women. The night before our trip we met on a campsite at Gooseberry Park, greeting one another with shouts of anticipation and eagerness for an adventure. Under candle and flashlight we pored over our maps and confirmed the route that some of us had carefully planned. The mileage from Snowbank to Sag was not great; in fact, we hoped to have time for side trips and meandering. The trip provided easy access to a variety of terrain of small lakes and large, of the western plain to the eastern hills and cliffs of the BWCA.

We broke camp early; we ate a loggerman's breakfast in Ely; we put in across our first lake. We quickly discovered that paddling together, our most experienced paddlers, Helen, seventy-eight, and Bonnie, sixty, easily outdistanced the younger and less experienced of us, one of whom had not canoed before. In midafternoon, a few lakes into our trip, a short, flat portage that we had depended upon did not seem to exist; we had to reopen a little-used trail over a high hill. Still in good spirits, we picked our way up the hill and through the trees with canoes on our heads and shoulders and packs on our backs. We reenergized ourselves by snacking on blueberries that were ripening in a patch of sun at the top of the hill. It took three round trips and what turned out to be two precious hours and the energy of adrenaline to transport all of our gear safely to the next shore. By then, we were muttering about "the portage from hell."

We had to make a decision: to camp then and there, or to cross several ponds and portages to the next large lake where we could make camp. Tired, but new to the trip and to one another, and having formed our habits by paddling with men, we plunged on.

We paddled toward the final portage in the sunset. The long, gradual but uphill, rocky portage led us by a rushing rapids and waterfall. We wished we had more time to enjoy the rapids, but night was falling and we needed to set up camp. Carrying a canoe on my head and knowing I was near the end of my energy, a likely time for an accident, I examined each rock directly before my feet before I stepped. As I watched, I noticed a lone wild iris that had somehow bloomed between the trail and the water. When I returned to get my pack, I stopped briefly by the iris who lived in such beauty by the waterfall. I was so tired, and I was concerned about the energy levels of the other women in the group. Yet the iris was too lovely, too transparently intimate, to pass without notice.

I paused to watch her, but she urged me on, reminding me that here in the wilderness, God is free to reveal how abundantly and generously she prepares the way for our journey.

❈ ❈ ❈ ❈

170

Feminist Reconstruction of the Premises of Pastoral Theology

Feminism has changed twentieth-century pastoral theology. Among men and women who learn and teach pastoral care and counseling, books of women's stories and pastoral care concerns have been collected and published; courses that include women's issues are taught. Secular theories that take gender seriously, such as the feminist psychologies of Carol Gilligan and Nancy Chodorow, are widely read and incorporated into feminist pastoral theologies. We can applaud the fact that over the course of several decades, images of sex roles in pastoral theology have been significantly transformed.

In the mid-1980s Carol Robb, a feminist theological ethicist, evaluated the strengths and weaknesses of various versions of sex role feminism. She appreciated the strength of sex role feminism for transformation of interpersonal gender roles, but she urged sex role feminists to look beyond interpersonal relationships to the political systems in which gender is constructed. Some feminist psychologists, such as Jessica Benjamin, have begun to do so. In a limited way feminist pastoral theologians have incorporated such interdisciplinary work into their writing and teaching.

If we chart such progress, we can see the general parallel in pastoral theology to the transformation of historical studies under the influence of women's history. Linda Kerber and Jane Sharron De Hart have charted the change in roughly the following way: first, occasional stories of women's history were collected; then, the stories were collected into a women's tradition; next, the tradition challenged the contours within which history was being done; finally, the basic set of assumptions upon which historical studies is based has changed (De Hart and Kerber, 1995, 4-6). To quote historiographer John O'Malley, who has watched these changes throughout his career, "History ain't what it used to be" (private correspondence).

In pastoral theology, the concerns of women have been collected (Glaz and Stevenson-Moessner, 1991; Stevenson-Moessner, 1996); women's traditions are being constructed (Couture and Hunter, 1995); theoretical reinterpretation has occurred (Graham, 1992). The premises of pastoral theology remain largely within correlations of psychology and theology, as was evident in the *Dictionary of Pastoral Care and Counseling* (Hunter, 1990). Thoroughgoing reconstruction of the premises upon which pastoral theology is based is yet to come. Social conditions, especially the increasingly strict requirements for licensing and supervision for pastoral counselors, are already severely limiting the possibilities for the next generation of pastoral theologians to follow the vocational trajectory of a Charles Gerkin or James Ashbrook, pastoral theologians who could maintain one foot in clinical practice while primarily devoting themselves to writing general pastoral theology. The situation is even more critical for feminist pastoral theologians who are called upon to articulate in theological education what interconnections exist among clinical pastoral counseling, general pastoral care, pastoral (and practical) theology, and women's studies (generally understood as feminist and womanist theology and ethics, and secondarily history and philosophy). Lest we find ourselves stuck in an undifferentiated morass, unable to communicate our discipline and its methods to our colleagues in theological education, the church, and society, we must reflect upon, and critically and theoretically reconstruct, who we are as feminist pastoral theologians and what we are about.

As feminists, we are accountable to our female students, our female colleagues, and the women with whom we engage in mutual care to represent their concerns in our theorizing. It is their questions, in connection with our own, that push us to the outward bounds of pastoral theology. Yet we believe that bringing our questions into the center of pastoral theology edifies the entire community. Based on this criterion for accountability, I conclude that the following premises are among those that must be rethought if we are to reconstruct pastoral theology:

1. that pastoral care can adequately address issues of gender, race, and class without paying attention to the social policies that keep women, especially poor women, in their place;
2. that the history of pastoral care can be told as the history of male clerics, without including as an equal and interdependent story the ongoing contributions of women to the caring ministries of the church through lay and parachurch associations;
3. that correlations between theology and social science are adequate foundations for pastoral theology, as long as the theologies and social sciences in question are judged to be ethically sound in their perspective toward women.

Pastoral theology has thought deeply about the role of gender, race, and class; however, the relation of pastoral care and counseling to social policy is an occasional, rather than central, topic (Couture and Hunter, 1995). In my teaching I addressed the second issue through a course that presented the caring ministries of women in the United States prior to the twentieth century and how those ministries were reshaped in twentieth-century culture; that course is reflected in publication only in the introduction to Stevenson-Moessner's *Through the Eyes of Women* (pp. 4-5). Neither premise has been treated adequately in relation to the theoretical framework in which pastoral theology does its work, in my work or elsewhere. This chapter is limited to exploring an alternative to the third premise only. I ask whether feminist pastoral theology needs aesthetics to interpret itself adequately to our various publics.

Pastoral Theology as an Art of Ministry: A Dormant Feminist Concern

We say that pastoral care is one of the arts of ministry. It rolls off the tongue without our even thinking about it. In a more serious moment, though, I wonder whether some feminist pastoral theologians seem "soft" or "unacademic" because who they are and what they are searching for are more akin to art than to social science? I think, for example, of women who make modifications in their classroom environments using music, candles, flowers, or incense. Or of women who delve into more specific "adjunctive therapies," such as dance, music, or visual arts—therapies that by definition of the *Dictionary of Pastoral Care and Counseling* are secondary to the "talking cure" but to them are central healing modalities (Hunter, 1990). Or of those women for whom natural beauty is an antidote to depression, such as a child locked in depression might find (Bondi, 1995, 92-96). Or of those for whom an embodied activity, from the hike to the health club, is central to self-care. In my own case, canoeing and fiddling have been embodied, nonrational, artistic activities that provide reliable preventives against spiritual dryness, depression, and professional sloth. These artistic activities have connected me gently with mysterious sides of myself, of other people, and of divine transcendence. Women tend to integrate these artistic searchings into their professional world more frequently than do men, in a way that makes women stick out like sore thumbs. Similarly, men's more recent search for themselves has engaged poetry, drums, and archetypes. When they search for themselves through the aesthetic experience, the world does not know what to make of them. If an aesthetic search is truly part of the human journey, a genuinely feminist pastoral theology will be aided by developing a theory of religious aesthetics that can provide a map to what might be going on when we do these things.

Yet pastoral theology has been strangely absent from whatever discussion of theology and the arts does exist. In 1987 in a study entitled *The Arts in Theological Education*, Wilson Yates conducted surveys and interviews to describe how art was actually included in the curricula of theological schools. His surveys showed that of all the areas involving practical theology and the arts of ministry, pastoral care was by far least likely to give any substantive attention to its relationship to the arts. Where art had become part of the course work in pastoral care, it was at that time used almost exclusively for the purpose of illustration. Yates concluded:

> One might ask why courses dealing with personality and interpersonal relationships do not draw more on film, video, and the novel given their heavy accent on relationships. It is also of interest that only one course [in twenty-one courses incorporating the arts in some manner in fifteen schools] treats the arts in a substantive fashion. Given the importance and extensiveness of this field in practical theology, the absence of any significant attention being given to the arts suggests that the field has failed to engage in any significant dialogue with the arts and their implications for pastoral care. (Yates, 1987, 37)

Furthermore, among the so-called classical disciplines, ethics was least likely to incorporate substantive attention to the arts in course work. About this finding, Yates asked:

> *Why, then, are the offerings not more extensive?* Ethics draws on non-theological
> disciplines, such as sociology, psychology and political science, for insights
> into cultural issues; why not draw on the arts, which provide in visual, dra-
> matic, musical and literary forms insights into the shape and character of
> culture? Ethics focuses on prophetic issues; why not deal with the arts,
> which have a rich tradition as bearers of the prophetic voice? Art theory
> has long examined the relationship of aesthetics and morality; why should
> ethics not contribute to that discussion? (Yates, 1987, 30)

In other words, Yates found that of all areas in the theological school curriculum, pastoral care and ethics were less likely to create a relationship to the
arts and plumb the potential in that relationship for theory or practice. Perhaps
that explains, at least in part, the reason that the arts have been so absent from
pastoral theology: pastoral theology has enjoyed an especially close relationship
with ethics. Pastoral theology has looked to ethics to evaluate the aims and ends
of the methods of transformation implied in the psychologies, as in the work of
Don Browning. It has also been assisted by ethics in reformulating the prophetic
ends that the field desires to uphold: an end to discrimination on the basis of
sex, race, or class. In so doing, it has frequently relied on the work of feminist
and womanist ethicists. But feminist and womanist scholars in pastoral care and
ethics have been trained in fields that most represent the dearth of work in aesthetics. In practice we have followed our instincts that say *that* the arts are
important to human transformation, but in theory we have not yet established
how they are important.

For various reasons pastoral theology has wanted to legitimate itself vis-à-vis
clinical psychology as a medical science. Our attempts at institutional legitimacy
are related to prior concerns: Schleiermacher fought to justify theology as a science in the university; Freud needed to legitimate psychoanalysis in the prominent medical science establishment in Vienna; Boison and Cabot recognized
that ministers needed to find a legitimate place for religion in the medical hospital. In so legitimating ourselves, we have reasoned our way across the elements close to art that are central in our craft: dream images and narratives.
Dream images and narratives are fundamental building blocks of our ability to
construct contextual theologies. Yet in our more theoretical work we have
rarely been able to admit that these represent a different kind of logic: one that
is artistic and intuitive. Yates wrote, "Even in our rational discourse theology is
dependent upon artistic elements—on the use of creative imagination and intu-
ition, on the use of mythic language and evocative symbols, on the use of
metaphor, on an awareness of the dramatic moment—which fashion it in the
ways of art as much as science" (Yates, 1987, 102).

Pastoral theologians' genuine need for institutional legitimacy has diverted
our attention from theorizing that our craft, while based on science, is also genuinely artistic in its fullest expression. When we cannot claim the elements that

are common in our work as the aesthetic work that they are, it is very difficult, if not impossible, to build bridges to other modes of art that might prove to be fertile ground in our theologizing, our wholeness, and our healing as human beings and persons engaged in an academic discipline.

Given these uncertainties regarding institutional legitimacy, pastoral theologians may also be disinclined to make theoretical connections with aesthetics in a philosophical world heavily dominated by Kantian compartmentalization. Kant argued for the separation of religion, ethics, and aesthetics as realms of discourse, and to an extent, modern scholarship mirrors this system. The way that a theologian, such as Frank Burch Brown, argues for a relationship between aesthetics and theology illumines some of the problems in relating aesthetics and pastoral theology. Burch Brown writes that aesthetica, or "the arts," are marked by three clusters of artistic traits: art is made to be appreciably aesthetic and often beautiful; art is made skillfully, knowledgeably, and creatively by human agents; art is made in forms that can express, fictively represent, and imaginatively transform "worlds" in a revelatory or prophetic way (Burch Brown, 102). In common parlance, however, art is often conflated with things beautiful without reference to its practical or transformative qualities.

Religious aesthetics is necessary to pastoral theology, first and foremost because of the transformative quality of aesthetica, secondarily because of the practices that aesthetic making invariably requires, and most remotely because of the formal significance of the qualities that we associate with beauty. Pastoral theology, in and of itself, is a discipline that engages in dependence and contingency, already seemingly of secondary significance in a world that simplistically values independence and self-sufficiency, in both philosophy and practice. To those who hold such assumptions, it seems that religious aesthetics deals with contingencies and so becomes a marginal discourse within philosophy, just as pastoral theology deals with contingencies and so becomes a marginal discourse within theology.

Yates's study also yields a clue to *why* it is so important to articulate the relationship implicit between pastoral theology and aesthetics. Feminist, womanist, and practical theologians have argued against the idea that contextual theology, or theology that reflects inductively on the here and now of human existence, is somehow second-class theology to systematic, doctrinal, or dogmatic theologies. When the latter represent the aristocratic citizens in the theological world, practical theology becomes applied theology—applying these theologies to concrete circumstances. Instead, as contextual theologians, we assume that these theologies represent the codified experience of persons in the past. When one theologizes *from* systems and doctrines *to* the lives of contemporary persons, we claim, one does so only at the risk of imposing such codes on persons whose lives are radically different from those of the past. That position does not require that we reject theological systems and doctrines as false, unhelpful, or unimportant to contemporary experience, nor does it reject the significance of theological and ecclesial tradition to contemporary people as some deconstructionist postmodernists would. Rather, many theologians simply want to establish the norm that inductive, contextual theological methods are finally as important as deductive, doctrinal methods toward creating theologies that truly respond to and reflect the experiences of diverse people. As such, pastoral *theology* is as fundamental as any other theological enterprise.

Yates found those scholars who were engaged in foundational theological and ethical analysis (in contrast to practical theologies and social ethics) to be most likely to incorporate substantive work in the arts into their scholarly reflection and courses. He identified four primary purposes they gave for doing so, purposes that resonate with the reasons we do pastoral theology:

1. concern with what the arts reveal regarding the religious and moral questions with which individuals and cultures struggle;
2. concern with the prophetic role of art and the judgments works of art make regarding the human community's own idolatry and injustice;
3. interest in the expressions of faith made through the arts, expressions of major traditional religions such as Judaism, Christianity and Buddhism, and various forms of civil and folk religions;
4. concern with the sacramental power of art to serve as a means by which renewal and grace, healing, and hope are experienced. (Yates, 1987, 25)

Pastoral theology, it seems to me, is deeply concerned with theological anthropology: with ways of being human; with ways that human beings are or tend to become distorted, alienated, or otherwise fragmented in their relations with themselves, with other people, and with God; and with transformation toward a more whole way of being, individually, in families, and in communities. If that is true, then we have much in common with those scholars who have incorporated the arts into their work.

Arguing for the relation of pastoral theology and religious aesthetics means creating a portage between two bodies of literature that exist on the margins of two dominant academic worlds of philosophy and theology. These various factors leave feminist pastoral theologians, who operate in yet another circle of contingency and marginality, with few resources to theoretically ground a portion of their work that they seem to intuit is significant.

A Portage Between Religious Aesthetics and Pastoral Theology: The Role of Aesthetics in Human Transformation Toward Love and Justice

Pastoral theology does not exist for the sake of the academic discourse of philosophy or even theology. Rather, pastoral theologians use academic discourse as a partial means toward another end—knowing God and transforming our knowledge of God into the "love of God with heart, soul, and mind, and love of neighbor as oneself." Pastoral theologians have primarily developed the use of language in the service of the Great Commandment, but we acknowledge in our reflections on pastoral and clinical therapeutic work that much pastoral care and counseling involves nonverbal interpersonal and intrapersonal communication. A significant amount of our work in clinical supervision amounts to learning to attend to and to synthesize linguistic, interpersonal, and intrapersonal knowledge. The arts represent nonverbal knowledge of other kinds — kinesthetic, spatial, and musical. Aesthetic experience synthesizes these various kinds of knowledge. Burch Brown argues that persons who practice Judaism and Christianity cannot live, or be transformed by and into, the Great Commandment without the fullness of aesthetic experience (Brown, 1989, 101-111), without engaging the total body, soul, heart, and mind.

Burch Brown discusses the relation of artistic traits mentioned above to the Great Commandment, concluding his analysis by describing how the arts engage body, heart, mind, and soul in transformation:

> This artistic capacity to envision, and in vision to transfigure this world or some hypothetical counterpart, evidently responds uniquely to an abiding human need. That is the need to discover, imagine, and come to grips with a world that can be thought and felt to matter, both in its goodness and beauty and in its evil and horror. . . . Precisely because we are embodied, thinking, passionate beings who want meaning and meaningfulness, truth and emotional satisfaction, we cannot be engaged wholly except through forms that imaginatively encompass and orient us within something like a world: something, moreover, as purposeful in its apparent purposelessness as we hope and trust life itself can be. (Brown, 1989, 109)

Burch Brown is arguing that the arts help people transform exactly those experiences that have so deeply concerned pastoral theologians — hopelessness, horror, tragedy, evil — and live beyond them in such a way that those experiences are not ignored but reimagined at their deepest level, and in the reimagining reconnect people with a hope, possibility, and actual reality of goodness and beauty. This goal, it seems to me, is at the heart of pastoral theology's ministry of presence, especially of its teaching methods that have exposed ministers to deeper experience of others in the world and that have encouraged ministers to explore their own experience theologically.

The arts engage the body in order to create a transitional world in which such imaginative transformation can occur. In part, the making of art requires bodily involvement. It takes a body to make music with an instrument or to shape the materials of the natural world with tools employed by the visual arts. It takes a central nervous system that commands the rest of the body into activity. The art that results becomes the expression of "the body's self-disclosure."

The arts also cause the mind to "think more," to think beyond the realm of the logical, measurable, and quantifiable. Art blurs the boundary between the real and the unreal. It blurs, in some respects, the line between the conscious and the subconscious, between waking and dreaming. When we are grasped by art, we are invited to reconsider our assumptions about what reality is.

The arts allow the heart to reconcile feeling and willing, to open the way so that actuality and the heart's desire can converge. In such transformation "art can become prophetic in mode, showing what is unjust or senseless, and possibly what is required in response. . . . For the heart, the world of the prophetic work" is morally, politically, or religiously charged (Brown, 1989, 110).

Such a powerful world is the one that is inhabited by the soul, traditionally what has had a central place in pastoral theology. "Because a world so charged is the sort of world that one enters or inhabits religiously, we can conclude that the worlds of artistic imagination can at times serve to reveal the realities significant to religion and the soul" (Brown, 1989, 110). Scripture itself, as revelation, is substantially artistic and, in addition, has been frequently mediated by aesthetic and artistic forms and engages one wholly.

This powerful world can be described in the pastoral theologian's common parlance of object relations theory. The artistic world reopens the child's place of play. It creates a transitional, imaginative space between realities. As infants, we created our sense of self in the gaze between ourselves and our primary caretakers. As toddlers, we practiced our abilities with transitional objects in the space between our growing sense of self and significant others. As adults, we continue to create and practice ourselves in the artwork that carries the complexity and sophistication of adult experience. As children, we needed a sense of a reliable world in order to develop a self that could live in the world's unreliabilities; as adults, regardless of the extent to which we have structured that reliability into a sense of trust and hope, we must ultimately face a world that will be reliable in ways that we wish it were not—it will inevitably present us with experiences of separation, loss, trauma, and transition. Art that captures the depth of this paradox, whether it is fine art, folk art, or our own art, gazes back at us and responds to our adult need continually to re-create hope, joy, and contentment in a world that is beyond our control. In part, to live into this world, we must live into the holding environment of culture, of which art becomes so revelatory. Art creates the transitional object—the art object—that mediates between ourselves and this environment and, in so doing, creates, shapes, and reconnects us (Winnicott, 1971, 95-103).

I encourage you to stop for a moment in your reading to imagine an object among the visual arts that most explicitly mediates between you and the Great Commandment. Then try to put into words the fullness of that communication. As you search your way to and from that experience, do you find that words, especially those of social scientific or philosophic logic, fail you? Do you discover that as hard as it would be, you would feel more satisfied expressing your experience in poetry or drama, translating the power of the experience into a linguistic art, than you would feel content describing it logically? Yet pastoral theologians, with a few exceptions (Capps, 1993; Doehring, 1995), have rarely taken it upon themselves to try to do so, much less to theorize about what they are doing. So doing, we encounter the problem of comparing apples and oranges: of philosophic and artistic modes of logic; of experience of humanity and God. The trail from the apple orchard to the orange grove is as long as we might have expected. We might decide that it is more realistic to continue to compare Jonathans and Galas—apples that might grow together in the same orchard. And yet the distance from the apple orchard to the orange grove is formidable only because we are so unused to walking it; our ancestors found it draining but far from impossible. We gain one important kind of knowledge in the analogies between apples and oranges; we learn something else comparing Jonathans and Galas. Apples and oranges give us breadth of vision; Jonathans and Galas give us depth. We need both (Rose, 1996, 15-22).

To know the Great Commandment is to know God's most expansive self-revelation—to discover, for example, on a clear night from a remote location that space between the familiar stars is filled with the dim but still brilliant light reflected from heavenly bodies. To know the Great Commandment is also to know God's most intimate self-revelation—to look down and notice the fossils under our feet on a sandstone path. The Great Commandment is mediated through humanity's ability to shape the materials of nature into a communication of God's expansive and intimate self-revelation into works of art. I think, for example, of the Lincoln Memorial. There, the stature of the man who shaped civil and religious ideals and whose character was simultaneously shaped by them rises above us even as his gaze falls upon us—the gaze that holds us for a moment in the depth of tragedy from which arises the ideal of "malice toward none and charity for all." Despite his shortcomings and our continuing faults, it is terrible to imagine the unrestrained hatred that might have been unleashed had he not promoted that particular ideal at that time. Such art holds before us the possibility of such an ideal at the lesser moments of our lives. The spiritual and therapeutic power of natural and human-created art as it mediates the Great Commandment is difficult to describe, even harder to contain, and therefore, impossible to quantify. Yet the transformational power of art becomes easier to ignore than to legitimate or to teach in a society or academic discipline that gives primary authority to what can be scientifically verified.

A Second Portage: The Role of Context

Context is an important element in the roles that art and pastoral theology play in transformation. How does the concept of context help us distinguish points of connection and distance between theology, psychology, and counseling? Once, the context of pastoral care and counseling was determined by the presence of a person who had a socially and ecclesially recognized ministry. Now, several demographic and ecclesial changes have required that the field of pastoral care broaden its understanding of the context of care and rethink its significance. John Patton, in *Pastoral Care in Context: An Introduction to Pastoral Care,* for example, describes three contexts of care that also represent developing understandings of care: classical, in which the major emphasis is on the message; clinical pastoral, in which the major emphasis is on what a minister must do, know, say, or be; and communal contextual, in which the major emphasis is on the interdependence of clergy and laity, congregations, gender, race, and class (Patton, 1993, 4). As women have entered pastoral care and counseling, our presence has pushed the field of pastoral care and counseling to reconsider the role of context. The presence of women created ambiguities regarding the context of care. Women had long been engaged in ministries of care that had not been officially recognized as pastoral care. Then, women became ordained in Protestant denominations. These women rapidly entered the specialties of chaplaincy and counseling. As the guilds of pastoral care and counseling became more ecumenical, women of Roman Catholic religious orders and laywomen and laymen asked the guilds to fully credential their caring ministries. This call occurred as Protestants were giving special attention to the priesthood of all believers and the equal worth of lay ministries and as Roman Catholics sought to concretize the reforms of Vatican II. Pastoral in pastoral care no longer meant care by the pastor through a personal attention or attitude toward care offered by a person endorsed by a religious institution. Now, the credentialing guilds in pastoral care and counseling recognize the ministry of men, women, clergy, and laity. As the ministries of laity have gained formal recognition as ministries of pastoral care, persons in pastoral care and counseling have had to rethink the meaning of context.

One way to think about the context of pastoral care is to think of the place where pastoral conversation occurs. Pastoral counseling usually refers to an activity conducted in a church building, in a building that extends church building space, or in a clinic specifically identified with religious practice. Chaplaincy provides an explicitly religious presence and activity in a secular institution such as a hospital, jail, or military establishment. In each case, the context in which pastoral care occurs may also incorporate various symbols that communicate a religious presence.

As pastoral care and counseling has become increasingly dominated by clinical and theoretical psychology, however, some have wondered whether a religious location really gives pastoral care a religious locus. What difference does it really make if clinical counseling occurs under the auspices of religion? Are we just deceiving ourselves? Should we not just recognize that religiously oriented pastoral care is one thing and clinical psychology is something else? Once our definition enters the world of the way that architecture and visual symbols communicate, pastoral counseling and clinical psychology may need an aesthetic theory to interpret what they are and do.

A similar turn toward understanding art in context has occurred for different reasons in aesthetic theory. We may also ask, How does context help us distinguish points of connection and distance between theology, aesthetics, and the arts? The discussion has ended up by a different means in theoretical distance between theology, aesthetics, and the arts, even though in practice we find constant commonalities. According to Gordon Kaufman, some theorists have argued that art is "a fully autonomous region of culture, with its own values, standards, modes of activity, and criteria for judgment" (1994, 13). For other theorists of religious aesthetics, art takes on meaning in a particular context. Kaufman suggests that art gains meaning "in and through complex interactions—and the meanings of those interactions as the artist creates the work—between artist and his or her world; and (in many successor events) in the complex interactions—and meanings of those interactions—between the art object and its many appreciators on subsequent occasions, and all the complexes of meaning specific to each of those interactions" (1994, 14).

The idea that art has meaning "for its own sake," he suggests, is peculiar to modern Western culture and is rarely found in other cultures, even in cultures that have produced "great art." Rather, he suggests that the meaning of art is discovered through the twin lenses of the artist's intention and the appreciator's apprehension. Relating to a work of art from these vantage points, we find that religious meanings in art may be explicit or latent. He writes, "We are not so in need of a 'theology of art' which explains what art 'really is' in some metaphysical sense as one which makes available to us criteria that can enable us to identify and to assess—as we focus on the art object in certain relevant contexts—what can appropriately be regarded as of religious (or, perhaps, specifically Christian) import" (1994, 15).

According to Kaufman, Paul Tillich's influential theology of the arts complicated the situation. Tillich thought that great works of art, by virtue of their spiritual power, always had theological import regardless of their setting. While this may be true, one can conclude from this statement that setting is irrelevant, leaving reflections on the arts to the metaphysical considerations. Kaufman argues that this position has assisted the separation of the arts and theology as realms that are unconnected by any common criteria, a distancing like that of clinical psychology and theology. I would argue that when theology and the arts are understood only in this uncontextualized relation, then as a culture we begin not only to truncate our theological interpretation of the fine arts but also to ignore the religious significance of folk art. We tend to consider the arts as a realm for esoteric specialists in which mere mortals cannot possibly involve themselves. We eliminate the entire realm of folk art as worthy of theological reflection, and severely limit the access that most persons, especially seminary students, have to increasing their knowledge of and participation in arts as a theological endeavor.

In a parallel fashion pastoral care and counseling increasingly relied on psychology to tell it "what it is" until pastoral care and counseling could in some cases be known only as religious because of its context in a designated religious space. For certain aims in counseling this may be appropriate, just as it is appropriate to interpret the spiritual import of great art on the basis of aesthetics alone. But when the theory of the relationship between theology and psychology is so distant that theology relates to pastoral care or counseling only because such counseling is religiously sponsored, then the riches of centuries of religious practice are lost to the healing of the spirit. We fail to understand the healing of the spirit as bound part and parcel with the practices of religious traditions—the riches of spiritual direction, prayer, and other "means of grace"—and fail to discern when the deep histories of people's religious tradition may be drawn forth for more holistic healing. In part, the reason pastoral care and counseling is so theoretically feeble in this regard is that these practices are more related to art than to the science of personality theory. To be fully confident of a holistic approach to their work, pastoral counselors would need a theory of the art of religious practice that is integrated with the theory of personality from which they operate.

Kaufman has alluded to the idea that a contextual approach to art makes cross-cultural interpretation more accessible. In pastoral care and counseling, a parallel statement may be doubly true. Pastoral counselors already acknowledge that people are not personalities abstracted from their society and culture, as some early personality theorists might have had it; rather the cultural and social contexts in which a person lives—including the meanings given to various cultural norms and social practices—deeply change how a counselor must intervene to be of assistance. Texts about pastoral care and counseling generally recognize this fact, but unfortunately, too few texts have plumbed the depths of what this means in the counseling situation as have texts in other fields, such as Doman Lum's *Social Work Practice and People of Color: A Process Stage Approach* (1986). Lum's work, influenced by Howard Clinebell, takes the religious practice of ethnic minorities as a strength to be built upon by the social worker as seriously as any other part of the client's background. Texts aimed toward pastoral care practitioners need to take as seriously religious practices across cultures.

Theories of context in cross-cultural pastoral care and counseling might also take the artistic traits of a culture seriously, especially where art exists in a culture in a more continuous relation between fine art and folk art, so that folk are more likely than in Anglo American culture to appreciate their culture's fine art. In so doing, Anglo practitioners of pastoral care and counseling might be taught ways to look differently at dominant culture for practices and artistic expressions of our own that we have failed to observe in ourselves and to understand them as central to our healing.

Pastoral theology provides the architectural blueprint for care and counseling. It may or may not comment on particular counseling practices or interventions, but it does suggest what persons involved in pastoral care and counseling should notice as they construct the milieu in which they work. Pastoral theology already contributes significantly to describing the various ethical boundaries that practitioners should observe. If we build theoretical bridges between pastoral theology and aesthetics, so that this relation has enough theoretical depth to provide a portage at the center rather than as adjunctive to the practice of care and counseling, we will have whole new strengths of human behavior to observe, to describe, and on which to build our healing practices. Such an endeavor may be aided by paying close attention to the pastoral theologies that ground other religious practices that have had a closer relation to aesthetics. Works of pastoral theology that rely heavily on theology and aesthetics, such as Don Saliers's *Worship as Theology: A Foretaste of Glory Divine* (1994), may reconnect us with the mystery of the human being, community practices, and their relation to the Divine—a mystery that personality theories have great difficulty keeping before us.

A Third Portage: Teaching and Learning

One of the most important places of transformation is the classroom, a place where pastoral theology and the arts naturally connect. Persons teaching pastoral theology and those teaching the arts in theological education, however, face significantly different hermeneutical problems. In the United States, twentieth-century culture became inhabited by general psychological concepts even as the arts lost their former acceptance. For example, since the 1970s public school systems have added courses in human relations, psychology, and sociology, even as courses in music, art, and drama have been deemed frivolous and have been eliminated. Seminarians and parish ministers have sometimes preached theologies that are almost indistinguishable from popular psychologies. In a culture increasingly dominated by psychology, pastoral theologians have had to teach psychology as a specialty, not because it was directly needful for ministry, but because, in order to teach what was necessary, we had to undo or reshape generalizations that students brought to seminary. At times, we have taught the psychological specialties in order to demonstrate to our colleagues that we were experts who could be distinguished from popular psychologists. Yet we have had to teach and write in such a way as to build a hermeneutical bridge between, on the one side, the psychologies that students and professional clergy merge with their theologies and, on the other, a more responsible way they will use theology and personality theory in their ministries. At times, our educational need to distinguish what we do from popular psychology may have resulted in our creating parish therapists

183

rather than helping ministers understand the role of psychology in the general pastoral care they would be called on to provide.

The cultural climate for the arts in theological education is almost a mirror opposite of that just described. Students and clergy have such a dearth of general cultural knowledge of the practice of, much less theories of, the arts that a conversation between theology and aesthetics can barely begin, except in rarefied situations. This void creates two effects: on a theoretical level, such a conversation may seem too esoteric and inaccessible to be useful; on a practical level, people with artistic inclinations are often too easily embarrassed to sing, dance, play, draw, or act because they have never had specific instruction.

As Yates's study pointed out, however, using the arts in the classroom to communicate pastoral theology would be natural. In my teaching, I relied heavily on extended role play, and I realized early on that the kind of role play I supervised was a form of dramatic improvisation. Role play functioned as drama in that it created an indirect means for students to experience, reflect upon, and transform their own emotions in a way that was appropriate for public communication. Drama creates a protective frame around experience: it begins, it moves from a problem through catharsis and resolution, and it provides closure. It seeks not to overwhelm the audience but to arouse emotions, to assist the audience to move through them, and then to resolve those emotions. For the actors, it requires an experience of deep sympathy of their own experience with the situation of another, so deep that they are able to reach into their souls to find experiences of commonality that portray that person. Dramatic form also promotes mastery over that sympathy for the actors and for the audience. Role play, as a form of folk drama, provides the protective frame of time, space, and ritual process of the stage and a predetermined way to enter and to exit the experience (Apter, 1991, 22). It allows the group to learn in the transition between paratelic and telic experience. Paratelic experience, or playful experimentation that does not focus on an immediate goal, frees the imagination to explore within safe space; telic, or serious goal-oriented experience, constructs insight and solidifies knowledge gained in the creative paratelic experience. Role play presents a situation in its multidimensionality and then allows students to talk about those dimensions, one by one. It provides a way for ministers to practice the skills of pastoral conversation and to involve themselves in a situation where the emotion is high but the stakes are relatively low, like doing something hair-raisingly adventurous in a dream.

The use of an art form such as drama in the classroom can provide education for freedom, in Maxine Greene's words, "to transform the indecent and overcome the unendurable" (1988, 86). In my classroom I saw time and again that it allowed students to confront their own wounding assumptions and relive their painful experiences in a safe, caring community and supervised setting. They learned where those previous experiences could endanger their ministries and, instead, used each experience transformatively and creatively. Carefully constructed, dramatic improvisation released the liberatory potential of which, according to Greene, the arts are capable. She writes:

> For those authentically concerned about the "birth of meaning," about breaking through the surfaces, about teaching others to "read" their own worlds, art forms must be conceived of as ever-present possibility. They ought not to be treated as decorative, as frivolous. They ought to be, if transformative teaching is our concern, a central part of curriculum, wherever it is devised. (1988, 131)

In teaching pastoral care through drama I want to stress that art entered the classroom at two levels. To teach pastoral care I used an art, dramatic improvisation, and might have used other arts as well. But I was also teaching an art. If we understand the practices of pastoral care and counseling as the practices of an art form with all that artistry entails—a theory or theology, a use of a tool for a further end, repeated practice in the use of that tool, and a creative, imaginative result—then we have freed ourselves from understanding the teaching of pastoral care and counseling as education in techniques: listening exercises and basic counseling skills. We free ourselves conceptually from the shroud that at times casts itself, in our own eyes and in the eyes of our colleagues, over our teaching—a shroud of technical reason, techniques that are recognizable only as a means, as interchangeable parts in an assembly line, a process that repeats itself toward a predetermined end.

Pastoral care is an art in that it is an activity that students must be prepared to practice, in thought and action, "on their feet." Reading a book about pastoral theology prepares a student minister for caring in actual situations about the way that reading a book on musicology prepares a student musician to play a violin in a concert. A book on musicology may well assist the musician to imagine ways to more fully interpret his or her music, but the process of imagining will be useless if the musician does not have the bodily practice with the violin to do in an instant what he or she imagines doing while reading the book. Ultimately, the student of pastoral care must be prepared to react with a thinking process that is as integrated as the thinking process that coordinates the fingers on the strings at a particular place in particular ways as the arm simultaneously draws the bow across the string at a particular speed and weight. Only regular practice will create this kind of learning. The study of musical theory, however, enhances and fine-tunes the practice far more than the audience ever knows. My reward in pastoral theological education comes when students return to the seminary and report about a moment in ministry, "When I needed it, it was all there." Then, I know they have learned what they need to know to begin their ministries and to be lifelong learners of pastoral theology and the practice of ministry.

We would rarely ask a person to play a musical instrument in church without having practiced, many times, in a safe space at home—an ill-prepared performance would be painful for the musician, the musical director, and the congregation. Yet our philosophy of theological education too frequently sends ministers into roles of religious leadership, asking them to perform with theory and personal experience—rather than with an opportunity to practice the art of ministry as carefully as a musician practices making music on his or her instrument under the watchful guide of a mentor and teacher. From those trained in the arts of ministry, does the church deserve any less?

❁ ❁ ❁

Our fourth day dawned drearily with a slow drizzle that was cozy and comforting. We had declared a layover day to allow our bodies and our spirits to reabsorb strength from one another and from our beautiful surroundings. We lounged in Leah's bug tent, sharing a homemade cinnamon apple coffee cake hot off the bake-packer stove. We had decided we could not make it to Ogishkemuncie, the large lake at halfway point. We had planned a twenty-four-hour window of opportunity during which we would meet Jeff and Jim, my brother and a friend who were shuttling the opposite direction from Sag to Snowbank to pick up our cars. But Leah had become sick, could not paddle, and now was coping with the side effects of medication—the meds had slowed her down as much as the original illness. In a mismatch of gender expectations, we thought that perhaps Jeff and Jim would paddle into our cove that morning. We thought they might be concerned that our having missed our meeting meant that we were having trouble and needed help. We were. We would have been grateful for their assistance through the six time-and-energy-consuming portages of the Kekekabic ponds that separated us from Ogish. But they had been watching for us from a visible campsite on Ogish, one of their favorite campsites ever, a three-tiered site from which they watched the same moon rise three times from different angles, ready to vacate when we arrived. It hadn't occurred to them to look for us. They thought that for some reason we had not declared earlier, six women on our own canoe trip wanted our female privacy.

As we rested that day, we reminisced about the joys of the previous days— the family of loons that held a party throughout the first night off our campsite, the full moon rising over the lake, the bald eagles on Thomas Lake, the geological formations in the cliffs that Leah, a geologist, could explain. We relived our ecstasy when we discovered that the last campsite on the lake was both airy and sheltered, nested in granite and pine, in a cove of its own—and that it was vacant, waiting for us to settle onto it. The Goddess does provide, and through a canoe trip she reminds us of how little we need some things and how much we need others. We talked about what we had learned about traveling as a group of women and wrote guidelines for paddling with women—new habits that we would re-create from our experience paddling apart from men. We agreed to pack lighter, more like backpackers than canoeists; to pick up a pack or a canoe with help, reserving our backs, not succumbing to the temporarily expedient temptation to pick up a heavy pack alone; and to pace ourselves differently, saving some of our strength for emergencies. After the trip, we clarified with Jim and Jeff that we thought we were traveling interdependently. A shuttle is a team, and when we missed our check-in point, we would have been reassured had they looked for us. In the intervening years, Jim has become a guide for differently abled persons and has adopted such disciplines, even with temporarily able-bodied groups. As women, when we reshaped the disciplines and habits of paddling to meet our own needs, our new habits contributed to the flourishing of all.

10

Womanist-Feminist Alliances

Meeting on the Bridge

Marsha Foster Boyd and Carolyn Stahl Bohler

Introduction

> In Dayton, Ohio, a bridge crosses the Great Miami River, which divides
> the city into the "West Side" and "East Dayton." The vast majority of the
> white population lives on the east side of that river; the black population
> lives on the west side. A tradition has grown up around that "Peace
> Bridge." Special events and walks for peace and unity are held there, or
> start there. In fact, European Americans and African Americans meet sev-
> eral times a year on that bridge. However, the bridge is there every day of
> the year. Most of the time whites stay on one side, blacks cross over and
> back.

We are two Methodist clergywomen (one African Methodist Episcopal, one
United Methodist), both professors of pastoral counseling at United Theological Seminary in Dayton, Ohio, where we live two blocks apart. We have
become dialogue partners within our professional discipline, in ministry, and
across the bridge of race. We have twice taught a course entitled Womanist and
Feminist Psychology and Theology, first in 1992 and again in 1997, and we
have co-led several workshops on race. As we prepared to teach our course for
the first time, we enrolled in a seminar entitled Friends and Allies: Black and
White Women Together, at Grailville, Ohio. This event assisted us to tell truth
to each other and to trust each other. We also sensed how we were uniquely
gifted by our professional locations to enable others to look at race matters in
heterogeneous as well as same-race settings.

The purpose of this chapter is to state what we have learned while teaching
with each other. These learnings cluster into three categories. First, we name a
set of womanist and feminist values that inform our teaching. Next, we make
observations about some recurring dynamics between African Americans and
European Americans. Finally, we analyze institutional attempts at dealing with
diversity. For us, when we work together, gender is often in the background —
race is in the foreground. We focus on race because white women and men
often want to escape that reflection.

One of the cardinal values of feminists and womanists is the creation of "safe
spaces" in which to do our work (DeMarinis, 1993). As theorists and practitioners, we need to make explicit our assumptions so that readers and parishioners might feel safer receiving the ideas. We have discovered that when we
teach together, we work primarily inductively, gathering ideas and values as we
proceed and naming them when relevant. Here, however, for the reader who is
not in actual dialogue with us, we name from the outset some of our value
assumptions. In a sense we are telling you who our friends are, i.e., some of those
people who have influenced us. Yet we have chosen to work from these values
not necessarily because "our friends" write about them articulately, but because
we see that the values work — they create a fertile learning environment.

Womanist and Feminist Values That Inform Our Teaching

Acknowledging Interdependence

Human beings are interdependent: we need each other in order to see a bigger picture and, in fact, to survive. Those who consider themselves to be independent and invulnerable are literally shortsighted.[1] Disciplines need broad-spectrum dialogue in order to move closer to relevant "truth." We all need to be reminded "of our blatant need for one another, young and old, large and small, female and male," writes Carolyn McCrary. She cites the West African Yoruban proverb, "The small hand of the child cannot reach the high shelf. The large hand of the adult cannot enter the narrow neck of the gourd" (Bailey and Grant, 1995, 159).

Pamela Couture, who traced the value of self-sufficiency in Christian denominations and American democracy, shows how laws in the United States such as those governing welfare and divorce have self-sufficiency as the goal. She argues that self-sufficiency is a misguided norm upon which to base policies (Couture, 1991, 25). The theological idea of shared responsibility or interdependence would be more faithful to Christian teachings (Couture, 1991). Toinette Eugene imagines that "to be truly free, womanists and feminists must live life in intimately connected relationships of integrity and justice-love" (Eugene, 1993, 10). Feminist and womanist pastoral theology assumes the value of interdependence, which fosters freedom, yet maintains connections.

Awareness of differences is not ignored, but is actually heightened, when interdependence is acknowledged. The little one is called to reach into the gourd; the tall one is needed for the shelf reaching. Susan Thistlethwaite maintains that awareness of difference must be respected as we maintain dialogue. Different-in-dialogue is an alternative to our current divide-and-conquer mentality in which one person or group independently seeks to gain dominance and pretends not to need others (Thistlethwaite, 1989).

Interdependence as a seriously practiced value is needed within and between institutions, too. For instance, womanists and feminists have seen the necessity of a well-traveled two-way path between the "academy" and the "church" (Miller-McLemore in Stevenson-Moessner, 1996, 10). Valerie DeMarinis demonstrates how the counselor can include not only family members, but also other significant people in the lives of the help-seeker: priests, ministers, even "cultural consultants." She takes seriously the academic interdependence of theology and spirituality in her "Critical Caring" model of pastoral counseling (DeMarinis, 1993).

Ecological wisdom underscores the immensity of interdependence between all species and the natural world. Frankly, black and white women and men working together seems like a puny effort toward acknowledging interdependence if one takes the perspective of the whole earth, which requires a dynamic interdependence of the entire ecosystem!

191

Thinking Interdisciplinarily

Clearly, there is a vast literature available for an interdisciplinary course that includes both psychology and theology. It takes a combination of hubris and humility for us to attempt such breadth of content, as well as the awareness that we will not "cover" the whole territory. However, as we teach together, we hold a bias toward an interdisciplinary approach because we see that the disciplines—like people—have a "blatant need for each other."

Two specific foci illustrate the need for an interdisciplinary approach: the image of God and christology. The image we hold of God affects self-esteem (Saussy, 1991). As Bons-Storm puts it, "How the Deity is represented is of the utmost importance for the strengthening of women's selfhood" (Bons-Storm, 1996, 129). Only when both disciplines—theology, dealing with God, and psychology, dealing with the self—are in dialogue will the ramifications for women be more fully illumined. The God-representation that is deeply embedded into the psyche—from its birth in us when we are young—is, psychologically speaking, our "living god" (Rizzuto, 1979). Theology can alter our theoretical view of God, yet psychology provides provocative questions about how people experience God in the first place.

Christology for womanists and feminists clearly has a theological foundation, yet our understanding of the significance of Jesus and Christ is informed by actual lives, both biblical and contemporary. Prominent womanists' and feminists' christologies are interdisciplinary. These theologies integrate the worldviews of the first century, which we meet in the Bible, the fact of the existence of evil and abuse throughout centuries, and contemporary psychological insights for transforming abusive patterns. Consequently, these christologies challenge some of the potential suffering and abusive implications of other male-developed christologies.

Delores Williams, who develops a poignant theology of wilderness, starting with Hagar's experience there, concludes that "the resurrection does not depend upon the cross for life, for the cross only represents historical evil trying to defeat good." She writes: "Perhaps not many people today can believe that evil and sin were overcome by Jesus' death on the cross. . . . It seems more intelligent and more scriptural to understand that redemption had to do with God, through Jesus, giving humankind new vision to see the resources for positive, abundant relational life" (Williams, 1993, 165).

Rita Brock argues that "the resurrection of an abandoned Jesus is a meaningless event. . . . The disciples of the Christa/Community at the cross . . . transformed the defeat of death into a wholeness of vision in the midst of pain and sorrow" (Brock, 1988, 100). Integrating object relations psychology into her understanding of feminist theology, Brock suggests that it was the community around Christ that took up—resurrected—the purpose and love of Jesus after his death (Brock, 1988).

Thistlethwaite appreciates Brock's christology, which emphasizes connectedness. However, Thistlethwaite, wary that white women more easily see connectedness with other women rather than destruction or differences, asserts that even in christology we need to be certain to maintain the awareness of destruction and evil at the heart of the cosmos, as well as to see connection and creativity (Thistlethwaite, 1989, 107).

When we teach, christology and abuse as well as God images and self-esteem are treated as interdisciplinary topics, enriched by knowledge of both psychology and theology. This interdisciplinary appraisal makes this work vital pastoral theology.

Honoring Subjectivity

When we teach together, we find that the use of videos is quite effective. We want the theologians and lived events of a wide variety of women to come alive for participants in class. Through the "Faces of Faith" videos, Hyun Kyung Chung, Ada Maria Isasi-Diaz, Sallie McFague, Rita Brock, and Renita Weems were present in our class.[2] In addition, students agreed to come more than an hour early to class on several occasions in order to see films: *Daughters of the Dust, Camille Claudel, Sankofa,* and *The Long Walk Home.*

We have observed that classroom discussions can easily shift to consider women "out there." In short, it is easy for class members to objectify those whom they are trying to understand or learn more about. By bringing a variety of women into class through video—contemporary theologians as well as those of other decades and geographical and social locations—we are making these women subjects and modeling the valuing of their experiences. We also work at communicating that we value the experiences of each woman in our classroom.

We want the people in our classes to realize that as people dialogue and interact with one another, each person holds subjective "truths." In other words, "truth" does not sit objectively somewhere to be grasped. If people experience themselves and others as having subjectivity, then they can more clearly notice objectification when it occurs in the past and present. For example, they would notice the objectification of African American women through stereotyping. Patricia Hill Collins, making this observation, writes: "Portraying African-American women as stereotypical mammies, matriarchs, welfare recipients, and hot mommas has been essential to the political economy of domination fostering Black women's oppression. Challenging these controlling images has long been a core theme in Black feminist thought" (Collins, 1991, 67).

When we teach together, we hold the assumption that women need to tell our stories among ourselves and get used to hearing our own voices, as well as listening to one another (Bons-Storm, 1996, 147). Women should not study ourselves as objects of another who defines us to ourselves, even if that other is a woman. We are subjects in our own right. As we work together in the classroom, we find it is impossible to teach wariness of objectification if we do not intentionally model that we honor each member as a subjective agent, and we trust that class members will do likewise.

Considering Power

Understanding power is essential to womanists and feminists because womanists and feminists need to decide for themselves how to claim wise power in order to be effective and healthy. Decades ago, Bernard Loomer articulated "Two Concepts of Power": (1) having the ability to produce an effect, to actualize, or the strength to influence, and (2) having the ability to be influenced as well as to influence, the power to sustain mutual relationships where each is affected by the other. Loomer, a white male, was clear that (white) males have defined power to be of the first type, that is, the power to make happen; however, he challenged his readers to consider the power of one who is able to receive others, to take them into one's own consideration. For Loomer, that one who can take in as well as to make happen is larger in stature, in what he calls "SIZE" (Loomer, 1976).

Using Loomer's analysis of power, emphasis upon subjectivity and interdependence generates an empowering presence for all persons involved. Thus, as we teachers receive the comments of students, we gain "power," and so do they. There is no scarcity of power—we all have more. In teaching together, our experience has led us to agree with Patricia Hunter, who names "an underlying fear that if a woman is able to claim her own power and name her passion, she may define herself in a way that excludes those who have traditionally been in power as defined by patriarchy. One of the limitations of patriarchy, to which Christians have succumbed, is to believe that some have power and some do not" (Townes, 1993, 193).

Rosita deAnn Matthews speaks of "Using Power from the Periphery." This means, for her, "using one's power to resist a threat by maintaining or establishing ethical principles and moral standards, and refusing to employ the aggressor's methods. Instead, the person chooses to redefine her involvement with the threat by establishing alternative ground rules within a larger framework" (Townes, 1993, 93). As we teach together and consider power with students, we work to focus upon establishing healthy relationships—between races and between women and men—with ground rules that assume there is plenty of power for all. There is no scarcity. The more capacity to implement and the more capacity to receive each person has, the more empowered all become.

Teaching Inductively

In teaching together, we start our courses with experiential exercises that focus upon truth telling and the development of trust. Farther into the course, after all have read some chapters in common, we focus as much on students' responses to and experiences of the ideas as we do to our clarification of the authors' views.

We have tended not to name our assumptions first, but to let them emerge as the class progresses. We ask for reflection/response papers or other types of creative works to be handed in at the end of each section of the course. These papers or other creative works are intended to value the subjectivity of the students. The students are asked to respond to the authors and the videos as well as to take their own initiative to explore at least one additional resource.

Recurring Dynamics Between African Americans and European Americans

Definitions First

We realize that dialogue cross-racially is far more complex than a two-race analysis, and that multiracial dynamics need to be addressed. However, given our expertise and limited purposes here, in this chapter we are discussing primarily black and white race relations. We use the terms *African Americans* and *European Americans* in parallel construction; to vary our terms, we also use *blacks* and *whites*.

When we teach together, we find that it is essential to begin by unpacking key definitions and assumptions regarding race in the North American context. The issues that surround race for those of us in the United States today in general, and those of us involved in pastoral theology in particular, began some five hundred years ago as various European nations sought to expand their sphere of influence and power by venturing out of Europe to "discover" other parts of the world—civilizations and peoples who had lived on their continents and in their lands for hundreds and thousands of years before these Europeans "discovered" them. To establish their superiority over the races they encountered, these Europeans claimed power "over" those they named as "others." (During that period, for example, racial categories were created by Europeans, e.g., Caucasoid, Negroid, and Mongoloid, to differentiate—and separate—peoples from one another.) We define racism as the institutionalization of power "over" others and the implicit assumption of the right to maintain that power.

We start from the premise that as whites passively accept this implicit assumption or accept unchallenged the benefits of the institutionalization of white power, whites are being passively racist. It is our observation through our years of teaching and working together that many, if not most, European Americans are not often conscious of their passive racism, and most who are white insist that they are not racist at all. We have observed that what they generally mean is that they are not engaging in *active* racism. For example, they are not members of the Ku Klux Klan; when they sell their home, they do not tell the Realtor not to sell to an African American client; nor do they use racial slurs in public or private. Yet they may engage in *passive* racism. For example, they may work at a place that does not actively recruit, hire, or promote African Americans; they may bank at an institution that "redlines" areas for housing loans; or they may hold—and spread to their children, friends, parishioners, or colleagues—unchecked assumptions about African Americans or African American culture and history that they see (or do not see) portrayed in the media or literature. To be *antiracist*, according to our definitions, European Americans must consciously and consistently think, act, and speak out against racism—it is a way of life, an active stance. It is impossible to be a passive antiracist!

African Americans can be prejudiced—holding assumptions based on race—but in our view African Americans cannot be racist in this culture because they do not have the institutionalized power "over" others to establish black superiority as an assumption or right. (We assume that this institutional power "over" others to establish superiority is still prevalent for European Americans, hence they can be racist.) Racism, with our definition, requires institutional power to dominate.[3]

Layers of Truth Telling—Emerging Trust

We are impressed with the positive effect of even very small efforts to talk with each other across the bridge of race. Several African American pastors expressed appreciation for an arena, in our seminary's Doctor of Ministry program, where it was safe to speak directly, with plenty of other African Americans present, to European American pastors. Most of those African Americans were pastors in settings where ecumenical dialogue meant that they were the only one or one of few black pastors in a community of white pastors. European American pastors said it had been years, if ever, since they had been in any dialogue about race with African Americans. Several indicated that this honest dialogue, for merely an hour, was "healing" of past experiences or fantasies about the other race, or about how members of the other race felt about them or perceived them.

These cross-racial dialogues are too rare; we believe that many such opportunities must be created. Most of Americans' discussion of and on race is not done in the context of truth telling to and with one another. Instead, we talk about each other with our "own kind." In family systems terms, this situation is an all-too-perfect example of rigid boundaries. Health in families—or communities—requires permeable boundaries, with direct avenues for dialogue among all members.

We have subtitled this chapter "Meeting on the Bridge." We started out conceptualizing what we were doing as bridge building and the goal as active bridge crossing. During our work, we have settled at least temporarily on the image of *meeting* on the bridge because we believe that bridges are already available. We need to use those bridges to meet each other. We hope that the bridges become thoroughfares, but in the meantime, let us at least meet.

In our classes, we have witnessed students' amazement that the two of us can disagree with each other, interrupt each other, supplement our ideas with each other's, and share our different viewpoints on a common experience or the thesis of a text. Honest dialogue across race is so rare. We Americans are amazed when we witness it—yet once we are accustomed to it, the truth telling can become as much a habitual way of being as avoidance, hiding, and hearsay had been. Dialogue does not require a miracle; it requires effort, genuine and persistent intent.

There are multiple layers of truth telling. At first it seems significant simply to face each other during a classroom exercise and say, "I am afraid of talking directly to you because . . ." Or "I am excited to have permission to talk with you because . . ." Then a person of one race manages to speak truth to one of another race not during an exercise in which truth is asked for, but during a moment of ordinary interaction.

For example, Marsha pointed out to Carolyn, when the two of us were talking, that Carolyn was doing what Marsha has termed "feigning naïveté;" that is, Carolyn was giving the impression to Marsha that she did not know what Marsha was talking about. In that moment, Carolyn, according to our definitions, was passively racist. She was not actively acknowledging—even in her own mind—racist behaviors of whites. Instead, she moved into a "naive" zone. Marsha was right; she knew Carolyn well enough to know Carolyn could understand and trusted Carolyn enough to tell her. Of course, Carolyn was embarrassed, but she gained a notch of trust in Marsha at that moment and Carolyn moved toward healthier psychological congruence (if that is measured in part by making repressed awareness conscious). Marsha could speak truth to Carolyn and still love her, and Carolyn could hear truth from Marsha and still love her. That event showed us that naming passive—or active—racism could be an opportunity for growth and grace in our relationship, not a cause for distancing, rejection, or resorting to stereotypes.

On another occasion, six years into our relationship, Carolyn gathered courage to ask Marsha whether she would come to a faculty social—a simple question for her to ask her white colleagues, but one that required a good deal of internal debate before Carolyn could manage to ask Marsha. Carolyn had been fretting over whether she would be too intrusive or whether Marsha would experience the question as criticism or a demand. Marsha explained how the African American colleagues called one another to ascertain whether they would be the only black present. For Marsha, faculty socials are not necessarily relaxing; they are often extra work, another "faculty assignment"—cross-cultural dialogue—in a way Carolyn does not experience. By Carolyn asking a direct question rather than wondering, and by Marsha providing a direct answer rather than hiding or camouflaging, another step in truth telling was taken. This is also an example of healthy human relations: direct communication rather than projection, guessing, or avoidance. However much we would hope that healthy relationships could risk such questions more quickly than in six years, it is worth the attempt whenever enough courage and trust develop.

Another example of truth telling between us occurred when Marsha mentioned the healthy paranoia of blacks' "protecting each other's backs" on campus. Carolyn at first wondered what this really meant. "Protecting from what? From whom?" Carolyn then began to see how she might also be one of those from whom blacks needed to be protected. For instance, she might "forget" or "not think" of implications for blacks when she voted on a seemingly minor faculty matter.

The layers of truth telling—and trust—deepen. Once Carolyn told Marsha she felt quite alone when she sided squarely with the black faculty in the midst of a decision-making struggle on campus in which African American and European American faculty members seemed on opposite sides. Marsha appreciated Carolyn's feeling of isolation, but she wanted Carolyn to understand the "cost" of her decision to vote with the African American faculty—that sometimes a "price is paid" for siding with those of another race. Marsha pointed out that Carolyn could be thought of as a "nigger lover" by their white colleagues. Marsha named a quandary that whites have sometimes experienced when they have, in U.S. history, sought to understand and dialogue with blacks. Carolyn realized that she needed to reestablish more dialogue with her European American colleagues, to grasp their viewpoints, that she needed to return to "her side" of the bridge for a while. Flexible boundaries and alliances, as suggested in family systems theories, are good for all in the system. Carolyn's relationship with Marsha did not need to pull her away from her white colleagues, and in fact resulted in pushing her back toward them to gain greater perspective.

European Americans' Educating Themselves: Mutual Dialogue When Mutually Beneficial

As we have worked together, we have noticed that European Americans consistently ask African Americans to educate them on race matters. African Americans often become exhausted, explaining the simplest facts about African Americans over and over again. Blacks can resent this demand from whites. By what right do European Americans perceive that they can request of any African American the time and energy—and wisdom—to educate them? Many European Americans, when asked what race they are, are perplexed that they even "have" a race. A surprising number of European Americans insist that they have no ethnic background; they just "are." To the extent that they believe that, they are seeing themselves as "normal" or "human" and others as "different." Using the adjective *European* reminds whites that they are not "just Americans." (Here again we regret our limitations, speaking only of whites and blacks; we need a more complex discussion with Asian Americans, Hispanic Americans, and Native Americans.)

As we move into a new millennium, with the opportunity for genuine diversity in many settings and the demography of our country changing rapidly, the urgency of European Americans' educating themselves on race matters is apparent. For the most part, they have been very lazy in this regard. European Americans have plenty of resources at their disposal to educate themselves about race in America if they put forth a minimum of effort. For example, they can read books by and about African Americans, take courses at almost any college, watch films (popular and educational), go to art galleries specializing in African American art, attend African American churches, shop in black neighborhoods, attend functions at African American schools, listen to various styles of African American music, eat and cook "soul" food, and observe or buy greeting cards and children's books with black images. In short, they can work at becoming at least bicultural rather than remaining proudly, naively, and dangerously monocultural.

All these forms of education are readily available to European Americans. African Americans have put forth effort to educate all people through these diverse means of instruction. European Americans need not act helpless, continually feign naïveté, or request of mere acquaintances who are black (or black colleagues whose expertise is not African American heritage) tutoring on African American history and culture. Whites need blacks to be colleagues, bosses, friends, neighbors, and students. When whites only ask blacks to be their tutors on race, they are not opening themselves as much as they could to the other expertise that particular African Americans are prepared to offer. Whites are seeing blacks solely as representatives of their race and experts on race. When European Americans educate themselves, they can approach African Americans as equals in mutual dialogue between educated persons. The dialogue could then be between equals and for mutual benefit.

In seminary classes, Carolyn has observed Marsha answer the most elementary questions on race ("What is the Middle Passage?" or "What do blacks want?") with immense patience and grace. In her role as educator, Marsha tries to answer. But sometimes Carolyn answers the question, showing that European Americans can and should know about and educate themselves with regard to race. On occasions, either of us will simply say that the question is one to which the student can find the answer in hundreds of books or search his or her soul for wisdom.

European Americans' Blindness and Desire to Be Healed

A woman risked grave punishment for breaking boundary taboos in touching Jesus' garment, yet she touched it because she wanted to be healed (Matt. 9:20-22; Mark 5:25-34; Luke 8:43-48). An audacious mother bested Jesus in an argument, undaunted even when likened to a dog, and she got healing for her daughter (Matt. 15:21-28; Mark 7:24-30). A widow importuned the judge until the judge wearied from the request and granted it (Luke 18:1-8). These women mentioned in the Bible actively sought out their own or their kin's healing.

European Americans should likewise actively seek out their own healing of racism, be it passive or active. African Americans are aware virtually all of the time that they are black in a culture in which whites are dominant. Whites are barely aware of their dominance and block it from their own awareness. European Americans who are sincere about wanting to be healed will have to *try to see* and try to motivate their friends to see.

For example, Carolyn taught a small group of pastors in southern Ohio who had recently responded to a survey taken by clergy in their district. She noted that the pastors, all of whom were white, responded that they had *no racism* whatsoever in their white churches. Granted that the pastors were probably functioning from a definition of racism that was closely equivalent to our active racist definition, any pastor who could believe that there is no racism in his or her church is blind.[4]

Dislike of difference, which European Americans could see if they tried to look from another perspective, abounds. When a local gym asks its members to be careful what they eat or what perfume they wear before coming to work out, because some patrons dislike the "odors," one might suspect dislike of difference. If that dislike of difference is legislated into a "rule" against certain smells, associated with persons of a certain race, that is racism. Those with power have assumed the right to name appropriate cultural fragrances.

Again, when a virtually all-white church imagines an integrated worship service to be just like "usual," but with a good many African Americans present, the church members are assuming the right to define *worship*. They are naming not just for themselves, but also for blacks. They are assuming the power and right to do that—unquestioningly. That is racist.

Another example may occur in a business. The business invests enormous efforts into formalizing principles and procedures that try to "avoid conflict" and maintain "order," and these "rules of order" are such that those who already have the say will maintain it. The desire to protect the status quo could be racist.

The term *politically correct* has had a pitiful influence upon European Americans. It removes the locus of responsibility from whites' own eyes, minds, and hearts, and places *righteousness* or *correctness* in some abstract transcendent realm—someplace where things are marked "correct" or "wrong." People who think of their behavior in terms of whether it is politically correct are, in Gestalt therapy terms, "giving their eyes away." They try to be "good" in the eyes of others, privately resisting honest soul-searching.

Whites should not ask others to tell them when they are being or doing something "wrong." To get others to monitor oneself is itself another expression of dominance. European Americans need to let the scales fall from their own eyes.

It may be embarrassing for whites to admit how blind they are, especially when they realize they have been deriving benefits from that blindness. Yet whites can seek to put on corrective lenses.

Using ourselves as examples, Carolyn tries to wear corrective lenses for race (knowing she can and does take them off plenty of times). Carolyn does not hand over to Marsha Carolyn's own eyes, by asking Marsha to watch out for Carolyn's racism. She does not make Marsha responsible for helping her to be antiracist. (Indeed, Marsha would not take on that responsibility!) However, in the friendship and collegial relationship, Marsha may mention some behavior of Carolyn's (or Carolyn might name Marsha's behavior) that warrants modification. In the example cited earlier, when Marsha challenged Carolyn with what she called "feigning naïveté," or pretending not to know or see some issue of race, which in fact Carolyn did know or see, Marsha was being a mutual friend, neither a monitor of political correctness nor a private tutor. Marsha had already established that Carolyn wanted to see and gained the trustworthiness to speak.

Sins of Omission

"I do not understand my own actions. For I do not do what I want, but I do the very thing I hate" (Rom. 7:15). In spite of this parallel confession of omitted as well as committed sins, our culture places significantly more emphasis upon committed sins. We have "committed" criminals, but those who "omit" action are omitted from comment, news, or punishment. (Child neglect is a sin of omission that is acknowledged.) When we humans act, we can make mistakes and sin. There is risk in action. Yet there is equal risk in nonaction.

Consider a father who is out of town, at the office, or simply not available for most of the ten years of his children's early childhood. He is likely to make very few sins of commission as a father. He will not explain the math problem incorrectly, say the wrong thing to a teacher, be in the other room when the child hurts himself or herself. The mother may commit many sins of commission. Yet there is one huge sin of omission the father commits: he omits himself from parenting!

Similarly, many whites frequently consider racism exclusively in terms of sins of commission (active racism). They imply that they do not sin when they say: "I do not teach my child to hate African Americans"; "I do not vote against taxes that support public schools"; or "I hire blacks." Yet they seldom consider their sins of omission: they do not generally teach their children about African American culture, worship, or history. They feel put out when they have to make some effort to understand an American who does not speak just like themselves. They do not notice the ways in which they do not hire or promote blacks. Many omit long-term dialogue with kindergarten teachers, principals, other parents, and school boards in order to achieve good public schools. Instead of whites, and blacks too in some cases, teaching their children that when there is a conflict, they can and must face it, those who can afford to may pull their children off the bus or out of the class, or enroll them in a private school. They think they have committed no sin, just made a "personal" or "family" decision, but they have committed a huge sin of omission. They have failed to help other human beings to find creative, positive solutions.[5]

Private schools serve a purpose, but the reason many whites (and some blacks) send their children to these schools is sometimes a sin of omission, a form of denial. We know white parents who enrolled their children in public kindergarten and went with their children on the first day of school. The first day was also the last. These parents explained, "I didn't mind the fact that the other kids were black, but they were just so much bigger than my son." Even if the white boy were small and other kids who were black were bigger, this immediate reaction is very likely an example of denial, not meaning what was truly felt, that black children seemed frightening or intimidating to the white parents.

A cardinal value of Christianity is self-transcendence, which requires being able to go beyond our own perspective to take another's point of view. Many of Jesus' actions were teaching moments of self-transcendence. Who will throw the first stone (John 8:1-11)? How much will the two laborers, the one who worked a few hours and the one who worked a full day, receive in pay (Matt. 20:1-16)? Yet we Christians too often stay rooted to our own points of view, thinking we have the only "reality." After we do this, we declare ourselves sinless. We do not wish to see what others see.

A major act of omission is the refusal to yield being in the position of having power "over" others. As stated earlier, there are healthy forms of power. We can maintain and express a healthy sense of our own power *and* receive the power of others, nondefensively. This cooperative giving and receiving of power is far more adaptive than using only power "over," whether in personal relationships, church, or politics; yet it is a rarity.

Effort for the Long Haul: Facing Ambiguity and Accepting Grace

For many whites in our culture, whenever they want to be free from dealing with racism, they can take a breather. They can choose at any time not to go near the bridge. Issues of race will seldom impinge upon them in a pervasive way. African Americans may find a haven in black churches, in the sanctity of family, or in the seeming sanctity of a white middle-class neighborhood, but elsewhere they have minimal freedom to put race aside when they are tired of dealing with it.

The process of meeting on the bridge—or possibly, creating thoroughfares on various bridges—will never be completed. Political correctness can be short-lived, until the political waters shift. But for those of us on either side of the bridge who choose to commit to antiracism work, the task is ours for the rest of our lives. However, this awareness of the need for a long-haul effort need not immobilize us. Resources from our faith are deep enough. In addition, we find that as we dialogue, we discover resources and solutions that were not on "our" side of the bridge!

Many theorists agree that maturity of faith and personality is found in the acceptance of ambiguity. When we face our own "shadows" of self-love, self-hate, racism, shame, and prejudice, then we grow in our level of tolerance for ambiguity.

In America today we cannot choose whether to be a pluralistic nation. We are. Early in the twenty-first century, European Americans will be a numerical minority in the United States. However, we can choose to embrace this diversity or not. Several blessings arise if we do. One is graceful appreciation, given to us by people of different races when we manage to hear them, speak with them, or risk some comfort level in our own community because we name what we see. European Americans should not expect appreciation to be given to them by African Americans or take any actions in anticipation of gratitude. But a result of "standing with" is often graceful appreciation. Likewise, African Americans cannot expect appreciation to be given to them by whites, or take actions to listen or to educate European Americans in anticipation of white gratitude. But a result of meeting on the bridge is sometimes graceful appreciation.

Family therapist Virginia Satir suggested that in a healthy family, any one member can enjoy watching the interaction of any other dyad or triad (Satir, 1967, 58). The one watching does not have suspicion, but savors the relationship of the others. In a similar way, if there are healthy race relations, European Americans can watch African Americans talking after a meeting, grateful that blacks have one another with whom to talk. African American faculty can receive the minutes from a meeting attended only by whites with the expectation that someone has considered how the decisions made in that meeting will affect blacks. From hymns chosen in worship to food for seminary lunches, from resources consulted for theology or history to knowledge of geography around the whole globe, we aim, in the long haul, for great movement from basic toleration of difference to thoroughfares across bridges.

Our Pastoral Theological Analysis of Institutional Attempts to Deal with Diversity

As we two have worked together over the last decade, we have analyzed institutional dynamics that we have witnessed, primarily, but not exclusively, in the seminary in which we teach. We write with the humble awareness that there are multiple perspectives on any "reality." We are keenly aware that people looking at the same institutions may write a completely different analysis.

Permeable or Rigid Boundaries?

During the 1960s and 1970s, a respectable number of white Americans were beginning to see the need for more ethnic diversity in "their" institutions. Whites seldom claim that their institutions are "white," but the very struggle to be diverse shows how truly white owned they are. In the midsixties, civil rights laws provided access to drinking fountains, and in 1967 Thurgood Marshall was admitted to the Supreme Court. Inclusion became the impetus for what were called "affirmative action" policies in the seventies. Americans were aware that whites excluded people of other races, and we as a country decided that we should redress the history of exclusion with intentional acts of inclusion.

Now, at the end of the century, seminaries, businesses, churches, and political arenas evidence a noticeable number of cases of "access." A few African Americans have joined faculties, become governors, and been elected bishops of white denominations. In some few settings there are more than a "token" number of nonwhites in what had been — and still are — predominantly white institutions. Up to now the personal sacrifices for European Americans have been minor. Some European American females and males did not get jobs or were not admitted to colleges, and they concluded that they would have been, had there not been affirmative action or the general desire for diverse access. It seldom occurs to European Americans that their predecessors or contemporaries were hired — and still are — in some measure because of their ethnicity.

Most whites naively expect blacks to want to participate in "integrated" institutions. However, a growing number of blacks are increasingly aware of the weaknesses of many "integrated" institutions in comparison to the benefits they realize when they choose to work or to worship in a predominantly black institution. Some middle-class African Americans who once attended predominantly white colleges or churches, or worked in white institutions, are now sending their children to historically African American colleges, attending African American churches, and working in predominantly black settings. European Americans who consider that they have worked hard to get blacks into their institutions are now sometimes worried or confused when these "token" African Americans leave. It seems like a revolving door: whites "give" access to blacks to enter the institution; blacks do enter, then leave after a number of years; whites search for other blacks to enter. (Of course, whites come and go, but this is less visible.) Whites fret that it takes a good deal of energy to have diversity at their institutions. Some whites wonder why their newfound colleagues leave. Aren't they grateful? Many of these European Americans actually enjoy and realize the benefit of some African American presence; others probably wish Americans would simply stop dwelling on race and "get back to" hiring and promoting people in a so-called (and we believe impossible) color-blind fashion.

Homeostasis and Second Order Systems Change

The boundaries of many institutions that had rigidly kept all but "exceptional" African Americans out, either with formal or informal rules, have become more permeable. A few blacks are in many institutions. In family systems terms, there has been "first order change." Things look a little different. However, once first order change occurs, a variety of issues emerge that disclose resistance to systemic change. Homeostasis looms large, and "second order change" is frustrated.

Some European Americans seem to be claiming or reclaiming ownership of institutions. This ownership is not necessarily financial, but includes the making and enforcing of rules and the creating of definitions. The process of claiming ownership is not necessarily even consciously sought after. In other words, some whites may not be aware of what they are doing, or they may be "feigning naïveté." European Americans, especially males who are in charge, may worry that their way of running the institution may be altered whenever more than a couple of persons of color, or women, have achieved access. They fear that "things might change."

The changes European Americans resist the most are called, in systems theory, second order change. Instead of just having people who look different sit on certain committees, an example of first order change, second order change might call into question the need for those committees. First order change brings African Americans to teach pastoral care or New Testament, instead of European Americans to teach the same courses. Second order change might alter how pastoral care or the Bible is taught; it might rearrange the disciplines or the requirements—or the fact that there are disciplines and certain requirements. First order change tenures some blacks in positions held previously only by whites, using the exact tenure rules and procedures. Second order change might scrutinize the tenure requirements to see whether they are relevant and meaningful.

According to systems theory, when change really threatens to alter the current arrangement of relationships, there is a powerful force for maintaining the current homeostasis. Consequently, in the transitional stage we in the United States are currently living through, behavior seems to focus upon shoring up rules, procedures, and policies to be sure that homeostasis is maintained. When homogeneity was more the rule, unstated trust held colleagues together. With heterogeneity comes the need for meticulousness in the place of trust. If there is to be any second order change, those who have been accustomed to having power "over" try at least to guarantee that the change will occur with the "due process" that they themselves have established.

European Americans, who still are in the majority in these institutions, may face real internal struggles: they say they want diversity, and think they genuinely mean it; but even as they mouth the words of inclusion, they cling more tightly to *principles* that restrict creative solutions than to a *process* that could make way for that very diversity. This is not surprising, for every individual and family facing a crisis experiences this dilemma. People want a creative solution because they are in pain. But they are accustomed to—and rather like some things about—the status quo.

It has been helpful in our seminary setting when white males have remembered exceptions to their rules in the past, for example, hiring white males who were pre-Ph.D. or reevaluating old tenure rules and creating new ones when a specific person was up for tenure. This makes it clear that exceptions were acceptable when the parties were virtually all white males, and that exceptions are not just made when questions of race or gender diversity arise.

Twenty-five years ago women seminarians were told that they could not use a female theologian as their choice for a systematic theology exam because there were no female "systematic theologians."[6] Now there are female systematic theologians who qualify to be the subject of such exams. In fact, some of those theologians are deans of seminaries. Today prospective faculty in various disciplines who are African American are expected to know what European Americans find "essential" to their discipline. If the African American approaches the discipline in a manner defined as Afrocentric, the European Americans may need to know whether this potential colleague knows the white (male) academic heroes (or heroines) well enough to suit them. Even if the candidate is well versed in what potential white colleagues require, the white colleagues may be wary that the discipline itself may be transformed, taught more from an African American perspective.

As blacks increase in presence to three or four on a small faculty, there is collegiality for African Americans among themselves. They can breathe easily with one another, relax from whiteness for a while. But whites can react out of fear—of the unknown—and project "plotting" in the place of collegiality for no good reason. At that point bridge meeting is crucial so that projection can be corrected.

African Americans who were accustomed to working hard to achieve access now need to discover ways to speak as colleagues, nondefensively. Some European Americans expect this equality and wonder what makes it so hard for African Americans to feel accepted. Some whites pretend not to see the presence of deeper barriers to full inclusion, to which they still cling. Blacks need time to gather their voices, to experience inclusion, and to act included.

When individuals or families face crises in which there are both pain and the desire to move forward, they can consult a therapist or their pastor. From a family systems perspective, the counselor considers his or her main task to enable the individual or family to safely try on new behaviors or attitudes. The counselor does not blame the client for "resisting change," but takes responsibility for considering other ways to undo the stuckness.

Several questions that we ask ourselves and other pastoral theologians are:

Who serves in this "therapeutic" capacity for institutions? Does a president, dean, CEO, or trustee take responsibility to focus on the homeostatis of an institution? Do colleagues name this to and for one another? What responsibility do pastoral theologians, who teach this very analysis on the individual and family level to students, have with their colleagues? If we took this responsibility seriously, how could pastoral theologians be heard?

Whites have all too often asked blacks: "Tell us how to include you." While blacks in a system can intervene in the homeostasis by altering their part of the cycle, for a genuine new creation to be born, blacks and whites will probably have to make the intervention together.

Retrenchment, Entrenchment, or the Struggle for the Birth of a New Creation?

As one looks at the current situation of race matters in the United States, one wonders if retrenchment, entrenchment, or a struggle for the birth of a new creation is happening.

If one holds to the analysis that seminaries and other institutions are in the midst of backlash or retrenchment, then we see parallels to the Jim Crow era. The time for gains made after the freeing of the slaves was brief. New laws established boundaries that made engagement across race very difficult. One might view the current period as a time during which white institutions credit themselves for having attempted access. By shoring up policies, they will now try to ward off any further transformation. If access dwindles, so be it. Whites can content themselves with the assurance that they have tried to be diverse. Meanwhile, African American institutions may experience a new vitality as blacks do not spend their energies trying to transform white institutions, but redouble their efforts to maintain and strengthen their own institutions.

If, on the other hand, we were to see the current situation as entrenchment, then we would argue that there never has been much effort or intent for inclusion of African Americans in European American institutions. There have been some different faces at the same desks whites might have occupied. Period. Whether out of desire for diversity or merely to look politically correct, whites have made cosmetic changes, but have not been able to budge from their position of ownership and privilege. More important, they never wanted or expected to make real changes.[7] The decades of apparent inclusion were simply entrenchment within the status quo; immobility has become apparent only as expectations have expanded to transformation beyond access.

If European Americans who have power to name and define their institutions are not retrenching to past strongholds and are not entrenched in possessive patterns never intended to be relinquished, then there is at least one other alternative—the birth of a new creation is in process. Rollo May argued that authentic creativity takes so much courage because it is an active battle with the gods that is occurring, the gods of conformity (May 1975, 22). Institutions that would be genuinely diverse in the twenty-first century must have the courage to god-wrestle. Currently, it is as if we in institutions have our fingers stuck inside a Chinese finger puzzle. We can relax and get released from past stuckness, freed to see what will be born, or we can tighten up, remain tense, and stay stuck.

To be new creations, institutions need, we believe, *full* inclusion at the trustee and administrative level as well as in the faculty and student population. People would need to take time to meet on the bridges that reach to all racial groups. We might need to decide who will work as institutional therapists with the role of attending to our resistances in order to foster creative solutions.

Early in this century, African Americans were forbidden from entering many white institutions, and they built black institutions. In more recent years they have knocked their heads against white walls where doors had been, and some African Americans have returned to black institutions, while others remain to create new doors and windows in those white walls. Simultaneously it is up to the current generation of whites to stand on tiptoe and to stay on those toes, no matter how uncomfortable, because that stretching will remind them to be conscious and intentional for the long haul. Pastoral theologians could be those who stand with a foot in theology and a foot in psychology, delving into the wisdom provided by each discipline in order to pronounce the prophetic call to meet on the bridge of race.

Notes

[1] As a group, women have highly developed the characteristic of vulnerability. Jean Baker Miller helped women more than two decades ago to see that this characteristic is essential to healthy living; and it is a strength, not a weakness, as many women have been told (Miller, 1976, 27-47).

[2] "Faces of Faith" videos are produced by EcuFilm, of The United Methodist Church, 810 Twelfth Avenue South, Nashville, TN 37203.

[3] Our racism and antiracism definitions are congruent with those of the Women's Theological Center in Boston, Massachusetts. They were adapted from a presentation given by Robert Terry in a conference, "New White Consciousness: Prerequisite for Change in America," sponsored by the Detroit Industrial Mission and New Detroit, Inc. Speakers Bureau, May 19–23, 1971. See Robert W. Terry, *For Whites Only* (Grand Rapids, MI: Eerdmans, 1970).

[4] It is equally blind to say that no one in the church has suffered any domestic abuse when racism and domestic abuse are pervasive in our culture.

[5] Once, when Carolyn's son was in the fourth grade, he was tripped by another

boy while getting off the school bus. The next morning the principal, to both boys' surprise, brought the two of them to her office to face one another in her presence. She had them talk with one another. Carolyn's son was surprised with how vulnerable the other boy was; that is, he was not just the "tough bully" he appeared to her son to be. That was a marvelous example of conflict resolution, for the two boys were able to make amends in a safe setting. That would not have happened if they had not both been back to school the next day and encouraged to speak to one another directly. It was a situation that taught each boy that conflicts could be faced and resolved.

[6] This was the case for Carolyn and several of her classmates at the School of Theology in Claremont as they prepared for the qualifying exams for the Doctor of Religion degree in 1972. There was active debate at the time to change the policy.

[7] Several years ago our seminary held a campuswide staff and faculty retreat in order to foster discussion. The facilitator asked us to form small groups to consider the question: How is our seminary like yogurt? Marsha's immediate answer was, "It's old and it's white." When Marsha shared this answer with her small group, the other group members painstakingly and vehemently defended the seminary's diversity decisions, good intentions, and so forth. Marsha contended then, and still contends, that though fruits or nuts are added to the yogurt or to the institution, neither is ever fundamentally altered. Any new people of color can be added or subtracted (like the flavor of the month); but the fundamental character of the institution, like the yogurt, remains old and white.

11

Feminist Values from Seminary to Parish

Jeanne Stevenson-Moessner

Ordering textbooks for a course on feminist theology is serious work. With sensitivity to seminarians' budgets, I proceed with caution when I hand my list to the bookstore. One particular semester, I had Marie Fortune's *Is Nothing Sacred? When Sex Invades the Pastoral Relationship* on the required list (Fortune, 1989).[1] It was only in hardback at the time and more expensive than other books on the list. Furthermore, it documented only one congregation ravaged by its pastor. At the end of the semester, I had to ask myself whether this in-depth case of one institution would be of help to my students in their pastorates. Some years later, at a seminary reunion, a former member of that feminist theology class, Sarah, approached me. She told me of her first church in a southern state where she was associate pastor, and she told me of the neighboring Protestant church in the city. One morning, there was a knock on her kitchen door. The pastor's wife from the other Protestant church stood there. In agony, she blurted out: "My husband has been having affairs with members in the church. I didn't know whom to tell, but I knew you would believe me." Sarah did believe her and helped the pastor's wife take appropriate steps in this case of clergy sexual misconduct. What Sarah said to me at the reunion was this: "After reading *Is Nothing Sacred? When Sex Invades the Pastoral Relationship*, I knew what to do. I knew I was prepared for that moment."

Feminist pastoral theology is not divorced from the world beyond the classroom. Feminist literature often comes from academicians and professors, but it is not estranged from the praxis of the parish, where many pastors will translate what they have heard, seen, and experienced in their seminary experience.

Based on two in-depth interviews with Paula and Stephanie, who identified and developed as feminists while in seminary, and on the case of Episcopal priest Cameron as documented in *The Stained-Glass Ceiling: Churches and Their Women Pastors* (Purvis, 1995), this chapter focuses on a central issue: How do feminist values translate *beyond* the halls of learning into the parish?[2] How do feminist values fostered in seminary apply to life in a congregation? Feminist values as they were perceived by these three ministers will be identified. Then, using case study methodology, the women will illustrate how they have developed these values in their congregations. Paula translates her feminist values into a difficult, dysfunctional setting where previous ministers had involved themselves in child molestation and financial fraud. Paula attributes her three and a half "successful" years in a church recovering from abuse largely to the fact that she brought feminist values to the process of ministry. She was chosen for this study because she not only identified herself at seminary as a feminist, but also took risks to support those who were hurt by the system. Likewise, Stephanie was chosen because of her clear identification as a feminist in a seminary setting where a cost was involved to so identify. Both women are gifted in their ability to articulate and translate what they perceive as "feminist values" learned or relearned in the classroom. Although Stephanie's parish setting is less sensational and more typical of what faces seminary graduates, her adaptation of feminist values such as mutuality and selective vulnerability aptly illustrates applied feminist theology. Episcopal priest Cameron in an urban Atlanta church demonstrates how power can be exerted in a nonauthoritarian way. The stories of these three women can only be cause for hope among those reconstructing pastoral teaching and theology.

A feminist educational methodology values each individual and the learning that individual can impart, empowers the constituency whether students in the classroom or parishioners in a congregation, encourages the ability to listen as well as speak, and establishes a safe environment for assertiveness and truth telling. A feminist reconstruction of pastoral theology offers what seminary graduate Paula has termed a "rearranging of the furniture."

Rearranging the Furniture

Paula formulated many of her feminist values while attending a Protestant seminary. In a number of the faculty who labeled themselves feminist or profeminist, she saw inconsistencies between their theory and practice. For example, while dazzling students with their charisma at the lectern and intimidating listeners with publications and the power of their academic position, they taught liberation theology, a theology that elevates the undervalued and sides with the underprivileged. Finally, in Paula's third year of seminary, a visiting feminist professor empowered her. This professor of education literally and metaphorically rearranged the furniture through experiential and participatory learning in the classroom. She took the desks, previously in straight lines, and redid the seating arrangement; in circular groupings students could look in one another's faces and engage one another in participatory learning. As Paula stated: "We knew in the middle of the semester . . . we had been placed in her care . . . an incredible moment when you know something miraculous is happening. She had this way of dotering around and appearing to be doing nothing, yet she was doing so much." In addition, a profeminist professor of biblical studies taught Paula a "hermeneutic of suspicion" or caution in accepting traditional interpretations of the Bible and a trust in her own instincts in reading Scripture. These two professors, whom Paula considered the most valuable to her learning, were not in Paula's opinion valued by the institution. She inferred that she could not be that valuable to the institution either, for she identified with their methodologies. These methodologies included "hearing a person into speech" (Morton, 1985, 207)[3] and even hearing the silence before the speaking (Bons-Storm, 1996, 58-59).[4] Paula, like her two role models, was drawn to those marginalized by the systemic evil she witnessed at a seminary that overempowered professors and underempowered students.

After leaving seminary, Paula took a call to underempowered parishioners. She chose a difficult, dysfunctional church that "no man in his right mind" would have taken: a dying and troubled church, an abused congregation, a church victimized by "white, male ministers." Children in the church had been molested by a former male minister who was later imprisoned eighteen months for his criminal behavior. Although this molestation occurred twelve years prior to Paula's installation as minister, it was the central issue that defined the church. The minister preceding the child molester was described as a "manic-depressive" involved in financial fraud. The minister following the child molester was a sociopath who ended up in jail. Paula was attracted to this church because it was an abused and hurting church. She had learned at seminary to identify with those on the underside of power. After a year in her first pastorate, Paula chose to enter therapy to take care of herself and to monitor her energy as she continued to minister in this high-risk situation.

Three and a half years had passed in this church at the time I interviewed Paula. She considered her ministry "successful" largely because of her feminist methodology of redistributing the power that is inherent in any structure. "Women working in the church demonstrate these differences just as much as women in the corporation. They want power in order to share with others and get the job done by collaboration" (Becker, 1996, 53). In Paula's words, the church had been accustomed to "abusive daddies" whom passive parishioners always expected to fix things. Paula showed the congregation that they had given their power away to men who abused it. First, she seized the power, then spent the next years giving it back to them. She took control as an ecclesial authority with the clear intent of restoring it to the people. She rearranged the furniture metaphorically and empowered the people in her care. No longer did parishioners sit intimidated in their straight lines in church as they literally looked up to the lectern. She taught them never to give their power away again. She showed them how to take care of themselves. This she sees as a type of "feminist mothering." "I have stayed with them; I have never left them." Her feminist methodology manifested itself in the following ways: she showed them how to pay attention to their surroundings; she broke the silences surrounding a history of abuse; she listened and listened, especially to the hushed voices. She heard the silence before the speaking. From the pulpit, she spoke out about the twisted history, especially the child molestation that had so defined the church. She named the evils. She engaged in truth telling. She became the church's advocate at presbytery, the regional and denominational body of accountability; in this way, she exhibited truth in action. Later, members of her congregation followed her lead and, using the denominational book of polity, challenged the regional governing body on points of accountability. Paula modeled for them a hermeneutic of suspicion, not confined to biblical studies, but redefined for the institutional church.

Paula's feminist values continued to permeate her ecclesial methodology. She planned a "healing service" in which fourteen parishioners "carried the pain" of the congregation and stood in on behalf of other survivors. These fourteen told the stories of abuse and recorded them for the first time in the church's minutes. "We rewrote the story" to include the abuse, states Paula. They named it, ritualized it, redeemed it. Old pairs of shoes were dumped in a pile to represent the old part of the journey—now over. The journey was not over, but the part of their history that had defined who they were as "the abused" was finished. They began by forgiving themselves, then by asking for forgiveness of the community with the old symbol of the brush arbor. Plans to restore the old sanctuary were begun. The first congregational vote failed. After an anonymous gift of $30,000 was received, the second vote passed. Years after Paula was called to another church, an interim insulted a member of the congregation from the pulpit. The session and the whole congregation said no and fired him. A feminist approach to ministry is committed to empowerment. This may require "rearranging the furniture."

The values that Paula saw modeled at seminary and tried to translate into her parish setting included the following: networking; engagement with and not disengagement from the congregation; empowerment of the constituency; hearing the parishioners; truth telling without breaking confidentiality; creation of a safe space; assertiveness; reliance on internal authority; listening; nondichotomizing of the sacred and the profane (for example, the pulpit becomes a place to name earthly evil); feminist "mothering," which honors self-other connections and boundaries. Having watched her feminist professor literally rearrange the furniture of the classroom to create circular groupings where students could see one another and engage themselves, Paula carried this observation from the seminary classroom into the parish setting where laity began to engage and empower one another. She continued to rearrange the furniture literally and metaphorically in her church. This metaphor of rearrangement was illustrated in the following ways: laity empowerment through experiential and participatory learning, networking, naming the evils that destroy personal dignity, fostering mutuality in relationships, and cultivating relational boundaries that do not merge, disengage, or overpower persons.[5]

Two primary issues arise for feminist pastoral theology from this case study: the stabilization of power and the maintenance of this stabilization, and the preservation of healthy self-other boundaries. Regarding the first issue, how would the seminary class conducted by Paula's feminist role model have maintained its distribution of power, first, between facilitator and students and, second, among students without someone to monitor the distribution? What checks and balances would there have been in Paula's congregation as the laity became empowered, to prevent a future takeover by a segment of the congregation or even a forceful individual? The maintenance of the mutuality in relationships that is sought as a value in feminist theory should be a concern in the reconstruction of a feminist pastoral theology.

Second, as feminists advocate solidarity with the underpowered, theologize from the viewpoint of the violated and exploited, advocate for the silent and listen to the silence, and especially as feminists face evil and name abuse, what prevents them from being overwhelmed? It is one matter to network in a city the size of Chicago or Atlanta. It is an entirely different situation to be in a small rural town as Paula was. A commitment to preserve resilient self-other boundaries and to protect the giver of care should be a concern in the pastoral field as evil systems are confronted.

> The pastoral caregiver has a critical role to play, as one who will explore with persons and groups the precarious and promising intersection between their need for boundaries, order, safety, and control, *and* their need for freedom, playfulness, imagination, and sacred mystery. But where does the pastor as caregiver stand in relation to the center and the margin? (Billman, 1996, 15)

"And Now That I Am in the Trenches"

Stephanie's analogy for life in the parish was "being in the trenches" in an embattled world. "And now that I am in the trenches, so to speak, I do have to find ways to put limits and have some boundaries because there's not enough time in the day for everything." Stephanie entered seminary as a second-career student; law had been her first career. After graduating from a Protestant seminary, Stephanie awaited her first call for five months. She was hired as a solo pastor in a small church of 125 people. She was the second woman to ever pastor that church.

As a feminist coming into seminary, Stephanie always believed in the equality of women and in the importance of relational values. "When I got to seminary, I began to struggle with a God who had been portrayed for most of my life as pretty hierarchical, pretty much a Godhead with all power, and a God who is 'Father.' And I had always struggled with that. . . . But I can now name a Trinity that, instead of being hierarchical with the Father and the Son and the Holy Ghost being underneath, . . . is very relational and integral and almost encircled and interrelated with each other, not just with each other but in the world."

Stephanie mentioned throughout the interview several feminist writers who had influenced her through their publications, two professors, and a support group on campus made up of feminists. One class in Christian education challenged her analytical and left-brain approach to learning and introduced her to art, music, and sensory experiences that altered the way she now conducts worship. Her image of God continued to shift away from an all-powerful, omnipotent Sovereign to a God in covenant relationship, a God changed by humankind as much as the reverse.

Stephanie was challenged to translate a nonhierarchical style of relationship into the parish. "It means that sometimes my boundaries aren't as sharp as sometimes the books say they should be. [I am] much more relational in the way I do ministry. In my teaching style, I never give lectures. . . . I think it affects my preaching, because I tend to do more narrative storytelling, reflective preaching rather than telling [people what to believe]. I don't see myself as the seer of truth that I then interpret to [the congregation]. Basically, I see us as struggling and working on truth together, working on what the Scripture is saying to us at this time. I think the biggest place it comes out is pastoral care. . . . I'm there at the hospital with people, sometimes holding them as they cry, trying to be a part of God's presence there with us in the room . . . not feeling any need to fix or change their life or give them a solution, but rather just to be there with them. And I share a lot of who I am with people. I try and be vulnerable. . . . People share with me things that I'm not sure they would share otherwise. And I think it's that sort of openness, a willingness to be in relationship with them that's two-way: not just me giving to them, but them giving back to me. It is a covenant relationship rather than me just being their minister who gives them the Word or their prayer."

With Stephanie's style of ministry, there emerged more of a mutuality in relationships than in a traditional model of ministry where there is often power exercised *over* people. With Stephanie, there was less of a boundary between pastor and parishioner. "As that boundary becomes less clear, one of the challenges is making sure that you're being appropriate, and not projecting. . . . When you make your boundary real clear, it's easier. And so one of the things that I am always struggling with is how that boundary looks. How do I stay healthy myself? How do I nurture myself? The line between being someone's friend and being someone's pastor can be really . . . a narrow line. And I'm always trying to remain somewhere in the middle, to be in relationship with [people] as their pastor, not as their best buddy."

One of the most common images of God among feminists is God as Friend, which reinforces the dilemma of boundaries as Stephanie described them. How "friend is defined" can also be a way out of the dilemma. Stephanie: "Sometimes we define friend as this sort of buddy, and it may not necessarily be a healthy relationship. Part of the role as pastor is to try to maintain relationship in a healthy way, but not encourage codependency. . . . At least I have experienced that that's sometimes easy to fall into. . . . Relationship is of such a higher priority than the boundary. If you're going to choose between them, the relationship ends up being the more important factor. One of the dilemmas that also comes in, not necessarily so much in pastoral care as in the worship setting, is the image of priest over against [versus] pastor. Some people need to hear you as their priest. This feels somewhat hierarchical, and I struggle with, for example, the assurance of pardon. Do you say 'our sins' or 'your sins'? Some people need the 'your.'"

Stephanie then talked about the role her feminism played in the hiring process. Her theological position on inclusiveness specifically impacted her favorable position on the ordination of gays and lesbians. Two churches in particular did not hire her on the basis of this issue. Stephanie related her openness and honesty in the interview process to her feminism. When she interviewed for an associate position, she ruled out heads of staff who expected someone nonassertive and self-effacing. One of the significant questions that would come up was about baptism. She asked them, "If I, as an associate, was in a relationship with a family, and they asked me to baptize their child, would this be acceptable to you as senior pastor?" If the heads of staff said no, Stephanie ruled them out as not offering the kind of team model she needed. She went on to comment on the importance of teamwork and networking: "One of the powers that I learned in law school and continued throughout my career has been the power of networking. . . . I may be disadvantaged in the world by my strong beliefs and my willingness to speak out on them, but in some ways, because I work hard to network, there's a real powerful group of women who support me. And because we've sought each other out and are willing to network, in some ways we're stronger than people who are reacting out of anger."

Stephanie remarked that she could have used help in seminary in finding ways to be effective with anger. As a feminist, she had hoped to learn more ways to use her anger rather than to let anger use her. "I think seminaries really need to help all people, not just women — or feminists — but all people to be more effective and not to let that anger be running them."

Seminary could have also trained her more in conflict management and feminist process. "We talk about process in grieving, but do we talk about the process of what happens when you are engaging in new ideas or in new concepts and then get in conflict?"

Stephanie also remarked that she could have learned more in seminary about models for implementing inclusive language and more participatory models in education. She had hoped for more help with boundary issues consistent with her feminist theology. She dismissed the hierarchical model, but is still having difficulty applying the egalitarian, relational, inclusive model of feminism to her parish ministry. "And now that I am in the trenches, so to speak, I do have to find ways to put limits and have some boundaries because there's not enough time in the day for everything. One of the things that I'm finding is that I get a lot of pastoral calls from people who aren't in my church."

Stephanie cited selective vulnerability as a feminist value and illustrated this approach to ministry with an example from her days in law practice. She cared for a friend dying of cancer and ran her law practice out of her friend's home. She confided this to some male colleagues who told her she would not be able to handle her practice as usual. They even hinted, given her "weakened condition" in the role of caretaker, that they might take advantage of the situation.

Stephanie said, "Well, you're right. You could do that, but I'm going to trust that you're not going to do that. And if I'm honest with you and you know why I'm doing this, you'll be more respectful." Within a year, she had eight calls from different male attorneys who called to tell her different things. "I never had a problem that summer. Later on that year they called, too. I remember one attorney in particular, whom I did not know well. He said: 'Stephanie, I just wanted to let you know my father died, and you're the only person I could think of that I could call and tell. I knew you would understand and wouldn't take advantage of the fact that I am really sad right now.' " Selective vulnerability involves conscious choice and wisdom on the part of the one holding the power to reveal.

The feminist values that emerge from Stephanie's interview that impact her pastoral methodology, as illustrated through her comments, are as follows: networking; mutuality and *selective* vulnerability; participatory learning; inclusiveness; truth understood subjectively; team-type model of ministry versus "head of staff"; honoring anger; finding and asserting the voice; conflict in community; maintaining boundaries; interrelationship modeled on trinitarian separateness and unity; collegiality versus competition. Stephanie's pastoral methodology embraces images of God that are applicable to this methodology, and a trinitarian formulation that honors boundaries, interrelationship, inclusivity, and vulnerability.

From the Viewpoint of Pew and Pulpit

In this chapter, the reconstruction of pastoral theology from a feminist perspective has been viewed largely from the pew and pulpit and from the pastor's or priest's office. Pastoral theology is applied theology. Thus far, from two Protestant pastors we have heard two narratives of feminist methodologies as their values within the parish context have been underscored. The pastoral is personal, yet in a collective context.

In supplement to the two interviews already offered in this chapter, Sally B. Purvis in *The Stained-Glass Ceiling: Churches and Their Women Pastors* offers a detailed case study of an Episcopal priest (Purvis, 1995). This ecclesiastical distinction is significant. "What we found was that a female priest is a somewhat different creature than a female pastor due to the differences in the theologies of ordination and the understandings and enactments the two traditions have of priestly or pastoral authority" (Purvis, 1995, 100). In her Episcopalian parish, the priest Cameron took control, yet exerted power in a nonauthoritarian way. She literally rearranged the furniture in the traditional worship space so that she as priest did not have to celebrate the Eucharist with her back to the congregation. The congregation was deeply involved in the renovation. The parental image of priesthood cast Cameron at times into the role of protective mother. One example occurred when the organist John was diagnosed with AIDS. Cameron was concerned to protect John not from viciousness but from oversolicitousness by well-intentioned parishioners. She then assumed the role of protective mother. As Cameron worked within a traditional hierarchy in the roles of both priestess and mother, Purvis adds to the discussion of feminist methodology and hierarchy by suggesting a "complex and comfortable juxtaposition of hierarchical and egalitarian authority structures" (Purvis, 1995, 48). Purvis maintains that not all hierarchies are oppressive, and in Cameron's church, "hierarchy functions very nicely alongside deep and pervasive egalitarian power and authority. The alliance is fragile, of course, and depends in part upon Cameron's desire to share power and authority with her congregation. If there were a more authoritarian leader, or even a more ineffectual one, the egalitarian nature of congregational life might recede" (Purvis, 1995, 45).

Even as the particular situation influences the theory as demonstrated by the cases in this chapter, the history and context of feminism and womanism developed throughout other chapters in this book also frame our wider discussion of pastoral feminist methodology. As feminists and womanists work to reconstruct pastoral method and pastoral teaching, we listen carefully to those "in the trenches" where the methodology is being utilized for survival. This is a circular methodology in which praxis and theory mutually empower each other. As pastoral theology is being reconstructed, the Paulas, Stephanies, and Camerons are critical players and colleagues in that reconstruction. We who are rewriting pastoral theology are under their influence as feminist values go from classrooms to parish, from parish to our classrooms.

Notes

[1] See Marie Fortune, *Is Nothing Sacred? When Sex Invades the Pastoral Relationship* (San Francisco: Harper & Row, 1989), which is a detailed case study of an average church with a stereotypical sexual offender. In the early 1980s, six women came forward with allegations. Evidence showed that many more women over a four-year period had been abused, raped, exploited, and harassed by the handsome, winsome pastor.

[2] These two interviews with pastors were first presented at the American Academy of Religion, Southeast region, in the Women and Religion section, "Womanist and Feminist Values in and Beyond the Halls of Learning," March 11, 1995.

[3] It was in working with severely retarded children, most of them with Down syndrome, that Nelle Morton described attentive listening. "Finally I think I learned to hear them to their own expressions of themselves" (207). This *attentive listening* she later applied to feminist theology.

[4] Riet Bons-Storm, Dutch theologian, mentioned this concept to me in personal

conversation in Atlanta, Georgia, in 1995. It goes one step farther back than Morton's "hearing into speech." It is hearing the silence before the speaking, especially with those who are not yet able to articulate their narrative. See also Riet Bons-Storm's *The Incredible Woman: Listening to Women's Silences in Pastoral Care and Counseling* (Nashville: Abingdon Press, 1996), 58-59. Bons-Storm describes an experienced event that "cannot be put into a self-narrative considered appropriate by the dominant belief system" as an *unstory*. These unstories cannot be told, and they stay "unworded" unless someone who understands and accepts these "unwordable experiences" can be found.

[5]See Carrie Doehring's extensive discussion on power dynamics and relational boundaries in *Taking Care: Monitoring Power Dynamics and Relational Boundaries in Pastoral Care and Counseling* (Nashville: Abingdon Press, 1995), 46. "Without a radical repentance, wherein eyes are opened to the extent of destruction caused by merged, disengaged, and overpowering dynamics, there will be no new life and no end of destruction."

Bibliography

Abbot, W. M. (Ed.). (1996). *The documents of Vatican II.* New York: Herder and Herder. Document cited: "Lumen Gentium, Dogmatic Constitution of the Church."

Ackermann, D. M., & Bons-Storm, R. (Eds.). (1998). *Liberating faith practices: Feminist practical theologies in context.* Leuven: Peeters.

Adams, C. J. (1994). *Woman-battering.* Minneapolis: Fortress Press.

Adams, C. J., & Fortune, M. M. (Eds.). (1995). *Violence against women and children: A Christian theological sourcebook.* New York: Continuum.

Alter, M. G. (1994). *Resurrection psychology: An understanding of human personality based on the life and teaching of Jesus.* Chicago: Loyola.

American Association of Pastoral Counselors. *AAPC: Membership Committee operational manual.* (1987). Fairfax, VA: AAPC.

Anderson, V. (1995). *Beyond ontological blackness: An essay on African American religious and cultural criticism.* New York: Continuum.

Apter, M. (1991). Danger and the protective frame. In J. H. Kerr & M. J. Apter (Eds.), *Adult play: A reversal theory approach.* Amsterdam, Berwyn, PA: Swets & Zeitlinger.

Arber, S., & Ginn, J. (1991). *Gender and later life: A sociological analysis of resources and constraints.* Newbury Park, CA: Sage Publications.

Armistead, M. K. (1995). *God-Images in the healing process.* Minneapolis: Fortress Press.

Bailey, R. C., & Grant, J. (Eds.). (1995). *The recovery of black presence: An interdisciplinary exploration.* Nashville: Abingdon Press.

Barbour, C. M., Billman, K., DesJarlait, P., & Dodge, E. (1994). Ministry on the boundaries: Cooperation without exploitation. In S. B. Thistlethwaite & G. F. Cairns (Eds.), *Beyond theological tourism: Mentoring as a grassroots approach to theological education.* Maryknoll, NY: Orbis Books.

Barnhouse, R. T., & Holmes, U. T. (Eds.). (1976). *Male and female: Christian approaches to sexuality.* New York: Seabury.

Bausch, W. J. (1984). *Storytelling: Imagination and faith.* Mystic, CT: Twenty-Third.

Becker, C. E. (1996). *Leading women: How church women can avoid leadership traps and negotiate the gender maze.* Nashville: Abingdon Press.

Belenky, M. F., Blythe, C., Goldberger, M., Tartule, N. R., & Mattuck, J. (1987). *Women's ways of knowing: The development of self, voice and mind.* New York: Basic Books.

Benjamin, J. (1988). *The bond of love: Psychoanalysis, feminism, and the problem of domination.* New York: Pantheon Books.

Billman, K. D. (1991). The paradox of sin and the bipolarity of shame. *Koinonia, 3.*

Bibliography

Billman, K. D. (1992). Integrating theology and pastoral care in ministry. *Currents in Theology and Mission, 19* (3).

Billman, K. D. (1993). Holy darkness, kindly light: Ancient gifts for ministry. *Currents in Theology and Mission, 20* (5).

Billman, K. D. (1996). Pastoral care as an art of community. In C. Neuger, (Ed.), *The arts of ministry: feminist-womanist approaches.* Louisville: Westminster John Knox Press.

Boff, L. (1987). *The maternal face of God: The feminine and its religious expressions* (R. R. Barr & J. W. Diercksmeier, Trans.). San Francisco: Harper & Row.

Bohler, C. S. (1977/1996). *Opening to God: Guided imagery meditation on scripture for individuals and groups* (Rev. and Expanded ed.). Nashville: The Upper Room.

Bohler, C. S. (1990a). Ministry as a helping profession: caring and system-transformation. *Journal of Theology, 94.*

Bohler, C. S. (1990b). *Prayer on wings: A search for authentic prayer.* San Diego, CA: Lura Media.

Bohler, C. S. (1990c). *When you need to take a stand.* Louisville: Westminster/John Knox Press.

Bohler, C. S. (1991). Sexuality and pastoral care. In H. W. Stone & W. M. Clements (Eds.), *Handbook for basic types of pastoral care and counseling.* Nashville: Abingdon Press.

Bohler, C. S. (1993). Essential elements of family systems approaches to pastoral counseling. In R. J. Wicks, R. D. Parsons, & D. Capps (Eds.), *Clinical handbook of pastoral counseling: Vol. 1* (Expanded ed.). New York: Paulist, Integration.

Bohler, C. S. (1994). Subjectively speaking. *Journal of Pastoral Theology, 4.*

Bohler, C. S. (1996, January). Where there was split and violence, let there be healing between sexuality and spirituality: A theological, pastoral perspective. In G. M. Cordner (Ed.), *Pastoral theology's and pastoral psychology's contributions to helping heal a violent world.* Sukarta, Indonesia: International Pastoral Care Network for Social Responsibility and DABARA Publishers (1996).

Bohler, C. S. (1996b). *God is like a mother hen, and much, much more.* Louisville: Presbyterian Publishing.

Bohler, C. S. (1997). God is like a jazz band leader: Location of divine and human power and responsibility—A call to pastoral theologians. *Journal of Pastoral Theology, 7.*

Bohn, C. R. (Ed.). (1995). *Therapeutic practice in a cross-cultural world: Theological, psychological, and ethical issues.* Decatur, GA: Journal of Pastoral Care Publications.

Boisen, A. (1936/1971). *The exploration of the inner world: A study of mental disorder and religious experience.* Chicago: Willett, Clark.

Bondi, R. (1995). *Memories of God: Theological reflections on a life.* Nashville: Abingdon Press.

Bons-Storm, R. (1991). The African American church as a healing community: Theological and psychological dimensions of pastoral care. *Journal of Theology, 95.*

Bons-Storm, R. (1996a). *The incredible woman: Listening to women's silences in pastoral care and counseling.* Nashville: Abingdon Press.

Bons-Storm, R. (1996b). Pastoral care. In L. M. Russell & S. Clarkson (Eds.), *Dictionary of feminist theologies.* Louisville: Westminster John Knox Press.

Bordo, S. (1988). Anorexia Nervosa: Psychopathology as the crystallization of culture. In I. Diamond & L. Quinby (Eds.), *Feminism and Foucault: Reflections on resistance.* Boston: Northeastern University Press.

Bordo, S. (1989). The body and reproduction of feminity: A feminist appropriation of Foucault. In A. M. Jagger & S. R. Bordo (Eds.), *Gender/body/knowledge: Feminist reconstruction of being and knowing.* New Brunswick: Rutgers University Press.

Bordo, S. (1993). *Feminism, Western culture, and the body.* Berkeley: University of California Press.

Bordo, S., and Jaggar, A. M. (Eds.). (1989). *Gender/body/knowledge: Feminist reconstructions of being and knowing.* New Brunswick: Rutgers University Press.

Boyd, M. F. (1991a). The African American church as a healing community: Theological and psychological dimensions of pastoral care. *Journal of Theology, 95.*

Boyd, M. F. (1991b). Theological implications of womanistcare. In L. H. Hollies (Ed.), *WomanistCare: How to tend the souls of women: Vol. 1.* Joliet, IL: Woman to Woman Ministries.

Boyd, M. F. (1997). WomanistCare: Some reflections on the pastoral care and the transformation of African American women. In E. M. Townes (Ed.), *Embracing the spirit: Womanist perspectives on hope, salvation, and transformation.* Maryknoll, NY: Orbis Books.

Boyd-Franklin, N. (1989). *Black families in therapy: A multisystem approach.* New York: Guiford Press.

Brenneis, R. L., Harbaugh, G. L., & Hutton, R. R. (1998). *Covenants and care: Boundaries in life, faith and ministry.* Louisville: Westminster John Knox Press.

Bringle, M. L. (1990). *Despair—Sickness or sin?: Hopelessness and healing in the Christian life.* Nashville: Abingdon Press.

Brock, R. N. (1988). *Journeys by heart: A Christology of erotic power.* New York: Crossroad.

Brock, R. N. (1995). Introduction. In R. N. Brock, C. Camp, & S. Jones (Eds.), *Setting the table: Women in theological conversation.* St Louis: Chalice Press.

Brown, F. B. (1989). *Religious aesthetics.* Princeton: Princeton University Press.

Brown, J. C., & Bohn, C. R. (Eds.). (1989). *Christianity, patriarchy, and abuse: A feminist critique.* New York: Pilgrim Press.

Bibliography

Brown, L. M., & Gilligan, C. (1992). *Meeting at the crossroads: Women's psychology and girl's development.* Cambridge: Harvard University Press.

Brown, S. R. (1982). Clergy divorce and remarriage. *Pastoral Psychology, 30.*

Browning, D. S. (1983). *Religious ethics and pastoral care.* Philadelphia: Fortress Press.

Browning, D. S. (1991). *A fundamental practical theology: Descriptive and strategic proposals.* Minneapolis: Fortress Press.

Browning, D. S. (1987). *Religious thought and the modern psychologies: A critical conversation in the theology of culture.* Philadelphia: Fortress Press.

Browning, D., Miller-McLemore, B., Couture, P., Lyon, B., & Franklin, F. (1997). *From culture wars to common ground: Religion and the American family debate.* Louisville: Westminster John Knox Press.

Bryant, C. (1995). Pastoral care and counseling in a cross-cultural context: The issue of authority. *Journal of Pastoral Care, 49* (3).

Bullis, R. K., & Mazur, C. S. (1993). *Legal issues and religious counseling.* Louisville: Westminster/John Knox Press.

Burbridge, L. C. (1993). Toward economic self-sufficiency: Independence without poverty. In B. J. Tidwell (Ed.), *The state of black America.* New York: National Urban League.

Burck, J. R., & Hunter, R. (1990). Pastoral theology, Protestant. In R. Hunter (Ed.), *Dictionary of pastoral care and counseling.* Nashville: Abingdon Press.

Butler, S. You shall betray me with a kiss. Public address delivered on October 5, 1989, at Boston University.

Cady, L. E. (1997). Identity, feminist theory, and theology. In R. Chopp & S. G. Devaney (Eds.), *Horizons in feminist theology: Identity, tradition, and norms.* Minneapolis: Fortress Press.

Cannon, K. G. (1995). *Katie's cannon.* New York: Continuum.

Cannon, K. G. (1998). *Black womanist ethics.* Atlanta: Scholars Press.

Capps, D. (1983). *Life cycle theory and pastoral care.* Philadelphia: Fortress Press.

Capps, D. (1984). *Pastoral care and hermeneutics.* Philadelphia: Fortress Press.

Capps, D. (1990). *Reframing: A new method in pastoral care.* Minneapolis: Fortress Press.

Capps, D. (1993). *The poet's gift: Toward the renewal of pastoral care.* Louisville: Westminster/John Knox Press.

Cardwell, S. W. (1967). MMPI as a predictor of success among seminary students. *Ministry Studies, 1.*

Cardwell, S. W. (1974). Theological school inventory: After ten years. *Journal of Pastoral Care, 28* (4).

Cardwell, S. W. (1982). Why women fail/succeed in ministry: Psychological factors. *Pastoral Psychology, 30* (4).

Cardwell, S. W. (1996). A struggle to achieve intellectual and affective congruence. *Journal of Supervision and Training in Ministry, 17.*

Cardwell, S. W. (1996). Seminary norms for the MMPI-2. *Journal of Pastoral Care, 50* (1).

Cardwell, S. W., & Hunt, R. A. (1979). Persistence in seminary and in ministry. *Pastoral Psychology, 28* (2).

Carr, Anne E. (1993). The new vision of feminist theology. In Catherine Mowry LaCugna (Ed.), *Freeing theology: The essentials of theology in feminist perspective.* San Francisco: Harper.

Cheston, S. E. (1993). Counseling adult survivors of childhood sexual abuse. In R. J. Wicks & R. D. Parsons (Eds.), *Clinical Handbook of Pastoral Counseling: Vol. 2.* New York: Paulist, Integration.

Cheston, S. E. (1994). *As you and the abused person journey together.* New York: Paulist.

Childs, B. (1990). *Short-term pastoral counseling: A guide.* Nashville: Abingdon Press.

Chodorow, N. (1974). Family structure and feminine personality. In M. Z. Rosaldo & L. Lamphere (Eds.), *Women, culture, and society.* Stanford, CA: Stanford University Press.

Chodorow, N. (1978). *The reproduction of mothering.* Berkeley: University of California University Press.

Chopp, R. S. (1989). *The power to speak: Feminism, language, and God.* New York: Crossroad.

Chopp, R. S. (1995). *Saving work: Feminist practices of theological education.* Louisville: Westminster/John Knox Press.

Clarke, R. L. (1986). *Pastoral care of battered women.* Philadelphia: Westminster.

Clebsch, W. A., & C. R. Jaekle (1983). *Pastoral care in historical perspective.* Englewood Cliffs, NJ: Prentice Hall.

Clift, J. D. (1988). Theory and practice of clinical supervision in pastoral counseling. *Journal of Supervision and Training in Ministry, 10.*

Clift, J. D. (1992). *Core images of the self: A symbolic approach to healing and wholeness.* New York: Crossroad.

Clift, J. D., & Clift, W. B. (1984). *Symbols of transformation in dreams.* New York: Crossroad.

Clinebell, H. (1984). *Basic types of pastoral care and counseling: Resources for the ministry of healing and growth.* Nashville: Abingdon Press.

Collins, P. H. (1991). *Black feminist thought: Knowledge, consciousness and the politics of empowerment.* New York: Routledge.

Cone, J. H. (1969). *Black theology and black power.* New York: Seabury Press.

Cone, J. H. (1972). *The spirituals and the blues: An interpretation.* New York: Seabury Press.

Cone, J. H. (1975). *God of the oppressed.* San Francisco: Harper & Row.

Cone, J. H. (1982). *My soul looks back.* Nashville: Abingdon Press.

Cone, J. H. (1984). *For my people: Black theology and the black church.* Maryknoll, NY: Orbis Books.

Bibliography

Cone, J. H. (1986). *A black theology of liberation* (2nd ed.). Maryknoll, NY: Orbis Books.

Cone, J. H., & Wilmore, G. S. (Eds.). (1993). *Black theology: A documentary history, 1966-1979.* (2nd and Rev. ed.). Maryknoll, NY: Orbis Books.

Congregation for the Doctrine of Faith (1990). (1990, July 5) Instruction on the ecclesial vocation of the theologian. *Origins 20,* (8).

Congregation for the Doctrine of Faith (1995). (1995, November 30) Response to the dubium of ordaining women to the ministerial priesthood. *Origins 25,* (24).

Congregation for the Doctrine of Faith (1996). (1997, February 3). Declaration on the question of the admission of women to the ministerial priesthood. *Origins 6,* (33).

Conn, J. W. (Ed.). (1986). *Women's spirituality.* New York: Paulist.

Cooper-White, P. (1991, February 20). Soul-stealing: Power relations in pastoral sexual abuse. *Christian Century, 108* (6).

Cooper-White, P. (1995). *The cry of Tamar: Violence against women and the church's response.* Minneapolis: Fortress Press.

Cooper-White, P., Coffey, M., Baltz, J., Sollom-Brotherton, J., Steele, M., Thornton, I., & Ulmer, N. (1994). Desperately seeking Sophia's shadow. *Journal of Pastoral Care, 48* (3).

Couture, P. D. (1990). If in a safe land you fall down: Why evaluations create so much turmoil and what supervisors can do about it. *Journal of Supervision and Training in Ministry,* (12).

Couture, P. D. (1991). *Blessed are the poor?: Women's poverty, family policy, and practical theology.* Nashville: Abingdon Press.

Couture, P. D. (1992). The context of congregations: Pastoral care in an individualistic society. *Journal of Pastoral Theology,* (2).

Couture, P. D. (1995a). Introduction. In P. D. Couture & R. J. Hunter (Eds.), *Pastoral care and social conflict.* Nashville: Abingdon Press.

Couture, P. D. (1995b). Partners in healing: Bridging pastoral care and public health through practical and pastoral theology. *Journal of Pastoral Theology,* (5).

Couture, P. D. (1995c). Single parents and poverty: A challenge to pastoral theological method. In P. D. Couture & R. J. Hunter (Eds.), *Pastoral care and social conflict.* Nashville: Abingdon Press.

Couture, P. D. (1996). Weaving the web: Pastoral care in an individualistic society. In J. Stevenson-Moessner (Ed.), *Through the eyes of women: Insights for pastoral care.* Philadelphia: Westminster John Knox Press.

Couture, P. D., & Hester, R. (1995). The future of pastoral care and counseling and the God of the market. In P. D. Couture and R. J. Hunter (Eds.), *Pastoral care and social conflict.* Nashville: Abingdon Press.

Couture, P. D., & Hunter, R. J. (Eds.). (1995). *Pastoral care and social conflict.* Nashville: Abingdon Press.

Daly, Mary. (1973). *Beyond God the Father: Toward a philosophy of women's liberation.* Boston: Beacon Press.

Daniels, D. B. (1991). Wholeness for caregivers. In L. H. Hollies (Ed.), *WomanistCare: How to tend the souls of women: Vol. 1.* Joliet, IL: Woman to Woman Ministries.

Dasher, J. E. (1996). Manna in the desert: Eating disorders and pastoral care. In J. Stevenson-Moessner (Ed.), *Through the eyes of women: Insights for pastoral care.* Minneapolis: Fortress Press.

Davis, A. (1981). *Women, race, and class.* New York: Random.

Davis, P. H. (1993). Women and the burden of empathy. *Journal of Pastoral Theology,* (3).

Davis, P. H. (1996). *Counseling adolescent girls.* Minneapolis: Fortress Press.

Dean, M. J. Paradox and promise: A theological and psychological view of humankind. *Journal of Pastoral Care, 39* (2).

Dean, M.J., & Cullen, M. L. (1991). Woman's body: Spiritual needs and theological presence. In M. Glaz & J. Stevenson-Moessner (Eds.), *Women in travail and transition: A new pastoral care.* Minneapolis: Fortress Press.

DeHart, J. S., & Kerber, L. (1995). *Women's America.* New York: Oxford.

Delaplain, L. (1997). *Cutting a New Path: Helping Survivors of Childhood Domestic Trauma.* Cleveland, OH: United Church.

DeMarinis, V. M. (1982). A theological investigation of interactions between death, dying, and caring: Research with hospice care-givers. *Harvard Theological Review, 75.*

DeMarinis, V. M. (1990). Movement as mediator of meaning. In D. Adams & D. Apostolos-Cappadona (Eds.), *Dance as religious studies.* New York: Crossroad.

DeMarinis, V. M. (1993). *Critical caring: A feminist model for pastoral psychology.* Louisville: Westminster/John Knox Press.

DeMarinis, V. M., & Grzymala-Moszczynska, H. (1995). The nature and role of religion and religious experience in psychological cross-cultural adjustment. *Social Compass, 42.*

Denham, P. L. (1982). Toward an understanding of child rape. *Journal of Pastoral Care, 36* (4).

Devor, N. G. (1994). Pastoral care for infertile couples. *Journal of Pastoral Care, 48* (4).

Doehring, C. (1992). Developing models of feminist pastoral counseling. *Journal of Pastoral Care, 46* (1).

Doehring, C. (1993). *Internal desecration: Traumatization and representations of God.* Lanham, MD: University Press of America.

Doehring, C. (1993). The absent God: When neglect follows sexual violence. *Journal of Pastoral Care, 47* (1).

Doehring, C. (1994). Life-giving sexual and spiritual desire. *Journal of Pastoral Theology, 4.*

Bibliography

Doehring, C. (1995). *Taking care: Monitoring power dynamics and relational bound-aries in pastoral care and counseling.* Nashville: Abingdon Press.

Doely, S. B. (Ed.). (1970). *Women's liberation and the church: The new demand for free-dom in the life of the Christian church.* New York: Association.

Dunlap, S. J. (1997). *Counseling depressed women.* Louisville: Westminster John Knox Press.

Dykstra, C., & Parks, S. D. (Eds.). (1986). *Faith development and Fowler.* Birmingham, AL: Religious Education.

Eagleton, T. (1983). *Literary theory: An introduction.* Minneapolis: University of Minnesota Press.

Ellen, C. (1990). Sexism. In R. J. Hunter (Ed.), *Dictionary of pastoral care and counseling.* Nashville: Abingdon Press.

Estadt, B. K., Compton, J. R., & Blanchette, M. C. (Eds.). (1987). *The art of clinical supervision: A pastoral counseling perspective.* New York: Paulist, Integration.

Estock, B. A. (1996). Hysterectomy and woman's identity. In J. Stevenson-Moessner (Ed.), *Through the eyes of women: Insights for pastoral care.* Minneapolis: Fortress Press.

Eugene, T. M. (1989). Sometimes I feel like a motherless child: The call and response for a liberational ethic of care by black feminists. In M. M. Brabeck (Ed.), *Who cares?: Theory, research, and educational implications of the ethic of care.* New York: Praeger.

Eugene, T. M. (1992). To be of use: Teaching womanist theology. *Journal of Feminist Studies in Religion, 8.*

Eugene, T. M. (1993a). Globalization and social ethics: Claiming the world in my eye. *Theological Education, 30* (1).

Eugene, T. M. (1993b). Liberation: Gender, race, and class. In A. F. Evans, R. A. Evans, & D. A. Roozen (Eds.), *The globalization of theological education.* Maryknoll, NY: Orbis Books.

Eugene, T. M. (1993c). Moral values and black womanists. In J. H. Cone & G. S. Wilmore (Eds.), *Black theology: A documentary history: 1980-1992: Vol. 2.* Maryknoll, NY: Orbis Books.

Eugene, T. M. (1993d, summer). Two heads are better than one: Feminist and womanist ethics in tandem. *Daughters of Sarah, 19* (10).

Eugene, T. M. (1994a). Multicultural ministry: Theory, practice, theology. *Chicago Theological Seminary Register, 84.*

Eugene, T. M. (1994b). While love is unfashionable: Ethical implications of black spirituality and sexuality. In J. B. Nelson & S. P. Longfellow (Eds.), *Sexuality and the sacred: Sources for theological reflection.* Louisville: Westminster/John Knox Press.

Eugene, T. M. (1995a). Swing low, sweet chariot!: A womanist response to sexual violence and abuse." In C. J. Adams & M. M. Fortune (Eds.), *Violence against women and children: A Christian theological sourcebook.* New York: Continuum.

Eugene, T. M. (1995b). There is a balm in Gilead: Black women and the black church as agents of a therapeutic community. In J. Ochshorn & E. Cole (Eds.), *Women's spirituality, women's lives.* New York: Haworth.

Eugene, T. M. (1996). In this here place, we flesh: womanist ruminations on embodied experience and expressions. *Daughters of Sarah, 22.*

Eugene, T. M. (1997). How can we forget?: An ethic of care for AIDS, the African American family, and the black Catholic church. In E. M. Townes (Ed.), *Embracing the spirit: Womanist perspectives on hope, salvation, and transformation.* Maryknoll, NY: Orbis Books.

Fackre, G. (1992). Sound doctrine in the church. The Second Annual Theodore Louis Trist, Jr., Memorial Lecture. Presented June 18, 1992, in St. Paul, MN.

Farley, E. (1983). Theology and practice outside the clerical paradigm. In D. S. Browning (Ed.), *Practical theology: The emerging field in theology, church, and world.* San Francisco: Harper & Row.

Farley, E. (1990). Practical theology, Protestant. In R. Hunter (Ed.), *Dictionary of pastoral care and counseling.* Nashville: Abingdon Press.

Farley, M. (1996). Relationships. In L. Russell & S. Clarkson (Eds.), *Dictionary of feminist theologies.* Louisville: Westminster John Knox Press.

Featherstone, M., & Hepworth, M. (1995). Images of positive aging: A case study of *Retirement Choice Magazine.* In M. Featherstone & A. Wernick (Eds.), *Images of aging: Cultural representations of later life.* London: Routledge.

Feldmeth, J. R., & Finley, M. W. (1990). *We weep for ourselves and our children: A Christian guide for survivors of childhood sexual abuse.* New York: HarperSanFrancisco.

Festinger, L. (1957). *A theory of cognitive dissonance.* Stanford: University Press.

Filippi, L. (1991). Place, feminism, and healing: An ecology of pastoral counseling. *Journal of Pastoral Care, 45* (3).

Finson, S. D., & Golding, G. (1996). *Bibliographic resources: Religion and child sexual abuse.* Milford, Nova Scotia, Can.: Creative Promotions and Print.

Fiorenza, E. S. (1983). *In memory of her: A feminist theological reconstruction of Christian origins.* London: SCM Press Ltd.

Fiorenza, E. S. (1984). *Bread not stone: The challenge of feminist biblical interpretation.* Boston: Beacon Press.

Fiorenza, E. S. (1992). *But she said.* Boston: Beacon Press.

Fischer, C. B., Brennema, B., & Benet, A. M. (1975). Introduction. In C. B. Fischer, B. Brennema, & A. M. Benet (Eds.), *Women in a strange land.* Philadelphia: Fortress Press.

Fishburn, J. (1991). *Confronting the idolatry of family: A new vision for the household of God.* Nashville: Abingdon Press.

Fortune, M. M. (1983). *Sexual violence, the unmentionable sin: An ethical and pastoral perspective.* New York: Pilgrim.

Fortune, M. M. (1984). *Sexual abuse prevention: A study for teenagers.* New York: United Church.

Fortune, M. M. (1987). *Keeping the faith: Questions and answers for abused women.* New York: Harper & Row.

Fortune, M. M. (1988). Forgiveness: The last step. In A. L. Horton & J. A. Williamson (Eds.), *Abuse and religion: When praying is not enough.* New York: Lexington.

Fortune, M. M. (1989). *Is nothing sacred?: When sex invades the pastoral relationship.* San Francisco: Harper & Row.

Fortune, M. M. (1991). *Violence in the family: A workshop curriculum for clergy and other helpers.* Cleveland, OH: Pilgrim Press.

Fortune, M. M. (1994, May). Therapy and intimacy: Confused about boundaries. *Christian Century, 111* (17), 18-25.

Fortune, M. M. (1995). *Love does no harm: Sexual ethics for the rest of us.* New York: Continuum.

Fortune, M. M. (1997, Autumn). After twenty years: A time to reflect. *Working Together.*

Fortune, M. M. & Graham, L. K. (1993). Empowering the congregation to respond to sexual abuse and domestic violence. *Pastoral Psychology, 41* (5).

Fortune, M. M. & Poling, J. N. (1993). Calling to accountability: The church's response to abusers. In R J. Wicks & R. D. Parsons (Eds.), *Clinical handbook of pastoral counseling: Vol. 2.* New York: Paulist, Integration.

Fortune, M. M., & Poling, J. N. (1994). *Sexual abuse by clergy: A crisis for the church.* Decatur, GA: Journal of Pastoral Care Publications.

Foucault, M. (1979). *Discipline and punish: The birth of the prison.* New York: Vintage.

Foucault, M. (1980). *Power/knowledge: Selected interviews and other writings 1972–1977* (C. Gordon, Ed.). New York: Pantheon.

Foucault, M. (1984). Nietzsche, genealogy, history. In P. Rabinow (Ed.), *The Foucault reader.* New York: Pantheon Books.

Frank, A. W. (1995). *The wounded storyteller: Body, illness, and ethics.* Chicago: University of Chicago Press.

Fraser, N. (1989). *Unruly practices: Power, discourse and gender in contemporary social theory.* Minneapolis: University of Minnesota Press.

Friedman, E. (1985). *Generation to generation: Family process in church and synagogue.* New York: Guilford.

Friere, P. (1970). *The pedagogy of the oppressed.* (M. B. Ramos, Trans.). New York: Herder and Herder.

Frye, Marilyn. (1995). Oppression. In M. Anderson & P. H. Collins (Eds.), *Race, class and gender: An anthology.* New York: Wadsworth.

Fulkerson, M. M. (1994). *Changing the subject: Women's discourses and feminist theology.* Minneapolis: Fortress Press.

Garrison, P. L. T., & Justes, E. J. (1990). Women, pastoral care of. In R. J.

Hunter (Ed.), *Dictionary of pastoral care and counseling.* Nashville: Abingdon Press.

Gebara, I. (1996). Ecofeminism. In L. Russell & S. Clarkson (Eds.), *Dictionary of feminist theologies.* Louisville: Westminster John Knox Press.

Gelo, F. (1997). Homophobia in the profession of pastoral counseling. *Journal of Pastoral Care, 51* (4).

Gerkin, C. V. (1984). *The living human document: Revisioning pastoral counseling in a hermeneutical mode.* Nashville: Abingdon Press.

Gerkin, C. V. (1986). *Widening the horizons: Pastoral responses to a fragmented society.* Philadelphia: Westminster.

Gerkin, C. V. (1997). *An introduction to pastoral care.* Nashville: Abingdon Press.

Gilkes, C. T. (1980). The black church as a therapeutic community: Suggested areas for research into the black religious experience. *Journal of the Interdenominational Theological Center, 8.*

Gill-Austern, B. L. (1981). A ministry of presence. In J. Weidman (Ed.), *Women ministers: How women are redefining traditional roles.* San Francisco: Harper & Row.

Gill-Austern, B. L. (1995). Rediscovering hidden treasures for pastoral care. *Pastoral Psychology, 43* (4).

Gill-Austern, B. L. (1996). Love understood as self-sacrifice and self-denial: What does it do to women? In J. Stevenson-Moessner (Ed.), *Through the eyes of women: Insights for pastoral care.* Minneapolis: Fortress Press.

Gill-Austern, B. L. (1997a). Responding to a culture ravenous for soul food. *Journal of Pastoral Theology, 7.*

Gill-Austern, B. L. (1997b). She who desires: The transformative power of subjectivity in women's psychological and spiritual experience." *American Baptist Quarterly, 16.*

Glaz, M. (1991). Theological rigor and covenantal law: foundations for pastoral supervision. *Journal of Supervision and Training in Ministry, 13.*

Glaz, M. (1995a). Can a healer be too wounded to heal? *Second Opinion, 20.*

Glaz, M. (1995b). Clinical pastoral education and supervision: Emerging issues and changing patterns. In P. D. Couture & R. J. Hunter (Eds.), *Pastoral care and social conflict.* Nashville: Abingdon Press.

Glaz, M., & Stevenson-Moessner, J. (Eds.). (1991). *Women in travail and transition: A new pastoral care.* Minneapolis: Augsburg Fortress.

Glover-Wetherington, M. A. (1996). Pastoral care and counseling with women entering ministry. In J. Stevenson-Moessner (Ed.), *Through the eyes of women: Insights for pastoral care.* Minneapolis: Fortress Press.

Goldenberg, N. R. (1979). *Changing of the gods: Feminism and the end of traditional religions.* Boston: Beacon.

Goldenberg, N. R. (1990). *Returning words to flesh: Feminism, psychoanalysis, and the resurrection of the body.* Boston: Beacon.

Goldenberg, N. R. (1994). Psychoanalysis and religion: The influence of theology on theory and therapy. *Pastoral Psychology, 40.*

Graham, E. (1995). *Making the difference: Gender, personhood and theology.* London: Mowbray.

Graham, E. (1996). *Transforming practice: Pastoral theology in an age of uncertainty.* London: Mowbray.

Graham, E. (1998). A view from a room: Feminist practical theology from academy, kitchen or sanctuary? In D. M. Ackermann & R. Bons-Storm (Eds.), *Liberating faith practices: Feminist practical theologies in context.* Leuven: Peeters.

Graham, E., & Halsey, M. (Eds.). (1993). *Life cycles: Women and pastoral care.* London: SPCK.

Graham, L. K. (1992). *Care of persons, care of worlds: A psychosystems approach.* Nashville: Abingdon Press.

Graham, L. K. (1997). *Discovering images of God: Narratives of care among lesbians and gays.* Louisville: Westminster John Knox Press.

Grant, J. (1989). *White women's Christ and black women's Jesus.* Atlanta: Scholar's Press.

Grant, J. (1993a). Black theology and black women. In J. H. Cone & G. S. Wilmore (Eds.). *Black theology: A documentary history: Vol. 1, 1966–1979* (2nd and Rev. ed.). Maryknoll, NY: Orbis Books.

Grant, J. (1993b). Womanist theology: Black women's experience as a source for doing theology, with special reference to christology. In J. H. Cone & G. S. Wilmore (Eds.), *Black theology: A documentary history: Vol. 2, 1980–1992.* Maryknoll, NY: Orbis Books.

Greene, M. (1988). *The dialectic of freedom.* New York and London: Teachers College Press.

Greer, J. M. G. (1993). Research in pastoral counseling: Definitions, methods, and research training. In R. J. Wicks, R. D. Parsons, & D. Capps (Eds.), *Clinical handbook of pastoral counseling: Vol. 1.* (Expanded ed.). New York: Paulist, Integration.

Greider, K. J. (1990). The authority of our ambivalence: women and priestly ministry. *Quarterly Review, 10.*

Greider, K. J. (1992). Congregational care: Lay leadership toward an expanded vision of pastoral care. *Impact, 29.*

Greider, K. J. (1997). *Reckoning with aggression: Theology, violence, and vitality.* Louisville: Westminster John Knox Press.

Griffin, G. B. (1992). *Calling: Essays on teaching in the mother tongue.* Pasadena, CA: Trilogy Press.

Gutierrez, G. (1973). *A theology of liberation: History, politics and salvation* (S. C. Inda & J. Eagleson, Trans.). Maryknoll, NY: Orbis Books.

Gutierrez, G. (1979). Liberation praxis and Christian faith. In R. Gibellini (Ed.) (J. Drury, Trans.), *Frontiers of theology in Latin America.* Maryknoll, NY: Orbis Books.

Gutierrez, G. (1993). Option for the poor. In I. Ellacuria & J. Sobrino, S. J. (Eds.) (R. R. Barr, Trans.), *Mysterium liberationis: Fundamental concepts of liberation theology.* Maryknoll, NY: Orbis Books.

Haight, E. S. D. (1995). What is pastoral about pastoral supervision? *Journal of Supervision and Training in Ministry, 16.*

Halligan, F. R. (1990). Womanchurch: Toward a new psychology of feminine spirituality. *Journal of Pastoral Care, 44* (4).

Harris, M. (1987). *Teaching and the religious imagination: An essay on the theology of teaching.* San Francisco: Harper & Row.

Harrison, B. W. (1985). "The power of anger in the work of love: Christian ethics for women and other strangers." In C. S. Robb (Ed.), *Making the connections: Essays in feminist social ethics.* Boston: Beacon Press.

Harrison, J. B. (1991). "WomanistCare: Responsibility and liberation." In L. H. Hollies (Ed.), *WomanistCare: How to tend the souls of women: Vol. 1.* Joliet, IL: Woman to Woman Ministries.

Hammer, M. L. (1994). *Giving birth: Reclaiming biblical metaphor for pastoral practice.* Louisville: Westminster/John Knox Press.

Hanson, K. R. (1996). Minister as midwife. *Journal of Pastoral Care, 50* (3).

Henderson, I. (1996). Matters close to the heart: Pastoral care to mastectomy patients." In J. Stevenson-Moessner (Ed.), *Through the eyes of women: Insights for pastoral care.* Minneapolis: Fortress Press.

Hennelly, A. J. (1995). *Liberation theologies: The global pursuit of justice.* Mystic, CT: Twenty-Third Pub.

Heyward, I. C. (1993). *When boundaries betray us: Beyond illusions of what is ethical in therapy and life.* San Francisco: HarperCollins.

Hiltner, S. (1958). *Preface to pastoral theology: The ministry and theory of shepherding.* Nashville: Abingdon Press.

Hochstein, L. M. (1986). Pastoral counselors: Their attitudes toward gay and lesbian clients. *Journal of Pastoral Care, 40* (2).

Hochstein, L. M. (1996). What pastoral psychotherapists need to know about lesbians and gay men in the 1990s. *Journal of Pastoral Care, 50* (1).

Hoke, R. G. (1997). Breast cancer: Pastoral crisis intervention. *Journal of Pastoral Care, 51* (3).

Holifield, E. B. (1983). *A history of pastoral care in America: From salvation to self-realization.* Nashville: Abingdon Press.

Holland, J., & Peter-Henriot, S. J. (1983). *Social analysis: Linking faith and justice* (Rev. ed.). Maryknoll, NY: Orbis Books, in collaboration with the Center of Concern, Washington, DC.

Hollies, L. H. (1990). A daughter survives incest: A retrospective analysis. In E. C. White (Ed.), *Black women's health book: Speaking for ourselves.* Seattle, WA: Seal.

Hollies, L. H. (1991). Caring through story-telling. In L. H. Hollies (Ed.),

WomanistCare: How to tend the souls of women: Vol. 1. Joliet, IL: Woman to Woman Ministries.

Hollies, L. H. (1992). *Inner healing for broken vessels: Seven steps to a woman's way of healing.* Nashville: Upper Room.

Hollies, L. H. (1997). *Taking back my yesterdays: Lessons in forgiving and moving forward with your life.* New York: Pilgrim.

Hollies, L. H. (Ed.). (1991). *WomanistCare: How to tend the souls of women: Vol. 1.* Joliet, IL: Woman to Woman Ministries.

Holliman, P. (1996). Mentoring as art of intentional thriving together. In C. C. Neuger (Ed.), *The arts of ministry: Feminist, womanist approaches.* Louisville: Westminster John Knox Press.

hooks, b. (1981). *Ain't I a woman?: Black women and feminism.* Boston: South End Press.

hooks, b. (1984). *Feminist theory: From margin to center.* Boston: South End Press.

hooks, b. (1990). *Yearning: Race, gender and cultural politics.* Boston: South End Press.

hooks, b. (1993). *Sisters of the yam: Black women and self-recovery.* Boston: South End Press.

hooks, b. (1994). *Teaching to transgress: Education as the practice of freedom.* New York: Routledge & Kegan Paul.

Hopkins, N. M., & Laaser, M. (Eds.). (1995). *Restoring the soul of a church: Healing congregations wounded by clergy sexual misconduct.* Collegeville, MN: Interfaith Sexual Trauma Institute and The Alban Institute.

Horney, K. (1950). *Feminine psychology.* New York: W. W. Norton.

Horney, K. (1973). *Neurosis and human growth.* New York: W. W. Norton.

Horton, A. L., & Williamson, J. A. (Eds.). (1988). *Abuse and religion: When praying is not enough.* New York: Lexington.

Hough, J., & Cobb, J. (1985). *Christian identity and theological education.* Atlanta: Scholars.

Huff, M. C. (1987). The interdependent Self: An integrated concept from feminist theology and feminist psychology. *Philosophy and Theology, 2.*

Hunsinger, D. V. (1997). *Theology and pastoral counseling: An interdisciplinary approach.* Grand Rapids, MI: William B. Eerdmans.

Hunt, R. A., Hinkle, Jr., J. E., & Malony, H. N. (Eds.). (1990). *Clergy assessment and career development.* Nashville: Abingdon Press.

Hunter, R. J. (1980). The future of pastoral theology. *Pastoral Psychology, 29.*

Hunter, R. J. (1995). The therapeutic tradition of pastoral care and counseling. In P. D. Couture & R. J. Hunter (Eds.), *Pastoral care and social conflict.* Nashville: Abingdon Press.

Hunter, R. J. (Ed.). (1990). *Dictionary of pastoral care and counseling.* Nashville: Abingdon Press.

Hunter, R. J., & Patton, J. (1995). The therapeutic tradition's theological and ethical commitments viewed through its pedagogical practices: A tradition in transition. In P. D. Couture & R. J. Hunter (Eds.), *Pastoral care and social conflict.* Nashville: Abingdon Press.

Hutcheon, B. (1989). *The politics of postmodernism.* New York: Routledge.

Imbens, A. & Jonker, I. (1992). *Christianity and incest* (P. McVay, Trans.). Minneapolis: Fortress Press.

Instruction on certain questions regarding the collaboration of the nonordained faithful in the sacred ministry of priests. (1997, November 27,). *Origins, 27* (24).

Jack, D. (1991). *Silencing the self: Women and depression.* Cambridge, MA.: Harvard University Press.

Jennings, Jr., T. W. (1990). Pastoral theology methodology. In R. Hunter (Ed.), *Dictionary of pastoral care and counseling.* Nashville: Abingdon Press.

Jewett, J., & Haight, E. (1983). The emergence of feminine consciousnes in supervision. *Journal of Supervision and Training in Ministry, 6.*

Johnson, S. C., & Spilka, B. (1991). Coping with breast cancer: The roles of clergy and faith. *Journal of Religion and Health, 30* (1).

Jones, R. L. (Ed.). (1991). *Black psychology* (3rd ed.). Berkeley, CA: Cobb and Henry.

Jordan, J., *et al.* (Eds.). (1991). Women's growth in connection: Writings from the Stone Center. New York: Guilford Press.

Journal of Pastoral Theology. (1993, Summer). Volume 3.

Justes, E. J. (1971). The church—for men only. *Spectrum 47.*

Justes, E. J. (1978). Theological reflections on the role of women in church and society." *Journal of Pastoral Care, 32* (1)

Justes, E. J. (1979). Role perceptions and the pastoral care of women. *Journal of Pastoral Counseling, 14.*

Justes, E. J. (1982). The role of theological reflection in future research on CPE. *Journal of Pastoral Care, 36* (2).

Justes, E. J. (1983). Implications of Thurman's ministry for pastoral care. In H. J. Young (Ed.), *God and human freedom: A Festschrift in honor of Howard Thurman.* Richmond, IN: Friends United.

Justes, E. J. (1993). Women. In R. J. Wicks, R. D. Parsons, & D. Capps (Eds.), *Clinical handbook of pastoral counseling: Vol. 1.* (Expanded ed). New York: Paulist, Integration.

Justes, E. J. (1994). We belong together: Toward an inclusive anthropology. In B. H. Childs & D. W. Waanders (Eds.), *The treasure of earthen vessels: Explorations in theological anthropology.* Louisville: Westminster/John Knox Press.

Kambon, K. K. K. (1983). Pastoral counselor: Role or function? A study of pastoral counseling and pastoring in the Roman Catholic tradition. Unpublished doctoral dissertation, Union Theological.

Kambon, K. K. K. (1992). *The African personality in America.* Tallahassee, FL: NUBIAN Nation Publishing.

Bibliography

Karaban, R. A. (1990). Cross-cultural counseling: Is it possible? Some personal reflections. *Pastoral Psychology, 38* (4).

Karaban, R. A. (1991). The sharing of cultural variation. *Journal of Pastoral Care, 45* (1).

Karaban, R. A. (1992). Cross-cultural pastoral counseling: method or hermeneutic? *Pastoral Psychology, 40* (4).

Karaban, R. A. (1993). Work in progress: Pastoral counseling as an emerging, professional, lay ministry in the Roman Catholic Church. *Journal of Pastoral Theology, 3.*

Karaban, R. A. (1998). *Responding to God's call: A survival guide.* San Jose: Resource Publications.

Kaschak, E. (1992). *Engendered lives: A new psychology of women's lives.* New York: HarperCollins.

Kaufman, G. D. (1994, autumn). Theology, the arts and theological education. In Waits, J. (Ed.), *Theological education: sacred imagination: The arts and theological imagination. Vol. XXXI.*

Keene, J. A. (1991). *A winter's song: A liturgy for women seeking healing from sexual abuse in childhood.* Cleveland, OH: Pilgrim Press.

Keller, C. (1986). *From a broken web: Separation, sexism, and self.* Boston: Beacon.

Keller, E. F. (1983). *A feeling for the organism: The life and work of Barbara McClintock.* San Francisco: Freeman.

Kemeza, M. D. (1996, November). Dante as guide and provocation. *Christian Century, 113* (34), 20-27.

Kendrick, L. S. (1994). A woman bleeding: Integrating female embodiment into pastoral theology and practice. *Journal of Pastoral Care, 48* (2).

Kerr, J. H., & Apter, M. (1991). *Adult play.* Berwyn, PA: Swets & Zeitlinger.

Kirkland-Harris, L. (1998). Partnership: A paradigm for pastoral counseling with African Americans. *Journal of the Interdenominational Theological Center, 25.*

Kornfeld, M. Z. (1998). *Cultivating wholeness: A guide to care and counseling in faith communities.* New York: Continuum.

Kristeva, J. (1979). Women's time (A. J. & H. Blake, Trans.). *Signs, 7.*

Kristeva, J. (1987). *In the beginning was love: Psychoanalysis and faith* (A. Goldhammer, Trans.). New York: Columbia University Press.

Lapsley, J. N. (1972). *Salvation and health: The interlocking processes of life.* Philadelphia: Westminster.

Lapsley, J. N. (1992). *Renewal in late life through pastoral counseling.* New York: Paulist Press.

Larsen, M. K. (1995). A feminist perspective on aging. In M. A. Kimble, S. H. McFadden, J. W. Ellor, & J. J. Seebor (Eds.). *Aging, spirituality, and religion: A handbook.* Minneapolis: Fortress Press.

Lebacqz, K., & Barton, R. G. (1991). *Sex in the parish.* Louisville: Westminster/John Knox Press.

Lester, A. (1992). *Coping with your anger: A Christian guide.* Philadelphia: Westminster.

Lewin, A. (1993). Mothercare. In E. Graham & M. Halsey (Eds.), *Life cycles: Women and pastoral care.* London: SPCK.

Liebert, E. (1992). *Changing life patterns: Adult development in spiritual direction.* New York: Paulist.

Liebert, E. (1995). The thinking heart: Developmental dynamics in Etty Hillesum's diaries. *Pastoral Psychology, 43* (6)

Liebert, E. (1996). Coming home to themselves: Women's spiritual care. In J. Stevenson-Moessner (Ed.), *Through the eyes of women: Insights for pastoral care.* Minneapolis: Fortress Press.

Loder, J. (1990). Theology and psychology. In R. Hunter (Ed.), *Dictionary of pastoral care and counseling.* Nashville: Abingdon Press.

Loomer, B. (1976). Two conceptions of power, *Criterion, 15,* 12-29.

Lorde, Audre (1984). *Sister outsider: Essays and speeches.* Freedom, CA: Crossing Press.

Lum, D. (1986). *Social work practice and people of color: A process stage approach.* Monterey: CA: Brooks/Cole Publishing Company.

Lyon, K. B. (1985). *Toward a practical theology of aging.* Philadelphia: Fortress Press.

MacDonald, C. B. (1969). Methods of study in pastoral theology. In W. B. Oglesby, Jr. (Ed.), *The shape of pastoral theology: Essays in honor of Seard Hiltner.* Nashville: Abingdon Press.

Manlowe, J. L. (1995). *Faith born of seduction: Sexual trauma, body image, and religion.* New York: New York University.

Marcellino, E. (1997). Grace under fire: Internalized homonegativity, self-concept and images of God in gay and lesbian individuals. *Journal of Pastoral Theology, 7.*

Marshall, J. L. (1994a). Pastoral theology and lesbian/gay/bisexual experiences. *Journal of Pastoral Theology, 4.*

Marshall, J. L. (1994b). Toward the development of a pastoral soul: Reflections on identity and theological education. *Pastoral Psychology, 43* (1).

Marshall, J. L. (1995a). Covenants and partnerships: Pastoral counseling with women in lesbian relationships. *Journal of Pastoral Theology, 5.*

Marshall, J. L. (1995b). Pastoral care with congregations in social stress. In P. D. Couture & R. J. Hunter (Eds.), *Pastoral care and social conflict.* Nashville: Abingdon Press.

Marshall, J. L. (1996). Pedagogy and pastoral theology in dialogue with lesbian/bisexual/gay concerns. *Journal of Pastoral Theology, 6.*

Marshall, J. L. (1997). *Counseling lesbian partners.* Louisville: Westminster John Knox Press.

May, R. (1975). *The courage to create.* New York: Bantam Books.

McCarthy, M. (1982). Family therapy: new paradigm, new challenge. In S. Kepnes and D. Tracy (Eds.). *The challenge of psychology to faith.* New York: Seabury.

McCarthy, M. (1990a). Discerning the ethical commitments implicit in models of supervision. *Journal of Supervision and Training in Ministry, 12.*

McCarthy, M. (1990b). A Roman Catholic perspective on psychiatry and religion." In D. S. Browning, T. Jobe, & I. S. Evison (Eds.), *Religious and ethical factors in psychiatric practice.* Chicago: Nelson-Hall.

McCarthy, M. (1992a). Empathy: A bridge between. *Journal of Pastoral Care, 46* (2).

McCarthy, M. (1992b). Growing into a professional self: a theory of pastoral psychotherapy. *Journal of Supervision and Training in Ministry, 14.*

McCarthy, M. (1993). Empathy amid diversity: Problems and possibilities. *Journal of Pastoral Theology, 3.*

McCrary, C. (1991). Interdependence as a normative value in pastoral counseling with African Americans. *Journal of the Interdenominational Theological Center, 18.*

McCrary, C. (1998). Wholeness of women. *Journal of the Interdenominational Theological Center, 25.*

McFague, S. (1982). *Metaphorical theology: Models of God in religious language.* Philadelphia: Fortress Press.

McHolland, J. (Ed.). (1993). *The future of pastoral counseling: Whom, how and for what do we train.* Fairfax, VA: American Association of Pastoral Counselors.

McKeever, B. C. (1991). Social systems in pastoral care. In H. W. Stone & W. M. Clements (Eds.), *Handbook for basic types of pastoral care and counseling.* Nashville: Abingdon Press.

McWilliams, F. C. (1996). Pushing against the boundaries of pastoral care: Clinical pastoral education in urban ministry settings. *Journal of Pastoral Care, 50* (2).

McWilliams, F. C. (1997). Voices crying in the wilderness: prophetic ministry in clinical pastoral education. *Journal of Pastoral Care, 51* (1).

Meadow, M. J., & Rayburn, C. A. (Eds.). (1985). *A time to weep, a time to sing: Faith journeys of women scholars of religion.* Minneapolis: Winston.

Meeks, S. H. (1980). The motherhood of God: A symbol for pastoral care. *Iliff Review, 37.*

Mercer, J. A. (1992). Legal and theological justice for abused adolescent girls. *Journal of Law and Religion, 9* (2).

Meyers, L. J. (1988). *Understanding an Afrocentric worldview: Introduction to an optimal psychology.* Dubuque, IA: Kendall/Hunt Publishing Company.

Miller, J. B. (1976). *Toward a new psychology of women.* Boston: Beacon.

Miller-McLemore, B. J. (1988). *Death, sin, and the moral life: Contemporary cultural interpretations of death.* Atlanta: Scholars.

Miller-McLemore, B. J. (1991a). Produce or perish: generativity and new reproductive technologies. *Journal of the American Academy of Religion, 59.*

Miller-McLemore, B. J. (1991b). Thinking theologically about modern medicine. *Journal of Religion and Health, 30* (4).

Miller-McLemore, B. J. (1992). Epistemology or bust: A maternal feminist knowledge of knowing. *Journal of Religion, 72* (2).

Miller-McLemore, B. J. (1993, April 7). The human web: Reflections on the state of pastoral theology. *Christian Century, 110* (11).

Miller-McLemore, B. J. (1994). *Also a mother: Work and family as theological dilemma.* Nashville: Abingdon Press.

Miller-McLemore, B. J. (1996). The living human web: Pastoral theology at the turn of the century. In J. Stevenson-Moessner (Ed.), *Through the eyes of women.* Minneapolis: Fortress Press.

Miller-McLemore, B. J. (1998). The subject and practice of pastoral theology as a practical theological discipline: Pushing past the nagging identity crisis to the poetics of resistance. In D. M. Ackermann & R. Bons-Storm (Eds.), *Liberating faith practices: Feminist practical theologies in context.* Leuven: Peeters.

Miller-McLemore, B. J. & Anderson, H. (1995). Gender and pastoral care. In P. D. Couture & R. J. Hunter (Eds.). *Pastoral care and social conflict.* Nashville: Abingdon Press.

Miller-McLemore, B. J., & Myers, W. R. (1989). The doctorate of ministry as an exercise in practical theology. *Journal of Supervision and Training in Ministry, 11.*

Mills, Lester O. (1990). Pastoral care (history, traditions, and definitions). In R. Hunter (Ed.), *Dictionary of pastoral care and counseling.* Nashville: Abingdon Press.

Moi, T. (1989). Feminist, female, feminine. In C. Belsey & J. Moore (Eds.), *The feminist reader: Essays in gender and the politics of literary criticism.* New York: Blackwell.

Moi, T. (1986). *The Kristeva reader.* New York: Columbia University Press.

Morrison, T. (1983). Interview with Claudia Tate. In C. Tate (Ed.), *Black women writers at work.* New York: Continuum.

Morton, N. (1985). *The journey is home.* Boston: Beacon.

Myers, L. (1988). *Understanding an Afrocentric world view: Introduction to optimal psychology.* Dubuque, IA: Kendall/Hunt.

Nason-Clark, N. (1997). *The battered wife: How Christians confront family violence.* Louisville: Westminster John Knox Press.

Nelson, S. C., & McWhirter, J. J. (1995). The regroup group: Career exploration in a church setting. *Journal of Pastoral Care, 49* (2).

Nelson, S. D. (1982). The sin of hiding: A feminist critique of Reinhold Niebuhr's account of the sin of pride. *Soundings, 65* (3).

Nelson, S. L. (1997). *Healing the broken heart: Sin, alienation and the gift of grace.* St. Louis, MO: Chalice.

Neuger, C. C. (1991). Imagination in pastoral care and counseling. In H. W. Stone & W. M. Clements (Eds.), *Handbook for basic types of pastoral care and counseling.* Nashville: Abingdon Press.

Neuger, C. C. (1991). Women and depression: Lives at risk. In M. Glaz & J. Stevenson-Moessner (Eds.), *Women in travail and transition: A new pastoral care.* Nashville; Abingdon Press.

Neuger, C. C. (1992). Feminist pastoral theology and pastoral counseling: A work in progress. *Journal of Pastoral Theology, 2.*

Neuger, C. C. (1993). A feminist perspective on pastoral counseling with women. In R. J. Wicks & R. D. Parsons (Eds.), *Clinical handbook of pastoral counseling: Vol. 2.* New York: Paulist, Integration.

Neuger, C. C. (1994). Gender: Women and identity. In B. H. Childs & D. W. Waanders (Eds.), *The treasure of earthen vessels: explorations in theological anthropology.* Louisville: Westminster/John Knox Press.

Neuger, C. C. (Ed.). (1996). *The arts of ministry: Feminist, womanist approaches.* Louisville: Westminster John Knox Press.

Neuger, C. C., & Holliman, P. J. (Eds.). (1991). Collegiality in pastoral care and counseling [Theme edition]. *Journal of Pastoral Care, 45* (4).

Neuger, C. C., & Poling, J. N. (Eds.). (1997). *The care of men.* Nashville: Abingdon Press.

New Century Hymnal, The. (1995). Cleveland: Pilgrim Press.

Nicholson, L. (Ed.). (1997). *The second wave: A reader in feminist theory.* New York: Routledge.

Niswander, B. J. (1976). Rebuilding a congregation through the house church. In A. L. Foster (Ed.), *The house church evolving.* Chicago: Exploration.

Niswander, B. J. (1987). The ministry of clinical supervision of pastoral psychotherapy: A process of professional formation. *Journal of Supervision and Training in Ministry, 9.*

Nobles, W. W. (1986). African psychology: Toward its reclamation, reascension, and revitalization. Oakland, CA: A Black Family Institute.

Nobles, W. W. (1991). African philosophy: Foundations of black psychology. In R. L. Jones (Ed.), *Black psychology* (3rd ed.). Berkeley, CA: Cobb and Henry.

Nouwen, H. (1972). *The wounded healer: Ministry in contemporary society.* Garden City, NY: Doubleday.

Oates, W. (1962). *Protestant pastoral counseling.* Philadelphia: Westminster.

Orr, J. L. (1991). Ministry with working-class women. *Journal of Pastoral Care, 45* (4).

Orr, J. L. (1997). Hard work, hard lovin', hard times, hardly worth it: Care of working class men. In C. C. Neuger & J. N. Poling (Eds.), *The care of men.* Nashville: Abingdon Press.

Palmer, P. (1983). *To know as we are known: A spirituality of education.* San Francisco: Harper & Row.

Palmer, P. (1997). *The courage to teach.* San Francisco: Jossey Bass.

Parks, S. D. (1982). Young adult faith development: Teaching is [sic] the context of theological education. *Religious Education, 77* (6).

Parks, S. D. (1984). Meaning and symbol in constructive developmental perspective. *Pastoral Psychology, 33* (2).

Parks, S. D. (1986a). *The critical years: The young adult search for a faith to live by.* San Francisco: Harper & Row.

Parks, S. D. (1986b). Imagination and spirit in faith development: A way past the structure-content dichotomy. In C. Dykstra & S. Parks (Eds.), *Faith development and Fowler.* Birmingham, AL: Religious Education.

Parks, S. D. (1987). Global complexity and young adult formation: Implications for religious and professional education. *Religion and Intellectual Life, 4.*

Parks, S. D. (1989). Home and pilgrimage: Companion metaphors for personal and social transformation. *Soundings, 72* (2-3).

Parks, S. D. (1990). Social vision and moral courage: Mentoring a new generation. *Cross Currents, 40* (3).

Parks, S. D. (1993). Pastoral counseling and the university. In R J. Wicks & R. D. Parsons (Eds.), *Clinical handbook of pastoral counseling: Vol. 2.* New York: Paulist, Integration.

Pattison, S. (1994). *A vision of pastoral theology.* Edinburgh: Contact Pastoral Monograph No. 4.

Patton, J. (1983). *Pastoral counseling: A ministry of the church.* Nashville: Abingdon Press.

Patton, J. (1985). *Is human forgiveness possible? A pastoral care perspective.* Nashville: Abingdon Press.

Patton, J. (1990). *From ministry to theology: Pastoral action and reflection.* Nashville: Abingdon Press.

Patton, J. (1993). *Pastoral care in context: An introduction to pastoral care.* Louisville: Westminster/John Knox Press.

Pellauer, M., Chester, B., & Boyajian, J. (Eds.). (1987). *Sexual assault and abuse: A handbook for clergy and religious professionals.* San Francisco: Harper & Row.

Pfäfflin, U. (1995). Displacement and the yearning for holding environments: Visions in feminist pastoral psychology and theology. *Journal of Pastoral Care, 49* (4).

Piercy, M. (1982). *Circles on the water.* New York: Alfred A. Knopf.

Plaskow, J. (1981). Woman as body: Motherhood and dualism, *Anima 8,* (1).

Poling, J. N. (1991). *The abuse of power: A theological problem.* Nashville: Abingdon Press.

Poling, J. N. (1995). Where I live is how I work. *Pastoral Psychology, 43* (3).

Poling, J. N. (1996). *Deliver us from evil: Resisting racial and gender oppression.* Minneapolis: Fortress Press.

Poling, J. N., & Miller, D. E. (1985). *Foundations for a practical theology of ministry.* Nashville: Abingdon Press.

Pope John Paul II. (1990, October 4). From the heart of the church. *Origins 20* (17), 265-276.

Bibliography

Pope John Paul II. (1998, July 16). To defend the faith. *Origins, 28* (8), 113-116.

Purvis, Sally B. (1995). *The stained-glass ceiling: Churches and their women pastors.* Louisville: Westminster/John Knox Press.

Ragsdale, K. H. (Ed.). (1996). *Boundary wars: Intimacy and distance in healing relationships.* Cleveland: Pilgrim Press.

Ramsay, N. J. (1991a). Pastoral assessment in the congregational genre. *Journal of Pastoral Theology, 1.*

Ramsay, N. J. (1991b). Pastoral supervision: A theological resource for ministry. *Journal of Supervision and Training in Ministry, 13.*

Ramsay, N. J. (1991c). Sexual abuse and shame: The travail of recovery. In M. Glaz & J. Stevenson-Moessner (Eds.), *Women in travail and transition: A new pastoral care.* Minneapolis: Fortress Press.

Ramsay, N. J. (1992a). Feminist perspectives on pastoral care: Implications for practice and theory. *Pastoral Psychology, 40* (4).

Ramsay, N. J. (1992b). The congregation as a culture: Implications for ministry. *Encounter, 53.*

Ramsay, N. J. (1995). A story of freedom's corruption: Sin as a response to the human condition. In R. Williams (Ed.), *Theology and the interhuman.* Valley Forge, PA: Trinity Press International.

Ramsay, N. J. (1998, fall). Compassionate resistance: An ethic for pastoral care and counseling. *Journal of Pastoral Care, 52* (3).

Ramshaw, E. J. (1987). *Ritual and pastoral care.* Philadelphia: Fortress Press.

Ramshaw, E. J. (1988). Ritual for stillbirth: Exploring the issues. *Worship, 62* (6).

Randour, M. L. (Ed.). (1993). *Exploring sacred landscapes: Religious and spiritual experiences in psychotherapy.* New York: Columbia University.

Rayburn, C. (1993). Prisons. In R. J. Wicks & R. D. Parsons (Eds.), *Clinical handbook of pastoral counseling: Vol. 2.* New York: Paulist, Integration.

Reid, K. G. (1994). *Preventing child sexual abuse: A curriculum for children ages five through eight.* Cleveland, OH: Pilgrim Press.

Reid, K. G. with Fortune, M. M. (1989). *Preventing child sexual abuse: A curriculum for children ages nine through twelve.* Cleveland, OH: Pilgrim Press.

Ress, M. J. (1990). Feminist theologians challenge the church." In A. T. Hennelly (Ed.). *Liberation theology: A documentary history,* 385-389. Maryknoll, N.Y.: Orbis Books.

Rixford, M. E. (1997). From the walls of the city: Disabilities as culture. *Journal of Pastoral Care, 51* (2).

Rizzuto, A-M. (1979). *The birth of the living god: A psychoanalytic study.* Chicago: University of Chicago.

Robb, C. (1985). A framework for feminist ethics, In *Women's consciousness, women's conscience: A reader in feminist ethics.* Minneapolis: Winston Press.

Robbins, M. B. (1981). The desert-mountain experience: The two faces of encounter with God. *Journal of Pastoral Care, 35* (1).

Robbins, M. B. (1990). *Mid-life women and death of mother: A study of psychohistorical and spiritual transformation.* New York: Peter Lang.

Robbins, M. B. (1996). Women and motherloss. In J. Stevenson-Moessner (Ed.), *Through the eyes of women: Insights for pastoral care.* Minneapolis: Fortress Press.

Robbins, M. B. (1997). The divine dance: Partners in remembering, revisioning, and reweaving. *Journal of Pastoral Care, 51* (3).

Roberts, J. D. (1974). *A black political theology.* Philadelphia: Westminster.

Robinson, Jr., E., & Needham, M. A. (1991). Racial and gender myths as key factors in pastoral supervision. *Journal of Pastoral Care, 45* (4).

Rose, G. J., M.D. (1996). *Necessary illusion: Art as witness.* Madison: International Universities Press.

Ruether, R. R. (1983). *Sexism and God-talk: Toward a feminist theology.* Boston: Beacon.

Ruether, R. R. (1986). *Women-church: Theory and practice.* San Francisco: Harper & Row.

Ruether, R. R. (1998). *Women and redemption: A theological history.* Minneapolis: Fortress Press.

Ruiz, B. C. (1994). Pastoral counseling of women in the context of intense oppression. *Journal of Pastoral Care, 48* (2).

Saiving, V. (1960). The human situation: A feminine view. *Journal of Religion, 2.*

Saliers, D. (1994). *Worship as theology: A foretaste of glory divine.* Nashville: Abingdon Press.

Satir, V. (1967). *Conjoint family therapy* (Rev. ed.). Palo Alto, CA: Science and Behavior Books.

Saussy, C. (1988a). Discovering goddess. *Pastoral Psychology, 36* (3).

Saussy, C. (1988b). Ministers and mutuality of relationship. *Quarterly Review, 8.*

Saussy, C. (1991). *God images and self-esteem: Empowering women in a patriarchal society.* Louisville: Westminster/John Knox Press.

Saussy, C. (1995). *The gift of anger: A call to faithful action.* Louisville: Westminster/John Knox Press.

Saussy, C. (1998a). From getting over getting older to getting on with getting older. *Journal of Pastoral Theology, 8.*

Saussy, C. (1998b). *The art of growing old.* Minneapolis: Augsburg.

Schlauch, C. (1995). *Faithful companioning.* Minneapolis: Fortress Press.

Schlauch, C. (1996). Mapping the terrain of pastoral psychology. *Pastoral Psychology, 44.*

Schroeder, W. W. (1995). The United Church of Christ: The quest for denomination identity and the limits of pluralism. In D. C. Bass & K. B. Smith (Eds.), *The United Church of Christ: Issues in its quest for denomination identity.* Chicago: Exploration Press.

Seligman, R. (1992). *Helplessness: On depression, development and death*. New York: W. H. Freeman and Co.

Segundo, J. (1976). *The liberation of theology* (J. Drury, Trans.). Maryknoll, NY: Orbis Books.

Sered, S. S. (1996, spring). Mother love, child death and religious innovation: A feminist perspective. *Journal of Feminist Studies in Religion 12* (1).

Sheares II, R. A. (1990). A covenant polity. In D. L. Johnson & C. Hambrick-Stowe (Eds.), *Theology and identity: Traditions, movements, and polity in the United Church of Christ*. New York: Pilgrim Press.

Shinn, R. (1991). *Confessing our faith*. Cleveland: Pilgrim Press.

Smith, Jr., A. (1982). *The relationship self: Ethics and therapy from a black church perspective*. Nashville: Abingdon Press.

Snorton, T. E. (1996). The legacy of the African-American matriarch: New perspectives for pastoral care. In J. Stevenson-Moessner (Ed.), *Through the eyes of women: Insights for pastoral care*. Minneapolis: Fortress Press.

Stevenson-Moessner, J. (1991). A new pastoral paradigm and practice. In M. Glaz & J. Stevenson-Moessner (Eds.), *Women in travail and transition: A new pastoral care*. Minneapolis: Fortress Press.

Stevenson-Moessner, J. (1996a). From Samaritan to Samaritan: Journey mercies. In J. Stevenson-Moessner (Ed.), *Through the eyes of women: Insights for pastoral care*. Minneapolis: Fortress Press.

Stevenson-Moessner, J. (1996b). Organicity and pastoral care: Theological interrelationships. *Journal of Pastoral Care, 50* (4).

Stevenson-Moessner, J. ed. (1996c). *Through the eyes of women: Insights for pastoral care*. Minneapolis: Fortress Press.

Stokes, A. (1985). *Ministry after Freud*. New York: Pilgrim Press.

Stone, H. (1994). *Brief pastoral counseling: Short-term approaches and strategies*. Minneapolis: Fortress Press.

Sturdivant, S. (1984). *Therapy with women: A feminist philosophy of treatment*. New York: Springer.

Surrey, J. (1991). The self-in-relation: A theory of women's development. In J. Jordan, et al. (Eds.), *Women's growth in connection*. New York: Guilford Press.

Tatum, B. D. (1997). Racial identity development and relational theory: The case of black women in white communities. In J. Jordan (Ed.), *Women's growth in diversity*. New York: Guilford Press.

Taylor, C. (1991). *The skilled pastor: Counseling as the practice of theology*. Minneapolis: Fortress Press.

Taylor, C. (1992, Summer). Black experience as a resource for pastoral theology. *The Journal for Pastoral Theology, 2*.

Thistlethwaite, S. (1989). *Sex, race, and God: Christian feminism in black and white*. New York: Crossroad.

Thornton, S. (1993, summer). Excerpts from a response to Roslyn Karaban. *Journal of Pastoral Theology, 3,* 67-70.

Tigert, L. M. (1996). *Coming out while staying in: Struggles and celebrations of lesbians, gays, and bisexuals in the church.* Cleveland: United Church.

Tong, R. (1989). *Feminist thought: A comprehensive introduction.* Boulder and San Francisco: Westview Press.

Townes, E. M. (Ed.). (1993). *A troubling in my soul: Womanist perspectives on evil and suffering.* Maryknoll, NY: Orbis Books.

Townes, E. M. (Ed.). (1997). *Embracing the spirit: Womanist perspectives on hope, salvation, and transformation.* Maryknoll, NY: Orbis Books.

Tracy, D. (1975). *Blessed rage for order: The new pluralism in theology.* New York: Seabury.

Tracy, D. (1981). *The analogical imagination: Christian theology and the culture of pluralism.* New York: Crossroad.

Trible, Phyllis, (1984). *Texts of terror.* Philadelphia: Fortress Press.

Troxell, B. B. (1993). Honoring one another with our stories: Authority and mutual ministry among United Methodist clergywomen in the last decade of the twentieth century. In R. Keller (Ed.), *Spirituality and social responsibility: Vocational vision of women in the United Methodist tradition.* Nashville: Abingdon Press.

Turner, C. W. (1997). Clinical applications of the Stone Center theoretical approach to minority women. In J. Jordan et al. (Eds.), *Women's growth in connection.* New York: Guilford Press.

Ulanov, A. B. (1971). *The feminine in Jungian psychology and in Christian theology.* Evanston, IL: Northwestern University.

Ulanov, A. B. (1972). Symposium: Do pastoral counselors bring a new consciousness to the health professions? *Journal of Pastoral Care, 26* (4).

Ulanov, A. B. (1973a). Self as other. *Journal of Religion and Health, 12* (2).

Ulanov, A. B. (1973b). The birth of otherness. *Religion in Life, 42* (3), 301-321.

Ulanov, A. B. (1975). Christian fear of the psyche. *Union Seminary Quarterly Review, 30.*

Ulanov, A. B. (1981). *Receiving woman: Studies in the psychology and theology of the feminine.* Philadelphia: Westminster.

Ulanov, A. B. (1986). *Picturing God.* Cambridge, MA: Cowley.

Ulanov, A. B. (1988). *The wisdom of the psyche.* Cambridge, MA: Cowley.

Ulanov, A. B. (1989). Vocation: Denying the denial. *Anglican Theological Review, 71.*

Ulanov, A. B. (1990). Religious devotion or masochism?: A psychoanalyst looks at Thérèse. In J. Sullivan (Ed.), *Experiencing Saint Thérèse today.* Washington, DC: ICS Publications.

Ulanov, A. B. (1992). The holding self: Jung and the desire for being. In F. R. Halligan & J. J. Shea (Eds.), *The fires of desire: Erotic energies and the spiritual quest.* New York: Crossroad.

Ulanov, A. B. (1994). *The wizard's gate: Picturing consciousness.* Einsiedeln, Switzerland: Daimon.

Ulanov, A. B. (1996). *The functioning transcendent: A study in analytical psychology.* Wilmette, Il: Chiron.

Ulanov, A. B., & Ulanov, B. (1975). *Religion and the unconscious.* Philadelphia: Westminster.

Ulanov, A. B., & Ulanov, B. (1982). *Primary speech: A psychology of prayer.* Atlanta: John Knox.

Ulanov, A. B., & Ulanov, B. (1983). *Cinderella and her sisters: The envied and the envying.* Philadelphia: Westminster.

Ulanov, A. B., & Ulanov, B. (1987). *The witch and the clown: Two archetypes of human sexuality.* Wilmette, IL: Chiron.

Ulanov, A. B., & Ulanov, B. (1991). *The healing imagination: The meeting of psyche and soul.* New York: Paulist.

Ulanov, A. B., & Ulanov, B. (1994). *Transforming sexuality: The archetypal world of anima and animus.* Boston: Shambhala.

Ulanov, A. B., & Ulanov, B. (1993). Counseling lesbians: A feminist perspective. In R. J. Wicks & R. D. Parsons (Eds.), *Clinical handbook of pastoral counseling: Vol. 2.* New York: Paulist, Integration.

Unterberger, G. L. (1989, December). Twelve steps for women alcoholics. *Christian Century, 106* (37).

Unterberger, G. L. (1992). Feminist works in progress: Excerpts from a response to Neuger. *Journal of Pastoral Theology, 2.*

United Church of Christ manual on ministry. (1986). New York: Office for Church Life and Leadership.

VandeCreek, L., & Glockner, M. (1993). Do gender issues affect pastoral education supervision? *Journal of Pastoral Care, 47.*

Voelkel-Haugen, R., & Fortune, M. M. (1996). *Sexual abuse prevention: A course of study for teenagers.* (Rev.) New York: Pilgrim.

Walker, A. (1983). *In search of our mothers' gardens: Womanist prose.* New York: Harcourt Brace Jovanovich, Harvest/HBJ.

Walker, A. (1986). *Revolutionary petunias and other poems.* San Diego: Harcourt Brace Jovanovich.

Watkins Ali, C. A. (1998). In the name of survival and liberation: A preface to pastoral theology in the African American context. Unpublished doctoral dissertation, University of Denver and Iliff School of Theology.

Way, P. A. (1963). What's wrong with the church: The clergy. *Renewal, 3.*

Way, P. A. (1964). Women in the church. *Renewal, 4.*

Way, P. A. (1968). Community organization and pastoral care: Drum beat for dialogue. *Pastoral Psychology, 19* (182).

Way, P. A. (1970a). An authority of possibility for women in the church. In S.

B. Doely (Ed.), *Women's liberation and the church: The new demand for freedom in the life of the Christian Church.* New York: Association.

Way, P. A. (1970b). The church and (ordained) women. *Christian Ministry, 1.*

Way, P. A. (1970c). Shattering the self-evidents: Toward a constructive view of field work and contemporary field education. *Criterion, 9.*

Way, P. A. (1972). Visions of possibility: Women for theological education. *Theological Education, 8* (4).

Way, P. A. (1975). New directions in theological education. Association of Clinical Pastoral Education 1975 Conference Proceedings. Minneapolis: Association of Clinical Pastoral Education.

Way, P. A. (1976). Truth and pastoral theology. *Pastoral Psychology, 24* (4).

Way, P. A. (1977, May 30-June 13) Homosexual counseling as a learning ministry. *Christianity and Crisis, 37* (9 and 10).

Way, P. A. (1980). Pastoral excellence and pastoral theology: A slight shift of paradigm and a modest polemic. *Pastoral Psychology, 29* (1).

Way, P. A. (1981). Women in theological education. Occasional Papers: #34. Nashville: The United Methodist Board for Higher Education and Ministry.

Way, P. A. (1983). The ecclesial contribution to the ethics/pastoral care dialogue. *Drew Gateway, 53.*

Way, P. A. (1984). The cultures of sexuality: Voices of the theological dialogue. Occasional Papers: #59. Nashville: The United Methodist Board for Higher Education and Ministry.

Way, P. A. (1990, January). Violence in the family: Theological perspective. Disciples Lecture, Vanderbilt Divinity School.

Weedon, C. (1997). *Feminist practice and poststructuralist theory* (2nd ed.). New York: Blackwell.

Wehr, D. S. (1987). *Jung and feminism: Liberating archetypes.* Boston: Beacon.

Weidman, J. (Ed.). (1981). *Women ministers: How women are redefining traditional roles.* San Francisco: Harper & Row.

Welch, S. (1985). *Communities of resistance and solidarity: A feminist theology of liberation.* Maryknoll, NY: Orbis Books.

Welch, S. (1990). *A feminist ethic of risk.* Minneapolis: Fortress Press.

Whitehead, J. D., & Whitehead, E. E. (1995). *Method in ministry: Theological reflection and Christian ministry.* Kansas City: Sheed and Ward.

Wiley, C. Y. (1991). A ministry of empowerment: A holistic model for pastoral counseling in the African American Community. *Journal of Pastoral Care, 45* (4).

Wiley, C. Y. (1995). Faith journey: How black women see God: Womanist theology in action. *Journal of Sacred Feminine Wisdom, 1.*

Williams, D. S. (1993). *Sisters in the wilderness: The challenge of womanist God talk.* Maryknoll, NY: Orbis Books.

Williams, D. S. (1993). Womanist theology: Black women's voices. In J. H.

Bibliography

Cone & G. S. Wilmore (Eds.), *Black theology: A documentary history, 1980-1992.* Maryknoll, NY: Orbis Books.

Wimberly, A. S. (1979). Configurational patterns in the function of the church for aging persons: A black perspective. *Journal of the Interdenominational Theological Center, 6.*

Wimberly, A. S. (1992). Reverence for life in severe and terminal illness: A theological ethical viewpoint. *Journal of the Interdenominational Theological Center, 20.*

Wimberly, A. S. (1994). Narrative approaches to viewing and addressing African American spirituality and sexuality: Toward a strategic pastoral theology. *Journal of Pastoral Theology, 4.*

Wimberly, A. S. (Ed.). (1997). *Honoring African American elders: A ministry in the soul community.* San Francisco: Jossey-Bass.

Wimberly, A. S., & Wimberly, E. P. (1995a). Congregation and academy. In N. F. Fisher (Ed.), *Truth and tradition: A conversation about the future of United Methodist theological education.* Nashville: Abingdon Press.

Wimberly, A. S., & Wimberly, E. P. (1995b). Pastoral care of African Americans. In M. A. Kimble, S. H. McFadden, J. W. Ellor, & J. J. Seeber (Eds.), *Aging, spirituality and religion: A handbook.* Minneapolis: Fortress Press.

Wimberly, A. S., & Wimberly, E. P. (1998). Narrative and personhood: A paradigm for hoping. *Journal of the Interdenominational Theological Center, 25.*

Wimberly, E. P. (1979). *Pastoral care in the black church.* Nashville: Abingdon Press.

Wimberly, E. P. (1991). *African American pastoral care.* Nashville: Abingdon Press.

Wimberly, E. P. (1994). *Using Scripture in pastoral counseling.* Nashville: Abingdon Press.

Wimberly, E. P., & Wimberly, A. S. (1986). *Liberation and human wholeness: The conversion experiences of black people in slavery and freedom.* Nashville: Abingdon Press.

Winnicott, D. W. (1971). *Playing and reality.* New York: Basic Books.

Winter, M. T., Lummis, A., & Stokes, A., with reflections by project consultants. (1994). *Defecting in place: Women claiming responsibility for their own spiritual lives.* New York: Crossroad.

Wise, M. M. (1991). Mother and daughter issues: Ties that bind and bless. In L. H. Hollies (Ed.), *WomanistCare: How to tend the souls of women: Vol. 1.* Joliet, IL: Woman to Woman Ministries.

Wren, B. (1995). I come with joy. In *The New Century Hymnal.* Cleveland, OH: Pilgrim Press.

Yates, W. (1987). *The arts in theological education.*

Young, I. M. (1985). Humanism, gynocentrism and feminist politics. *Women's Studies International Forum, 8* (2).

Young, Pamela D. (1990). *Feminist theology/Christian theology: In search of method.* Minneapolis: Fortress Press.

Contributors

Carolyn Stahl Bohler has been the Emma Sanborn Tousant Professor of Pastoral Theology and Counseling at United Theological Seminary in Dayton, Ohio, since 1982. She is the mother of two teenagers and an ordained elder in The United Methodist Church. She is the author of the following books: *CHIPS & SALSA: Children in Plays — Short and Lively Sacred Action*; *Opening to God: Guided Imagery Meditations on Scripture, Completely Revised and Expanded*; *God Is Like a Mother Hen and Much Much More*; *When You Need to Take a Stand*; and *Prayer on Wings: A Search for Authentic Prayer.*

Marsha Foster Boyd is the Academic Dean of Payne Theological Seminary in Wilberforce, Ohio, a seminary of the African Methodist Episcopal (AME) Church. She is the first female Academic Dean at any AME seminary and the first full-time female faculty member at Payne. Dr. Boyd is also a tenured faculty member in Pastoral Care and Counseling at United Theological Seminary in Dayton, Ohio, on leave to serve at Payne. She has taught at United for eight years.

Pamela D. Couture is Associate Professor of Pastoral Theology at Colgate-Rochester Divinity School in Rochester, New York. She is author of *Blessed Are the Poor?: Women's Poverty, Family Policy and Practical Theology*, coeditor of *Pastoral Care and Social Conflict*, and coauthor of *From Culture Wars to Consensus: Religion and the American Family Debate.* She is an ordained elder in The United Methodist church and educational consultant to their Bishop's Initiative on Children and Poverty.

Carrie Doehring is Assistant Professor of Pastoral Psychology at the School of Theology and Graduate School of Boston University, a clinical supervisor of doctoral interns at the Danielsen Institute, and has a part-time ministry in a United Church of Christ congregation. She is author of *Internal Desecration: Traumatization and Representations of God* and *Taking Care: Monitoring Power Dynamics and Relational Boundaries in Pastoral Care and Counseling.* She is married and has two sons.

Susan J. Dunlap is Assistant Professor of Pastoral Theology at Duke Divinity School. She has written *Counseling Depressed Women*, a feminist theological account of the incidence and care of depressed women. Her research now focuses on construals of the body in pastoral care literature on care for the sick. As a Presbyterian pastor, she has served churches in the Baltimore area.

Brita L. Gill-Austern is Associate Professor of Pastoral Care and Practical Theology at Andover Newton Theological School, an ordained United Church of Christ minister, and the mother of three boys. She served parishes for eight years in Pennsylvania and California. She is a contributor to the volumes *Through the Eyes of Women* and *Tending the Flock: Congregations and Family Ministries.* She has also published articles in journals in her areas of research: the psychology and spirituality of women, models of congregational care, and spiritual resources for healing.

Kathleen J. Greider is Associate Professor of Pastoral Care and Counseling at Claremont School of Theology. She is ordained by The United Methodist Church, a certified member in the American Association of Pastoral Counselors, and has previously worked in in-patient psychiatry and parish ministry. Her publications include *Reckoning with Aggression: Theology, Violence, and Vitality.*

Gloria A. Johnson, an ordained minister in the Presbyterian Church (USA), is Director of Kaleidoscope Pastoral Counseling Center in Claremont. She has served as parish minister, hospital chaplain, and school chaplain. She is currently a Ph.D. student in Theology and Personality at the Claremont School of Theology.

Roslyn A. Karaban is Associate Professor of Ministry Studies at St. Bernard's Institute in Rochester, New York, and a pastoral counselor at Samaritan Pastoral Counseling Center, also in Rochester. She is a Roman Catholic laywoman committed to expanding the roles available to women in the church. She is the coeditor (with Deni Mack) of *Extraordinary Preaching: Twenty Homilies by Roman Catholic Women* and author of *Responding to God's Call: A Survival Guide* and *Complicated Losses, Difficult Deaths: A Practical Guide for Ministry to Grievers* (forthcoming 1999), all with Resource Publications.

Kristen J. Leslie, lecturer in Pastoral Care and Counseling at the Yale University Divinity School, is ordained by The United Methodist Church. She has been a local parish minister, a college chaplain, a pastoral counselor, and a rape crisis counselor. She is completing her Ph.D. in Theology and Personality at the Claremont School of Theology.

Bonnie J. Miller-McLemore is Associate Professor of Pastoral Theology and Counseling at Vanderbilt University Divinity School, an ordained minister in the Christian Church (Disciples of Christ), a certified member in the American Association of Pastoral Counselors, and the mother of three boys. Her publications address major cultural issues and include *Death, Sin and the Moral Life: Contemporary Cultural Interpretations of Death; Also a Mother: Work and Family as Theological Dilemma;* and, most recently, a coauthored volume, *From Culture Wars to Common Ground: Religion and the American Family Debate.*

Christie Cozad Neuger, an ordained United Methodist Minister, has served as parish pastor, hospital chaplain, pastoral counselor, and professor. She is a diplomate in the American Association of Pastoral Counselors and currently serves as Professor of Pastoral Care and Pastoral Theology at United Theological Seminary of the Twin Cities. She has recently published two books, *The Arts of Ministry: Feminist-Womanist Approaches* and *The Care of Men* (coedited with James Poling). Her book, *A Narrative Approach to Pastoral Counseling with Women,* is in preparation.

Jeanne Stevenson-Moessner, an ordained Presbyterian minister (PCUSA), is

Assistant Professor of Pastoral Theology and Spiritual Formation at the University of Dubuque Theological Seminary. She is a certified member of the American Association of Pastoral Counselors and counsels one day a week at a community mental health center. Her dissertation for the University of Basel, Switzerland, was titled *Theological Dimensions of Maturation in a Missionary Milieu.* She coedited *Women in Travail and Transition: A New Pastoral Care* and edited *Through the Eyes of Women: Insights for Pastoral Care.* She is the mother of two children.

Carroll A. Watkins Ali, an ordained minister in the Christian Church (Disciples of Christ), is a Training Director in the Denver District Attorney's Office for a federally funded grant designed for a nationwide project to provide seamless service to victims of crime. A certified member of AAPC, she also has a part-time practice in pastoral counseling and serves as an on-call Chaplain at the Children's Hospital in Denver. She has served as an associate pastor in Denver and earned her Ph.D. in Religious and Theological Studies at the University of Denver and the Iliff School of Theology. She is the author of *Survival and Liberation: Pastoral Theology in African American Context* (forthcoming 1999).

Index